WHY?

WHY?

The Deeper History Behind the September 11th Terrorist Attack On America

2nd Edition
Expanded and Updated

J.W. Smith

Copyright © 2003 by J.W. Smith

We believe all ideas should have maximum exposure. Thus for any properly cited individual quotation up to 500 words no permission is necessary.

By expanding upon parts of this manuscript, or nesting your work within the framework of this in-depth study, you can present a clearer picture while producing a book in six months as opposed to 6-to-10 years. Permission will be granted by the author (ied@ied.info) and the manuscript will be sent by email to those who present a serious and scholarly outline of a proposed book utilizing this foundation.

The author, The Institute for Economic Democracy, and their officers and supporters, specifically retain full rights to this work and other published research by this author so that others may use it, correct it, expand upon it, and produce an ever-more powerful and workable plan for world development and elimination of poverty.

Published jointly by: The Institute for Economic Democracy
& The Institute for Economic Democracy
Group Discounts, Classroom/University Bookstore Discounts
www.ied.info/cc.html

Publisher's Cataloging-in-Publication
(Provided by Quality Books, Inc.)

Smith, J.W., 1930-
  Why? the deeper history behind the September 11th[th] terrorist attack on America / J.W. Smith.--2nd[nd] ed.
  p. cm.
  Includes bibliographical references and Index.
  ISBN: 0-9624423-6-4 (hbk)
  ISBN: 0-9624423-7-2 (pbk)

  1. September 11 Terrorist Attacks, 2001—Causes.
  2. Economic history. 3. Free enterprise—History. 4. Free trade—History. 5. Capitalism—History.
  6. International economic relations—History. Terrorism --Prevention. 8. Equality. I Title

HV6432.7.S65 2003   330.9
                       QB102-200998

Book cover designed by John Cole, www.johncolegrf.com

This book is printed on acid free paper

Table of Contents

Introduction   **1**
Subtle-Monopolization is a Remnant of Feudal Property Rights

1. The 1,300-Year Battle between Christians and Muslims   **10**
The Crusades • The Rise of the Ottoman Empire • The Rise of the West and Decline of the East • The Decline of the Ottoman Empire • Claiming the Spoils • Redrawing the map of the Islamic World and Installing their Rulers • The Secret Agreements exposed • Oil Monarchs are paid well to protect the Interests of Western Empires • A Battle over Resources and the *Wealth-Producing-Process* • Controlling the *Wealth-Producing-Process* starts with Control of Land

2. Resource-Poor Wealthy Nations and Resource-Rich Impoverished Nations.   **24**
The Origin of *Plunder-by-Trade* • Never did a Nation Develop under Adam Smith Free Trade • All Successful Nations Developed under Friedrich List's Principles of Protection of Tender Industries and Markets • America's Freedom is based on Economic Freedom • America chose to ally with its Cultural and Religious Cousins • History Validates Friedrich List

3. The CIA Establishes the Greatest Propaganda Machine in History   **38**
Inoculating America, and much of the World, against philosophies of Full and Equal Rights • Corporate-Funded Think-Tanks reinforce the CIA's *Mighty Wurlitzer.* • McCarthyism yet stills many Minds in Academia and the Media • Eliminating the Washingtons, Jeffersons, Madisons, Lenins, Gandhis, and Martin Luther Kings of Emerging Nations • Imposing Beliefs upon Citizens Having Free Speech and a Free Press • Access to Resources and Control of the *Wealth-Producing-Process* was threatened • Controlling Elections Worldwide • Destabilizing Internal Political Groups • Most Professors and Intellectuals are locked into Protecting Empire • Protecting Wealth and Power through Creation of Enemies • The Inquisitions • The Eradication of the Knights Templar • The Inquisitorial Suppression of the Illuminati

4. Destabilizing Emerging Democracies Worldwide   **66**
Destabilizing a Newly-Free Iran • Containing Iraq • Containing Indonesia • Containing Libya • Containing Vietnam • Containing Nigeria • Destabilizing Guatemala • Destabilizing Chile • Destabilizing El Salvador • Destabilizing Nicaragua • Angola, Mozambique and other Frontline States

• Containing Cuba • The Korean War: A *Strategy-of-Tension* to gain Citizen Support for Suppressions of Breaks for Freedom

5. Containing and Destabilizing the Soviet Union and Eastern Europe — 84

The Costs to the Soviets were Enormous • Errors in Soviet Planning • Cold War I: The Official Enemy was Communism • A Sensible Restructuring Plan for Russia • Could the Soviet Union have avoided the Cold War? • Afghanistan, the Final Straw that Collapsed the Soviet Union • The 'Official' Enemy is now Terrorism

6. It was Yugoslavia's Turn to be destabilized — 102

Taking over the Media of the Defeated Serbia • Reality as opposed to the Thunder of the *Mighty Wurlitzer* • *Policies-of-State* to Control Resources and the *Wealth-Producing-Process* • The gains to *Imperial-Centers-of-Capital* are Huge • Turning the Screws Tighter • A NATO Alliance all the way to Russia's Border • Collapse of the *Invisible Borders* between the High-Paid Imperial Center and the Low-Paid Periphery

7. Inequality Structured in Law — 122

Free Food is Horribly Expensive • Financial Warfare • Equal Trade as opposed to Unequal Trade • Capital destroys Capital • Sincerely Sharing the *Wealth-Producing-Process*

8. Equal Rights in Domestic Economies — 143

Regaining Rights to a Modern Land Commons • Regaining Rights to a Modern Technology Commons • Regaining Rights to a Modern Money Commons • Creating a Constant-Value Currency

9. Reclaiming the Information Commons — 155

Eliminating Political Corruption by the Wealthy and Powerful • An unseen and unfelt Money Transaction Tax • Converting Wasted Time to Free Time • That Population can be stabilized without Coercion has been proven

Conclusion: Give Full Rights to all People and Terrorism Disappears — 160

Five Primary Guidelines for a World at Peace • *Democratic-Cooperative-Capitalism* • Powerful Nations giving up their Superior Rights • These are Historic Moments • Restructuring to an efficient Internal Economy • Enormous Savings Possible abandoning Subtly-Monopolized Economies • Restructuring all Societies to a Life of Leisure • Peace through Full Citizenship and Full Rights

Appendix I: A Practical Approach for Developing Poor Nations and Regions — 174
Appendix II. An Hour of Work as the World Money Unit — 175
About the Author — 196

Acknowledgements

I wish to thank the many great authors and reporters cited who have laid out reality so clearly. Without their dedication to truth, there would have been no way to find one's way through the maze of misinformation.

Petr Kropotkin had to flee for his life when he exposed European aristocracy in much the same way as this work exposes our financial and corporate aristocracy today. I trust I will not have to flee.

Friedrich List was jailed for his exposure of the fraud of Britain promoting free trade. Every nation that developed successfully did so following the guidelines laid down in his classic written in 1883, rhetoric that they developed under Adam Smith free trade notwithstanding (see Chapter 2). I trust I will not go to jail for exposing that the same fraud is being imposed upon the world today.

Ralph Borsodi's insights were crucial for understanding money. Later authors whose insights into current events were invaluable to me were: Michel Chossudovsky, Jared Israel, William Blum, Sally Covington, Jared Diamond, James Fallows, Jeff Faux, William Greider, Susan George, Sean Gervasi, Michael Kettle, Philip Knightley, Mark Lane, Christopher Layne, John Loftus, Arjun Makhijani, Milton Mayer, Ralph McGehee, William McNeill, Seymour Melman, Yousai Mohammad, George Monbiot, Michael Parenti, L. Fletcher Prouty, Ellen Schrecker, John Stockwell, Lester Thurow, and William Appleman Williams. Their crucial insights and many more too numerous to mention provided to the deeper history of this book.

Ray Miklas and Pete Gannon (stuffguys.com) kept my computers running. Special thanks go to Anup Shah, Bernie Maopolski, William Kötke, John Bunzl, and Jeff and Diane Jewell. As the subject of this book is of such high interest to all people in every country, all worked hard for its timely release. It would not have been possible without them. Special thanks go to Mieczyslaw Dobija's research on money originating as an accounting unit of productive labor.

Special mention must be made of Feisal Mansoor and Jeanne Thwaites of Sri Lanka and Mochamad Effendi Aboed of Indonesia. Professor Andrej Grubacic of Yugoslavia, Professor Radh Achuthan, Professor Michael Rivage-Seul, Cosmas Bahali of Tanganyika, Daniel Blackman, John Leonard, and reporter Dmitry Yanovich from Belarus.

I owe a deep debt to Professor Robert Blain of the Southern Illinois University, Professor Glen T. Martin of International Philosophers for Peace, and Professor Walter Davis of Kent State University. Most important are the groups, both those internationally established and those who are regional, who have banded together to support this research. Marie Gunther, http://4thefixbooks.com, brought all this together.

I sincerely thank all for their input. I alone remain responsible for any errors that remain.

Acronyms

Central Intelligence Agency (CIA)
Coordinating Committee for Multilateral Export Controls (Cocom)
Counterintelligence Program (COINTELPRO)
European Community (EC)
Federal Bureau of Investigation (FBI)
Free Trade Area of the Americas (FTAA)
General Agreement on Trades and Tariffs (GATT)
General Agreement on Trades in Services (GATS)
German Central Intelligence Agency (BND)
Gross National Product (GNP)
International Monetary Fund (IMF)
Kosovo Liberation Army (KLA)
Military Professional Resources (MPRI)
Most Favored Nation (MFN)
Multilateral Agreement on Investments (MAI)
Multilateral Trading Organization (MTO)
National Agreement on Free Trade of the Americas (NAFTA)
National Endowment for Democracy, (NED)
National Security Council Directive (NSC, NSD)
National Union for Total Independence (UNITA)
NATO Alliance High Representatives to Bosnia-Herzegovina (HR)
North Atlantic Treaty Alliance (NATO)
Organization for Economic Cooperation and Development (OECD)
Office of Strategic Studies (OSS)
Organization of Oil Exporting Countries (OPEC)
Partnership for Peace (PfP)
Popular Movement for the Liberation of Angola (MPLA)
Proto-Indo-Europeans (PIE)
Quadrilateral Group of Trade Ministers (QUAD)
Regional alliance of Eastern provinces of former Soviet Union (GUUAM)
Seven leading Western Countries (G7)
Socialist Workers Party (SWP)
Special Operations Command (SOCOM)
World Trade Organization (WTO)

WHY?

Also by J.W. Smith

Cooperative Capitalism: A Blueprint for Global Peace and Prosperity

Economic Democracy: The Political Struggle of the Twenty-First Century, 3 editions

The World's Wasted Wealth 2

The World's Wasted Wealth

Introduction

On 9/11/2001, terrorists hijacked four American passenger jets minutes apart, flew two of them into the New York World Trade Center twin towers, and flew one into the Pentagon. The fourth crashed when heroic passengers battled the hijackers at the plane's controls.

The question most asked was WHY? Americans were stunned. In newspapers, on radio, in news magazines, and on TV there were thousands of hours of open discussions, all trying to understand WHY?

The more obvious reasons why America is hated were discussed. Was it American support for Israel as the Jews terrorized the Palestinians into fleeing so as to reclaim their homeland of 2,000 years ago? Was it the Western embargo and continued assault on Iraq? Was it American troops and weapons on sacred Muslim soil? Was it all of these?

We look at the deeper reasons and study in depth the proposition that restructuring to a peaceful world is really quite simple once one understands the oppressive economic and foreign policies which impoverish other nations, which have caused anger throughout the world, and which remain conveniently ignored.

The United States of America is a great country. It was founded on the great ideals of freedom of speech, freedom of thought, freedom of movement, and freedom from oppression. These were considered extremely radical for their time. This author cherishes those values as much as anyone else and believes firmly that the war against terrorism must be waged. But that war cannot be permanently won without understanding and removing its causes.

Almost every book is written with a view to being *politically correct*. As we are attempting to look reality right in the eye, we cannot worry about such niceties. Our research is simply finding the truth in history for there is much hidden history that does not square with justice, with ethics, or with doing what is right. That part of Western history must be fully understood if we are to understand the terrorist attacks on America.

It is important to note that most *policies-of-state* which we will be addressing that are unethical and unjust were put in place by good people, no different than ourselves. These *managers-of-state* are locked into a system of unequal trades which began in the Middle Ages. The very life-blood of powerful societies flows through those arteries of unequal trade and conscientious leaders could not disrupt that flow of commerce without creating a severe crisis.

However, the gains in technological efficiency from restructuring to a more efficient economy under *democratic-cooperative-capitalism* provide the opportunity for a historic shift to ethical state policies of equal and fair trade.

That transition alone, if it develops, will quickly reduce violence, terrorism, and wars and their elimination, once the benefits are shared, will wipe out most poverty. After all, only an additional $40-billion a year is needed to provide clean water and sanitation, maternity and child care, basic health, nutrition, and education for all while the money spent on arms annually is $800-billion. The wealth destroyed by war is surely an equal amount, and the wealth production forgone by these wasteful efforts is by far the greatest losses of all.

Many within the media know very well why America is hated so much. If they research seriously they cannot help but become aware that America has a hidden foreign policy which suppresses the freedoms and rights in other countries, those very freedoms and rights that are cherished for its own citizens. We discuss in depth in Chapter 3 how ideology, peer pressure, job security, self censorship, and protection of wealth and power do not permit an in-depth analysis of these suppressive foreign policies.

Once self-censorship has been practiced for any length of time, the media are entrapped in a *social-control paradigm* (a belief system) they themselves help create. Once a belief is firmly in the social mind, even a conscientious major media outlet cannot expose the truth because they would not be believed and would lose customers and advertisers in droves. Thus self-censorship remains firmly in place.

When a national security crisis such as the 9/11/2001 terrorist attack on America which triggered this book erupts, a self-censored media must still remain silent or be branded as traitors and supporters of the terrorists; witness Bill Maher's temporary loss of his TV show, *Politically Incorrect*.

Maher stated that terrorists who flew those planes into buildings were not cowards as everybody was saying. The real cowards were those who sent missiles into Yugoslavia from a safe haven 2,000 miles away. He temporarily lost his show for pointing out an obvious truth. Not even a show titled *Politically Incorrect* can dare be too politically incorrect. This is why the closest any media guest—or political leader, foreign or domestic—ever came to exposing the deeper history we are addressing were soft statements like, "American foreign policy is partly to blame."

We had immense media coverage on the "war against terror." However, the range of discourse itself was quite narrow. We had amazing details on what was happening, how leaders were responding, how citizens were reacting, how the economy was faring and so on. But we have little discussion on the deeper causes which, if known by most, could have led to changes in foreign policy and elimination of the causes of those attacks. Only by discussing this deeper history can America realize the terror of its foreign policy as viewed through others' eyes. This book presents that in-depth discussion.

People are good and this includes America's leaders but there is a reason why America has persisted in such a violent foreign policy. Enormous wealth and power is dependent upon maintaining a system of unequal trades and this inequality needs protection to continue. The secrets of *plunder-by-trade*, well hidden from mainstream history, are still operational today and we address them in depth in Chapters 2 and 7.

The rights and freedoms of you and I are not the issue at all, they never really were. The issue is, as it has been throughout history, the protection of wealth and power—the struggle for the control of resources and the *wealth-producing-process*.

Broadening the issue to encompass the rights and freedoms of all people, we will be discussing a world development policy (*democratic-cooperative-capitalism*) in which both the rich and poor countries can win; a win-win policy as opposed to today's win-lose or even lose-lose policies.

Because what can only be described as "wholesale" state terrorism to protect wealth and power is so well hidden from Western nations' own citizens, our third chapter presents an outline of how Western state terrorism was left out of the civics, sociology, and history books and the daily news. We deal in no conspiracy theories. We study the well-documented and historically accurate facts of what is likely the greatest propaganda machine in history. Looking past that propaganda, we look at and analyze the institutional and systematic use and abuse of power that *creation of reality* is designed to hide.

In Chapters 4 through 6, we address the more violent assaults on what can only be called innocent people wishing to be free and in control of their own destiny. It was this wholesale terrorism that America's worldwide propaganda machine was designed to hide.

State terrorism is not simply mindless violence; its causes are buried deeply in economic history. So we next lay the deeper economic history of those past centuries on the table. Western society went from plunder-by-raids to *plunder-by-trades* centuries ago and today's *plunder-by-trade* is the unspoken reason for world violence today—just as plunder of another society's wealth has been the cause of wars for centuries.

It is the same battle over wealth that caused the 9/11/2001 terrorist attack on America. Those terrorists simply had no other weapons except suicide bombs. The last half of the 20th-Century saw the greatest peacetime transfer of wealth in history from the already-impoverished to the already-wealthy. It is worth noting that the 9/11 terrorists attacked America's most visible symbol of world trade, the World Trade Center, and the most visible symbol of the military might which enforces the unequal rules of world trade, the Pentagon.

Philosophers understand that societies dare not tell the truth about themselves. The reason is that societies try to be altruistic but simply cannot relinquish the amenities of life, produced by the labors of others that they have become accustomed to. Thus they present to themselves, to their children, to their students in the universities, and to the world, the face of a moral and altruistic society while the truth is far from that. The truth is powerful societies are doing almost the exact opposite of what they claim. Witness again the immense wealth transferred from the already poor to the already rich over the past half century.

A good example of lying to oneself and the world to protect both one's image and one's advantage is the very foundation philosophy the world economy supposedly functions under—Adam Smith free trade. The truth is, as addressed in Chapter 2, that no country ever developed under Adam Smith's free trade philosophy as interpreted by neo-mercantilists (i.e. unrestricted, survival-of-the-fittest capitalism). Instead, virtually every wealthy country developed successfully under Friedrich List's philosophy for protection of tender developing industries and markets.

Britain imposed Adam Smith free trade upon the world even though she developed under protection (Chapter 2). So long as the undeveloped world could be made to believe in and follow Adam Smith's free trade philosophy (as interpreted by neo-mercantilists), they would unwittingly hand their wealth to Britain of their own free will. The old imperial nations broke themselves battling over the world's wealth (World Wars I and II) and America took over the job of imposing Adam Smith free trade upon the world. Of course the mighty American military is there to force back in line any who would not accept that philosophy.

Western society must lie to itself because its own population will not tolerate injustice in its name. It must also provide a cover story to the world because the citizens of the world would not tolerate the theft of their wealth if they fully understood that the primary mechanism of this theft was the very philosophy being imposed upon them. Thus it was necessary to set up the greatest propaganda system in history (Chapter 3), backed by massive military might, to impose a corrupted Adam Smith free trade philosophy upon the world.

Imposing a philosophy on the impoverished world antithetical to their best interests could not have been done in one sweep. The process grew as technological development and world trade grew and the world was never given the opportunity to establish any other economic and trading system. World trade was monopolized at the start of the industrial revolution under the philosophy of mercantilism and the wealthy and powerful simply never abandoned monopolization, rhetoric and the teachings in universities notwithstanding. Every attempt to establish a more equitable system was suppressed by massive military power backed by an equally massive propaganda system.

How could there possibly be propaganda in a society with a free press and free speech? It is because most of the rewards within a society's educational system go to those whose philosophies protect and expand that system. Not only will a professor or media personality not receive any of those rewards if he or she were to lay out the truth, they would be totally ostracized, much the same as speaking out against one's religion in church.[a] Thus professors and major media personalities, even most on the so-called left, stay politically correct. Being interested only in the bottom line truth we will be documenting that all the essentials of mercantilist *plunder-by-trades* are in force today hiding under the cover of Adam Smith free trade.

All wealth comes from combining plentiful labor and capital with scarce natural resources and most of those resources are in the impoverished former colonies, now known as the developing world. To ensure this wealth flowed primarily to themselves, the strongest empires gained control of natural resources (primarily through establishing and protecting puppet governments) and dictated the rules of unequal trade. The key is to gain control of the *wealth-producing-process* and guide most of the wealth to themselves. The old imperial nations eventually broke themselves battling over the world's wealth (World Wars I and II) and they no longer had the power to maintain control of their puppet governments. Those former colonies were then able to make their break for freedom.

The only major accumulation of wealth remaining was in America. The old imperial nations of Europe handed the baton to their American cousins to suppress the world's break for freedom and thus protected their continued access to those resources and control of the *wealth-producing-process*. Although America had enough resources to remain wealthy, under the thunderous rhetoric of the Cold War, and for the same purpose as Britain (i.e. to protect access to those scarce resources and control the *wealth-producing-process*), Americans took over the job of imposing Adam Smith free trade upon the world in exactly the same way—propaganda backed by a massive military.

Partly to hide their own guilt, partly because speakers and writers do not know this deeper history, and primarily because we have been told all our lives how altruistic we are, the citizens of the powerful West still believe they are trying to help the world rise above poverty. But the truth is far simpler. Utilizing labor and capital, all wealth is processed from scarce natural resources most of which are in the impoverished world, and powerful nations must control those resources and the *wealth-producing-*

---

[a] The story is too big for a summary. Chapter 3 explains how the media was controlled and one will find more there on control within the university.

process. That is the secret of their wealth and power and the cause of poverty in weak nations.

All wealth is processed from natural resources. Check a globe and note the tiny area of land taken up by the old imperial nations of Europe. Where are their natural resources? They have few. Where are Japan's resources? Almost none exist on those islands? Where are Taiwan's resources? Where are South Korea's Resources? Hong Kong's? Singapore's? Those resources are primarily in Africa, South America, the collapsed former Soviet Union, the Middle East, North America, and Australia. Only Indonesia, Malaysia, and China amongst the formerly rapidly developing countries have substantial resources.

To counter fast expanding socialism, the powerful West protected the economies of virtually every one of those resource-poor countries through protecting their access to resources and markets. Though still a communist nation, China was allowed into the protected group only under the understanding that she would restructure to a capitalist economy.

After the collapse of the Soviet Union, the West, no longer fearing another developing center of capital, withdrew those protections. As a result, even while totally under centralized control, Japan's economy immediately went flat and then started dropping. Then, in 1997, currencies on the periphery of empire collapsed. Even having put protections in place against that currency collapse, Malaysia's economy shrank 25%. Thailand's economy was hit even harder. The South Korean economy shrank drastically. With no protections in place, the resource-rich Indonesian economy totally collapsed. With controls firmly in place (Friedrich List protection), China's economy has held steady.

Until the 9/11/2001 terrorist assault on America, the imperial centers strengthened financially while the periphery of empire was collapsing and the money was flowing back to the imperial centers. Those collapses stemmed from the withdrawal of protection for Japan and the "tiger economies" following the collapse of the Soviet Union.[a] That is financial and economic warfare.

Through economic warfare, financial warfare, covert warfare, and overt war, powerful nations throughout history have obtained weaker nations' resources for a fraction of their true value. The simple cause of world terrorism is that the wealth of powerful nations was stolen, and is still being stolen, from weak nations. The collapse of the periphery, as the center strengthens, speeds up this wealth appropriation process exponentially (Chapter2).

The alert in the developing world understand this. Their nations have a long history of being plundered in various forms and are more aware of

---

[a] Rollbacks of labors' rights within the developed world are a further concentration of that wealth.

what is really happening today than we in the developed world are likely to be. Some, as a result, are very angry.

But, upon learning where their wealth comes from, citizens of the wealthy world need not despair. We go on to address how subtle-monopoly capitalism can be restructured to *democratic-cooperative-capitalism* and utilize the wealth once wasted in economic wars, financial wars, covert wars, and overt wars to produce industry for developing regions. With that industry, these regions can build their own economic infrastructure and consumer products; even as the economies of the wealthy world are protected.

If the world is to have peace and security, if terrorism is to be eliminated, there is no choice but to share natural resources and permit each other to share fairly in the *wealth-producing-process*. If the powerful continue to control the world for their own selfish ends, the same 20% will be wealthy and insecure while the other 80% will remain impoverished and insecure. The mere *existence* of terrifying nuclear, chemical, and biological weapons of mass destruction is a ticking time bomb that must be defused by sharing the world's resources and the fruits of the *wealth-producing-process*. If we do not, the entire human race is at risk.

This book, our earlier books, and books we have yet to write are geared to pointing the way towards *democratic-cooperative-capitalism* so we can attain peace, security, and prosperity for all. After all, it is the impoverished countries' resources—their natural wealth—which is transformed, as per the wealth appropriation formula in Chapter 2, into the manufactured wealth (economic infrastructure and consumer products) and capitalized wealth (the financial wealth) of the powerful world.

The world's manufactured and capitalized wealth is produced from natural wealth so the impoverished countries which own those natural resources are entitled to their fair share. Only with such equality will the anger of the dispossessed subside and terrorism fade into history.

Subtle-Monopolization is a Remnant of Feudal Property rights

Social customs are a form of law. It is well recognized that social customs are huge obstacles for societies to evolve efficiently. The fact that the debris of *residual-feudal exclusive* titles to nature's wealth severely reduces the efficiency of capitalism is not even considered.

We are taught that monopolization has been eliminated by law. This is not true. Laws are designed by the powerful, for their protection, they have specifically designed subtle monopolization into the laws of capitalism. Under *residual-feudal exclusive* title to nature's wealth a tiny minority monopolize natural resources and the wealth produced. As Western societies evolved from full-fledged feudalism (absolute exclusive title), the entrenched powers and the newly powerful only granted *residual-feudal monopoly* rights to a few more people.

The basic principals of monopolization were never abandoned, that we are taught they were notwithstanding. We have full rights only in the sense that each has a chance at becoming a wealthy monopolist. But only a calculable few can attain those monopoly rights. This is not visible to Americans and Europeans because of the large percentage that has a high standard of living and thus appears to have full rights.

But, unrealized by the masses and most in academia, that high standard of living is only through the purchase of the wealth of weak nations for a fraction of its true value, and the distribution of that appropriated wealth through the massive expenditures on the military (the multiplier factor) which is the final arbiter to maintain the system of laying claim to others' wealth. This translates to an economic system not viable in times of peace. The powerful today are fighting to retain their *residual-feudal exclusive* property rights just as historic feudal powers fought to maintain the monopolization of wealth based on their *feudal absolute exclusive* property rights.

All this will become visible as we demonstrate how, through abandoning those remnants of feudal exclusive property rights to nature's wealth and restructuring to *democratic-cooperative-capitalism*, economic efficiency will increase equal to the invention of money, the printing press, and electricity. As we describe today's internal economies and global trade, we ask the reader to take note of the close connection current subtle-monopoly laws have to the up-front monopoly laws of feudalism. Today's wars are protecting a monopolized *wealth-producing-process* just as aristocracy fought to retain the monopolies which was the source of their wealth and power. Today's partial democracies are only a stepping stone towards full freedom and full rights for all as the last remnant of *residual-feudal exclusive* titles to what is properly social wealth is converted to *conditional* titles that recognize everyone's rights to their share of nature's bounty.

The efficient economy we are describing will not happen until true democracy is established. At each point in the centuries-long march to full rights and full democracy, the powerful have structured the laws for their protection. The rights of the masses were only considered when a crisis threatened. Full rights were not attained even after revolutions. There was simply too much debris of *residual-feudal monopoly* law and monopoly custom to clean away.

Theoretically we have democracy today but we actually have only partial democracies with the potential of full democracies. But we are getting closer. The very meaning of democracy is subverted by those subtle-monopolies. Once democratic-economic-democracy eliminates those *residual-feudal exclusive* titles, a full democracy will emerge.

This book borrows heavily from *Economic Democracy: The Political Struggle of the 21st-Century*. We felt the fundamental thesis of a modern commons and *residual-feudal* property rights in *Cooperative Capitalism: A Blueprint for Global Peace and Prosperity* was so important that, to give those readers the benefit, we inserted it into this manuscript and that of later editions of *Economic Democracy: The Political Struggle of the 21st-Century*. Each book has its own focus which gains strength when built upon the central theses of our magnum opus, *Economic Democracy,* and that of *Cooperative Capitalism*. Though there is duplication, we trust our readers will recognize the need of later concepts to fit within this little discussed world view and bear with us.

We highly recommend that our readers pick keywords and key people and countries off these pages and run Internet searches on Google. One will be surprised at what has been missed in the news and history books and each search only takes minutes. With those sources right at the reader's fingertips, in a few years authors will insert only a few citations. A search for alternative views on subjects on the evening news will be a great education. One will quickly learn that he or she has been poorly informed by their media.

1. The 1,300-Year Battle between Christians and Muslims

Although neither Christians nor Muslims will acknowledge it, for 1,300 years they have been locked in a battle over who will control people and nations.

If we are to understand the 9/11/2001 terrorist attack on the World Trade Center in New York and the Pentagon, using hijacked airplanes and passengers as guided missiles, we must know the history behind the efforts of the world's powerbrokers to control the resources of the world and lay claim to its wealth, especially to that of the volatile Middle East.

The Crusades

News and talk shows searching for answers to the World Trade Center and Pentagon bombings occasionally mentioned the Crusades which were Christian attempts to gain control of Christian shrines located in the center of the Muslim world and which broke out periodically over a period of 175 years, 1095-AD to 1270-AD. The Muslims eventually won those early struggles. The Crusades are therefore victories to Muslims and a matter of pride, not anger, for Muslim zealots.

Those Crusades are important to our story only because they are recorded in current history books. What is more important and is neglected by history books is the later crushing of the Muslim East by the Christian West. In this first chapter we tell that story of plunder-by-raids back and forth between the Christian West and the Muslim East and the eventual crushing of the East. The control of Christian shrines of the Crusades evolved into economic struggles. These *economic crusades* claiming weaker nations' wealth through *plunder-by-trade* are addressed in later chapters.

Of significance to this history is that, simultaneous with their battle with Western Christians, Eastern Orthodox Christianity faced the brunt of Muslim power for centuries and provided enormous protection to the "West.". Under assault from both Muslims and Western Christians, Eastern orthodox populations almost disappeared from the heart of their culture, around Constantinople and in the Eastern Balkan countries.

The remnants of Orthodox Christianity are now centered in the Slavic regions of Eastern Europe. A hint to the pressures faced by the Eastern Orthodox culture is that the word slave is derived from their Slav culture being a source of slaves for both Muslims and Western Christians.

The Rise of the Ottoman Empire

The Roman, Byzantine, Spanish, Portuguese, Dutch, French, English, and Ottoman empires all demanded tribute from their outlying provinces and continually consumed this wealth—and eventually wealth from the center—defending against encroachment by competing empires.

The Romans extended their empire around the entire Mediterranean Sea and parts of the Bible record battles resisting subjugation in the peripheral province of Israel. After 300 years of Rome persecuting Christians, during the 4th-Century AD, Emperors Constantine and Theodosius saw the advantage in allying with their adversaries, made Christianity the Roman state religion, and "forbade the worship of ancient pagan gods."[a]

Over the next 1,100 years, as the Roman Empire in the West was overwhelmed by barbarians, the people of Turkistan—who had a long history of conquest and defeat, back and forth, with China, Mongolia, Europe, Persia, Mesopotamia, and Egypt—accepted the Islamic religion. They formed an alliance with other Arabs and Muslims, defeated, and then ruled, much of the Byzantine (Eastern) half of the "Holy Roman Empire." This was the Islamic/Ottoman (Turkish) empire, which reached its zenith under the rule of Suleiman the Magnificent in 1550 AD [b]

By the 8th-Century, just 100 years after the death of Mohammed, the Arabs had converted most of North Africa to the Muslim faith, crossed the

---

[a] George Ostrogorsky, *History of the Byzantine State* (New Jersey: Rutgers University Press, 1969), p. 53; J.M. Roberts, *The Triumph of the West* (London: British Broadcasting Company, 1985), p. 67. A potentially powerful Egypt can only have been a serious threat to Rome. The knowledge of the world was in the Library of Alexandria and knowledge is power. The alliance of Christianity and Rome and the burning of the Library of Alexandria and execution of every educated Egyptian all in the 4th Century needs to be looked at closely. It parallels closely later alliances of church and state to destroy. All powers write history to hide their intrigues and all such hidden histories will be, and are, denied. The exposé's in this book will also be denied.

[b] The former Byzantine Empire was the eastern half of the Holy Roman Empire. They were once one empire ruled by co-emperors, one in Rome and one in Constantinople. Whenever one emperor died, the other named his replacement. Over several centuries, Hellenic culture overwhelmed the efforts to transpose Latin culture into the Balkans and Asia minor and the two empires became culturally separate (Ostrogorsky, *Byzantine State)*. This established the Christian "East" and Christian "West" that still divide the Western world today.

Straits of Gibraltar, and overrun Spain. They then entered France, but were decisively defeated by the Christians at the Battle of Tours (Poitiers) in 732 AD. For 700 years, from the 8th-to the 15th-Century, the Spanish Christians slowly pushed the Muslims back and, during the reign of Queen Isabella in 1492, the same year Columbus reached the Americas, they drove the Muslims off the peninsula.[1]

While that 700-year battle was being fought, Muslims remained firmly astride the trade routes to the silks of China and the spices of the Far East. Searches for another route were attempts to envelop the Muslims in a giant pincer movement (containment). Portugal's coinage minted from African gold was even called the "Cruzada" (the Crusade).[2] While Christians prevailed in Western Europe, the Muslims were growing stronger in Eastern Europe.

The success of the Turkish people up to this time was due to their warlike heritage, superior cannons, and the cohesive strength of the Islamic faith. But, as with all extended empires, the greater the distance from its center, the more difficult it became to defeat and control other societies. Though they had defeated Byzantium in the East, Muslims were still face to face with the Western half of the former Holy Roman Empire and its common bond of Christianity.

As "the center of gravity of the Western world [shifted] from the Mediterranean to the Atlantic seaboard," a series of defeats marked the turning point of Islamic/Ottoman fortunes in the East.[a] The first came in 1571 when, in a three-hour battle, a Christian fleet "composed of 208 Venetian, Spanish, Genoese, and papal galleys" destroyed 90% of the Ottoman fleet of 260 ships in Greece's Bay of Lepanto.

For the next 100 years, the Turks tried to regain their momentum and expand deeper into Europe. But they suffered a horrendous defeat in 1683 trying to take Vienna and, weakened by that setback, lost several other cities, including Athens, to the Christians. At this time Russia, under Peter the Great, joined the Holy Alliance against the Turks. The inexorable crushing of the Islamic/Ottoman Empire by the Christian Empire had begun.[b]

Leaders of these religions may not acknowledge that such a struggle took place but those who have been impoverished, because they have seen

---

[a]At this time, large amounts of silver and gold were being plundered from the Americas. This not only furnished the money that is credited with starting the Industrial Revolution, it seriously devalued Turkish money required to buy the tools of war. Thus the treasures gathered for centuries by the people of the great Aztec, Mayan, and Inca cultures were transported to Christian Europe and provided the muscle that overwhelmed the Islamic empire (Jack Weatherford, *Indian Givers* [New York: Fawcett Columbine, 1988], p. 16).

[b]The actual plan to envelop and crush the Islamic empire began 200 years earlier with Portugal's exploration of the west coast of Africa, which led to the discoveries of Vasco da Gama and Columbus (Roberts, *Triumph of the West,* Chapter 6, especially p. 180).

their natural wealth turned into the real wealth and capitalized wealth of the powerful, understand it very well. As many Christian nations are among the exploited, the motivations and methods are financial and economic, not religious. However, an alliance of church and state gave both religious and secular leaders enormous control and power over the people. During the first 800 years of this struggle both Christians and Muslims were ruled jointly by church and state.

The Rise of the West and the Decline of the East

The Christian and Muslim worlds were relatively equal until the West stole all the gold and silver that the American Indians had mined over several thousand years. This provided greater wealth for the West and drove down the value of the East's gold and silver. The East (Muslims) now had far less money and the West (Christians) far more money. The West could now outspend the East in both war and technology.

In the 16th-Century Luther broke with Roman Catholic Christianity and the West started its slow (yet incomplete) evolution to democracy and freedom. The big breaks toward liberalism and democracy: the American and French Revolutions came late in the 18th-Century. The crushing of the feudal Muslim East was imminent just 100 years later.

As Jared Diamond outlines, control of the world's resources and technology—and expansion of societies through financial, technical, and military superiority—is not only as old as history, it is history.[3] The building by the West of the Suez Canal and what railroads there were in the East is evidence of the West's technical, financial, and military superiority. Add the wealth being plundered from the Americas, Africa, and Asia to that being taken from Muslim regions and the Muslim East was obviously in for the rapid decline relative to the Christian West that history records.

Just as Christian fundamentalism and feudal governments held back the development of Western culture and technique during the Dark Ages and Middle Ages, the Muslim retention into the 20th-Century of feudal forms of government retarded, and continues to retard, its cultural and technical development. But we also must remember that, as will be documented below, the West overthrew emerging Muslim democracies and installed and protected those puppet feudal governments ever since the Ottoman Muslim Empire was crushed 85 years ago.

So long as they are denied equality in technology and trade, the wealth of the East will flow to the West. Muslims retreating into the protection of their religion remains the last bastion of protection for Muslim culture.

The Decline of the Ottoman Empire

The battles between Christians and Muslims ebbed and flowed for another 100 years, and as America won its freedom and the French their revolution, the Muslim Empire steadily gave ground. By the middle of the 19th-Century, the collapse of the Ottoman Empire was imminent, and European powers started positioning themselves to claim the spoils. France sought to maintain influence in Jerusalem, Egypt, Algeria, and later, Tunisia. Her building of the Suez Canal (1859-1869) conflicted with Britain's plans to control the land and sea routes to Asia.

While jockeying for position in the Middle East, France and England joined forces to prevent Russian expansion from getting out of hand in the Balkans (Crimean War, 1854-1856). But 10 years later, while England was occupied with the conquest of India, Russia pushed the Turks out of most of Europe. Those gains to Russia were largely lost when Britain recalled some of her troops from India and, in concert with France, denied Russia those military and political gains.

Claiming the Spoils

Turkey was humbled by these military defeats and, just as dependent countries today must do, turned to countries with capital (France, England, Russia, Germany, and Austria) for loans to build a modern infrastructure. "European interests were willing to supply the networks and systems which the Ottoman Empire lacked but of course wanted to own them, preferably on the basis of exclusive concessions."[4] The result, as told by Jaques Benoist-Mechin, is worth quoting at length:

> Each loan was granted on condition of guarantees and security. Each country had its own banks, monopolies and controllers. Banks, railways, mining companies and forestry, gas and water works were all foreign built, run and owned. France had seen to it that the tobacco monopoly had been [turned] over to her in 1883 as well as the docks at Beirut and Constantinople (1890), Smyrna (1892), and Salonica (1896). In 1890 followed the rights to exploit natural resources at Herklion and Salenica as well as running the Jaffa-to-Jerusalem Railway; in 1891 the Damascus-Homs and Mudanya-Bursa railway rights; in 1892 the rights to the Salonika-Constantinople Railway and in 1893 to the Smyrna-Kasaba Railway. The English had a healthy share in the "Ottoman Bank." Through the mediation of an Armenian, Calouste Gulbenkian, they obtained sole oil rights in Mossul in 1905. The Russians enjoyed various privileges, had secured the rights to all customs duties in Constantinople and in Black Sea ports. The Germans had secured the rights to free port docks at Haider Pasha (1899), railway shares and a municipal transport monopoly, and the docks at Alexandrette (1905). Through the operations of diverse combines the foreign powers sucked the wealth out of the country. The share of the national income which did not flow directly into the Sultan's coffers went to London, Paris, Viennese or Berlin banks. ... European capitalism was at its zenith at the time and drank the blood of its victim. "With such perfect organization the people were deprived of the fruits of its labour. Nothing was left for the abandoned cities, the treeless forest which had been overfelled, for the fields parched by drought, for the people themselves, who had neither doctors nor teachers."[5]

Foreigners now handled even the management of state finances:

> The impressive bank officials and foreign dignitaries in their elegant palaces on the Bosporus were mightier than the Sultan and the Grand Vizier.... [But] the only thing they had in common was the conviction that "the empire and its millions of subjects had only one raison d'être: to throw up enough earnings to be able to pay interest every six months to the innumerable holders of Ottoman certificates of indebtedness, whose number was increasing at a giddy pace."[6]

Besides the wealth wasted internally on their outdated feudal form of government, foreign military might forced the signing of unequal trade contracts that consumed more wealth. "[E]verything in Turkey which [was] clean, sturdy and beautiful [was] from somewhere else."[7] It only remained for the violent upheaval of WWI to dissolve the once mighty empire.

Redrawing the map of the Islamic World and Installing their Rulers

The provinces of Algeria and Tunisia were the first to break away (1830 and 1881). Though nominally still a Turkish province and coveted by France, Egypt was effectively taken over by Britain in 1881. In 1911, Italy invaded Libya and—pressured by the Balkan states of Bulgaria, Greece, Montenegro, and Serbia attacking from the West—Turkey made peace with the eastern invaders and lost control in Africa as it rushed to defend its western provinces.

Italy now took an interest in Libya while the ostracized German nation saw its chance to gain power vis-à-vis France, England, and Russia by becoming an ally of Turkey. They built the Berlin-to-Baghdad Railway and trained the Turkish army. In 1912, the war in the Balkans cost the Ottoman Empire almost all territory west of the Bosporus. Much was regained in 1913 when the Balkan nations could not agree on the division of the spoils and went to war amongst themselves.[8]

It was later English, French, and Russian covert efforts to destabilize Germany's trading partner—the Austro-Hungarian Empire—that led to WWI. Turkey felt that "if the Allies won the war, they would cause or allow the Ottoman Empire to be partitioned, while if Germany won the war, no such partition would be allowed to occur."[9] To quote Karl Polanyi, it was the collapse of the balance of power that led to WWI. Before that alliance with the besieged Ottoman Empire Germany was

> reinforcing her position by making a hard and fast alliance with Austria-Hungary and Italy.... In 1904, Britain made a sweeping deal with France over Morocco and Egypt; a couple of years later she compromised with Russia over Persia, that loose federation of powers was finally replaced by two hostile power groupings; the balance of power as a system had now come to an end.... About the same time the symptoms of the dissolution of the existing forms of world economy—colonial rivalry and competition for exotic markets—became acute.[10]

Just as British diplomats had long feared, "the scramble to pick up the pieces [of the Ottoman Empire] might lead to a major war between the European powers," WWI erupted.[11] Christopher Layne provides an analysis:

> Backed by Czarist Russia's pan-Slavic foreign policy, Serbia attempted to foment unrest among Austria-Hungary's restless South Slavs, with the aim of splitting them away from Austria-Hungary and uniting them with Serbia in a greater South Slav state—the eventual Yugoslavia. The Austro-Hungarians knew that this ambition, if realized, would cause the breakup of the Habsburg empire (and in fact, did so). In Vienna, Serbia came to be regarded as a threat to Austria-Hungary's very existence. On July 2, 1914, the Austro-Hungarian Foreign Minister, Count Berchtold, told Emperor Franz Josef that to remain a great power, Austria-Hungary had no alternative but to go to war against Serbia. In July 1914, Austria-Hungary believed it could survive only by defeating the external powers that were exploiting its internal difficulties.... Austria-Hungary's rulers, having weighed the balance, decided that "the risks of peace were now greater than the risks of war."[12]

Turkey joined on the side of the Triple Alliance (Germany, Austria-Hungary, Italy), and with the defeat of that alliance, as had been secretly agreed on in 1916, the Middle East was divided among the victorious powers with Britain "adding nearly a million square miles to the British Empire."[a]

> The promise of self-determination implicit in Lenin's diplomacy and President Wilson's "Fourteen Points" of January 1918, made it no longer possible for Britain and France to impose direct colonial rule over the Arab lands they had agreed to partition in 1916. They therefore came up with a proposal whereby these same areas would be ceded to them by the League of Nations as their "mandates" under the fiction that these territories were being prepared for future self rule. Iraq, Palestine, and Transjordan came under British mandate, Lebanon and Syria under that of France.... [Egypt's monarchy] was set up only to facilitate British control; it was overthrown by the Egyptian army in 1952.... [Since that time,] Syria, Jordan, Lebanon, and Iraq have had to struggle hard to establish their legitimacy. Meanwhile, the Arabic speaking states of North Africa continued as colonies: Algeria, Morocco, and Tunisia under the French, and Libya under the Italians. They became independent only after the Second World War. A small piece of land

---

[a] Fromkin, *A Peace to End All Peace*, pp. 26, 401. Modern Turkey was the only piece of the old Ottoman Empire to nominally keep its freedom. In 1919, "two Greek divisions had landed at Smyrna on the Aegean coast of Turkey, and some Italian forces at Adalia, farther south, in an initial step toward the execution of the Allied plan for dismembering the Ottoman Empire." Mustapha Kemal renewed the battle and, in a bloody two-year war, drove the occupiers out of Turkey (Edmond Taylor, *The Fall of the Dynasties* [New York: Dorset Press, 1989], pp. 387-91). Except for the volatile loyalty of religion, that impoverished country, nominally and very precariously allied with the West today, is all that remains of that once mighty *Eastern* Empire.

called Kuwait also continued to exist under colonial rule, as a British protectorate.[13]

The father of Islamic Modernism, Jalal al-Din al-Afghani (1838-1897), traveled the Muslim world warning that Britain, France and Russia were colluding with Middle Eastern rulers and robbing the local people through sweetheart deals for exploitation of natural and commercial resources. His predictions came true. After WWI the borders and the leaders of virtually all Arab states were decided upon by Britain and France.[a] Many assigned monarchs were not even locals; they were from tribes of other regions. On April 27, 1920, at the Conference of San Remo following the collapse of the Ottoman Empire,

> Britain and France finally concluded a secret oil bargain agreeing in effect to monopolize the whole future output of Middle Eastern oil between them.... Two years later when under pressure from their own puppet (King Feisal) for Iraqi independence, Britain's Prime Minister, Lloyd George commented] "If we leave we may find a year or two after we departed that we handed over to the French and Americans some of the richest oilfields in the world."[14]

European Christian Empires now claimed massive amounts of the wealth of the old Muslim Ottoman Empire. But one must remember that the Islamic empire had tried for centuries to conquer Christian Europe and the powerbrokers deciding the fate of those defeated people were determined that these countries should never be able to organize and threaten Western interests again.

With centuries of mercantilist experience of divide and conquer, Britain and France created small, unstable states whose rulers needed the support of their Western masters to stay in power. The development and trade of these states were controlled and were meant to never again be a threat to the West. These external powers then made contracts with their puppets to buy Muslim resources cheaply, making the feudal elite enormously wealthy while leaving most citizens in poverty.[15] Forty percent of Saudi Arabians, in what should be per capita the richest country in the world, are illiterate.

Once small weak countries are established, it is very difficult to persuade their rulers to give up power and form those many dependent states into one independent, economically viable, nation. Conversely, it is easy for outside powerbrokers to support an exploitative faction to maintain or regain power.

---

[a]Italy had backed out and the new Soviet Union rejected all such violations of sovereignty—including control of the Dardanelles and Bosporus Straits, which would have given them the warm water ports we were later told they would go to war for. It was the Soviets, after their revolution, who laid on the table the secret agreements of Britain, France, Italy and Russia (signed during the WWI, 1916) to crush and divide the Ottoman Empire.

If such manipulation of small nations was admitted to, the neo-mercantilist world would fall apart. The fiction of sovereign governments, equal rights, fair trade, et al., must continue. Any obvious effort to control the world has always invited immediate widespread rebellion. A language called "diplomacy" has been created to hide such realities.

The Secret Agreements exposed

After the Russian Revolution in 1917, the new Soviet government exposed to the world Britain's, France's, Italy's, and Russia's secret agreement signed one-year earlier to carve up the Middle East and many other such secret agreements were exposed. President Woodrow Wilson was determined to thwart them and proposed the League of Nations under which colonialism would eventually be dismantled. He personally assumed the role of U.S. negotiator for that purpose.

Being a head of state gave President Wilson the right to chair the peace conference and set the agenda. This caused great anxiety among the colonial powers of Europe. But Lloyd George, the British negotiator and designer of the Middle East partition that President Wilson found so offensive, was able to thwart Wilson's every move to grant those territories independence. With a shift in elections at home, President Wilson could not even obtain the consent of the United States to join and lead the League of Nations. His great hopes for world peace were thus stillborn.[16] The suggestions described in this work outline how President Wilson's dream of world peace can be achieved by giving full political and economic rights to all people of the world.

World War II consumed the wealth of the colonial governments of Europe and the disenfranchised world started to break free from their shackles. Some of the installed puppets became increasingly independent and others were overthrown. The last direct control in the Middle East was abandoned in the early 1970s when Britain "grant[ed] independence to Oman and the small sheikdoms that would become Bahrain, Qatar, and the United Arab Emirates."[17] Granting independence is a misnomer. Most of these feudal governments stayed in power only at the whim of the nation which put them in power. That lack of political independence denied those nations economic independence. Under today's power relationships, true independence can only come through having the power to protect equality of trades with other nations.

Oil Monarchs are paid well to protect the Interests of Western Empires

Their own selfish interests denied Middle East Muslim monarchs and heads of states the option of bargaining for equality of trades. (As we will see, equality of trades means establishing efficient industries, an efficient economic infrastructure, having equal access to markets, and equally-productive labor equally paid.) The dependence of feudal governments upon Western arms to suppress democratic movements which could overthrow them required sweetheart deals which enriched those feudal monarchs and Western traders at the expense of a nation's impoverished citizens.[18] Surely those impoverished had an equal right to nature's wealth within their borders? The alert in the Muslim world were aware of this conflict of interest and it was under this suppression of freedom and rights by their own leaders, in collusion with the West, that terrorism by religious extremists was born.

The old Soviet Empire had a long common border with the Middle East. The West therefore feared those two regions joining forces. If that had happened the Middle East would have had the weapons to protect their resources and the power to negotiate equality in trades. The natural resources of the Soviet Union and the Middle East together would have been comparable to those held by the West. Most of the world's reserves of oil were within the borders of those two empires and by raising oil prices, a good part of the West's wealth could have been claimed by the East. This is the explanation for the West's large military expenditures to maintain control in that region. That also explains the occupation of Iraq in 2003. If such nations obtained the major weapons of war, the *imperial-centers-of-capital* would lose their power to control the world's resources and the *wealth-producing-process*.

We must remember that, when the Soviet Union rejected the secret agreements to carve up the Middle East, they released all title and right to resources outside their borders. Soviet philosophy was to develop within their borders utilizing their own resources. That, of course, was a philosophy for peace.

Western policies were created, as we address below, to deny industrialization on the periphery of empire. Soviet policy, on the other hand, was to industrialize countries that had declared their independence. As the Soviets had plenty of oil, the Arabs, by establishing their independence, stood to gain considerably by establishing their independence and industrializing.

A Battle over Resources and the *Wealth-Producing-Process*

Equal rights mean all people sharing the world's resources and having equal opportunities within the *wealth-producing-process*. Battling over the world's wealth is consuming the world's resources. As all wealth is processed from natural resources, aggressive nations are destroying the very wealth they are battling over.

World War II is an excellent example. If those warring nations had recognized the simple moral reality that all people are entitled to their share of resources and the wealth created, the immense wealth destroyed by that war would have remained and would have produced more wealth. The savings from avoiding that one epic struggle alone could have developed the rest of the world to a sustainable level and eliminated poverty.

Through sharing the world's wealth most excuses for wars vanish. If we abandon those wars and cooperate in protecting all societies (this also means protecting the resources and the environment), there is plenty on this earth for all. As we will be demonstrating, the efficiency gains from restructuring to *democratic-cooperative-capitalism*, and thus avoiding those wars, would equal the invention of money, the printing press, and electricity.

Controlling the *Wealth-Producing-Process* starts with Control of Land

Western Christian nations controlling Muslim nations through puppet governments they put in power, Christian military forces based close to Muslims' most sacred religious site (Mecca) attacking Muslim nations, the Jewish enclave controlling the second most sacred Muslim site—the al-Aqsa Mosque in Jerusalem—coupled with the continued expansion of Jewish settlements on Palestinian land with the backing of Christian powers looks to Muslims very much like, and it is, an extension of the Crusades when Christians captured the Holy Land. (Note: Fundamentalist Christian Grace Digital Media operates America's TV beamed into Iraq under the War on Terror.)

Though it is very relevant, one does not need to look to a history of the Crusades to understand today's terrorism carried out by enraged Muslims. All people will fight to the death for their land. They must, their land is their livelihood. The loss of it threatens their very existence as a people. Thus Palestinians fight with their only remaining effective weapon, suicide bombs. The Middle East is controlled by proxy and Christian military power. To many of the over 1.2-billion Muslims in the world, they view terrorizing those suppressing them as the only means left to defend their lands and their people.

The massive funds spent by feudal oil monarchs for arms and their high living could just as well have produced industry and a modern economic infrastructure within Muslim nations. With that development those countries could have produced consumer wealth for their citizens. An industrialized Middle East would have meant democracy, education, and loss of feudal control.

The oil monarchs are not going to give up their power, as a modern economy would require, so there is little industry built in the Muslim world. Unemployment is high and the noose of unequal trade squeezes tighter. Though the feudal monarchs are still wealthy, the people feel their poverty and many understand well that the squandering of their patrimony of oil reserves being used as spending money will eventually create even more impoverishment. That denial of control of their destinies creates anger.

America says it is being targeted because of its freedoms, quality of life, and immoral lifestyle. If that were so, why are Sweden, Denmark and Holland not being terrorized? They are just as free, their standard of living is equal, and even Americans find aspects of their lifestyle immoral.

Besides the 1,300-year history we have just outlined, *managers-of-state* know well why others are angry. In Chapters 5 and 6 we will be discussing how the terrorist training camps in Afghanistan were established by America's CIA to train terrorists to do to capitalism's competitors what was done to New York's World Trade Center and the Pentagon. American bombs destroyed training camps that America built and, as America hunts down worldwide the still-active elements of the 35,000 terrorists trained in those camps, the War on Terrorism is killing terrorists that America trained.

But these American-trained terrorists were only a small part of the massive assault upon capitalism's competitors. The entire world is familiar with the devastation of a few acres at New York's World Trade Center. But few are aware that every building over one story high in an essentially defenseless North Korea faced the same devastation by Imperialism. Fewer than three thousand were killed in New York while 4-million were killed in Korea, half of whom were women and children. Between 12-million and 15-million worldwide were killed and hundreds of millions died due to destruction of their economies as capitalism successfully suppressed the post WWII breaks for freedom of the former colonial world.

We cannot be sure exactly what the deepest secrets of the current War on Terrorism are, but this we are sure was known by the powerbrokers: (1) Terrorists had already attacked American embassies and infrastructure overseas; (2) and that they were going to attack targets within mainland America. After all, terrorist efforts generate a lot of phone traffic and ECHELON, the software for America's electronic intelligence gathering service, intercepts and analyzes (through keywords picked out by powerful computers) virtually every message in the world that is sent through space and much of what is sent by ground. Obviously dangerous messages lead to detailed analysis of all traffic to and from those phone numbers. Over time, almost all terrorist cells and a rough outline of their plans become known.

We know the current prime target of the War on Terrorism, Osama Bin Laden, worked with the CIA and Pakistani Intelligence in establishing and operating those terrorist training camps in Afghanistan. So long as he and Al-Qaeda members were terrorizing capitalism's competitors, they were classed as "freedom fighters." As soon as they turned their training to blowing up American political and economic emblems, they were relabeled 'terrorists.' Terrorists, of course, are what they were all along. Western media has simply ignored the destruction of the political and economic infrastructure of its economic competitors by these same terrorists.

So much terrorism of others has been neglected by the media and, as Chapter 3 documents, there has been so much distortion of reality by the greatest propaganda system in history that figuring out what is real is very slippery. We do know Osama Bin Laden praised the terrorist attacks on America. But so did Western leaders praise all their terrorist attacks on their competitors. We do know that Al-Qaeda is dedicated to the destruction of America. But America trained them to terrorize and destabilize both Afghanistan and the Soviet Union and millions (Afghani, Soviets) were killed in the process as opposed to the few thousand killed so far as these terrorists turned on their trainers and benefactors.

We do know that every empire creates enemies to justify expansionist and suppressionist policies. We know that excuses for war are created so as to gain the political backing of a nation's citizens and permitting attacks causing the deaths of citizens is a *strategy-of-tension* that has proved effective. History is rife with examples but America has its destruction of the battleship Maine in Havana which rallied citizens for the Spanish American War and Pearl Harbor which rallied them for WWII.

We also know that the West feels they must control the vast oil fields around the Caspian Sea. Virtually all the former Eastern provinces of the Soviet Union have joined NATO's "Orwellian-named Partnership for Peace (PfP) military bloc." Major wars have been fought over fewer resources and those former Soviet provinces will receive arms from, and be doing training maneuvers with, NATO troops.

Going deeper, economies on the periphery of empire are in deep trouble and the imperial centers are threatening to stall or even collapse. Oil was below $10 a barrel, the imperial centers lost control, and it rose to over $30 a barrel. Gaining control of Iraqi oil is expected to again drop prices below $20 a barrel, maybe below $10, and restart Western economies. Researchers should look close at this as the primary purpose of the 1993 war against Iraq. They will have to look deep, this will not be the analysis recorded in history.

We discuss what is a known to point out that there is much more to terrorist attacks on America than Osama Bin Laden and Al-Qaeda. Such terrorists must be neutralized but so must the massive violence, suppressions and oppressions of the West that we discuss in Chapters 4 through 6 be abandoned.

The one aspect of this history that stands out is how American trained terrorists were freedom fighters when terrorizing and destabilizing competitors and terrorists when they turned on America. Hiding America's complicity in imposing severe violence upon others through tagging others with buzzwords of friends (freedom fighters) or enemies (terrorists) is an enormously effective propaganda tool.

When there is no oppression by an imperial center and societies have control of their own destinies, any dissident who inflicts harm on innocent people would gain no followers. In a reasonably just world, terrorists would have nowhere to hide even within their own culture. There would be very few of them and no need to activate an army to find them. Most people of all cultures are good and their own society would disown them.

However, if the economic injustice and suppressions of others' destiny continues, those suppressed will understand. The current terrorist networks will be devastated, but only one dedicated terrorist can do serious harm to citizens traveling outside the borders of the *imperial-centers-of-capital*.

In the next chapter we show how resource-poor, yet powerful, nations become wealthy and resource-rich weak nations remain impoverished. It is a matter of simple math and power. We next demonstrate how inequality of pay for equally-productive work creates an exponential gain in wealth for a well-paid nation and an exponential loss of wealth for a poorly-paid nation. Those inequalities of trades, and thus those exponential gains to the *imperial-centers-of-capital*, are maintained by economic, financial, and military power.

Endnotes

[1] Ralph V.D. Magoffin and Frederic Duncalf, *Ancient and Medieval History* (New York: Silver Burdett and Company, 1934), pp. 449, 673. See also Barnet Litvinoff, *The Burning Bush* (New York: E.P. Dutton, 1988), pp. 53-4, 74-5, 80-5, 199.

[2] Roberts, *The Triumph of the West*, p. 180.

[3] Jared Diamond, Guns, Germs, and Steel: The Fates of Human Societies (New York: W.W. Norton, 1999) and The Third Chimpanzee: The Evolution and Future of the Human Animal (New York: HarperCollins, 1992).

[4] David Fromkin, *A Peace to End all Peace* (New York: Avon Books, 1989), p. 46.

[5] Jaques Benoist-Mechin, *The End of The Ottoman Empire* (ISBN 3-89434-008-8, no publisher or date noted), p. 104; see also, Fromkin, *A Peace to End All Peace*, esp. pp. 46-48, 95.

[6] Benoist-Mechin, *End of the Ottoman Empire*, p. 104.

[7] Benoist-Mechin, *End of the Ottoman Empire*, p. 104.

[8] Benoist-Mechin, *End of the Ottoman Empire*, pp. 162-63.

[9] Fromkin, *A Peace to End All Peace*, p. 66; Christopher Layne, "America's Stake in Soviet Stability," *World Policy Journal* (Winter 1990-91): esp. pp. 66-67; Karl Polanyi, *The Great Transformation* (Boston: Beacon Press, 1957), p. 19.

[10] Polanyi, *Great Transformation*, p. 19.

[11] Fromkin, *A Peace to End All Peace*, pp. 28-29; see also pp. 49, 66.

[12] Layne, "America's Stake in Soviet Stability," pp. 66-67.

[13] Feroz Ahmad, "Arab Nationalism, Radicalism, and the Specter of Neocolonialism," *Monthly Review* (Feb. 1991): pp. 30-31.

[14] Fromkin, *A Peace to End All Peace*, pp. 509, 534. See also Noam Chomsky, "Oppose the War," *Z Magazine* (Feb. 1991): p. 62; Said K. Aburish, *A Brutal Friendship: The West and the Arab Elite* (New York: St. Martin's Press, 1998);

[15] Fromkin, *A Peace to End All Peace*, esp. pp. 45, 49, 50, 74-75, 139, 192-95, 264, 286-88, 392, 401, 410, 493, 506, 512-14, 462, 562. See also Elie Kedourie, *England and the Middle East* (London: Bowes and Bowes, 1956).

[16] Fromkin, *A Peace to End All Peace*, pp. 253, 257, 262, 389-402.

[17] Stephen Shalom, "Bullets, Gas, and the Bomb," *Z Magazine* (Feb., 1991): p. 12.

[18] Aburish, *A Brutal Friendship*).

2. Resource-Poor Wealthy Nations and Resource-Rich Impoverished Nations.

Every neo-liberal economic formula is built on assumptions. Those assumptions are a severe distortion of reality:

> In direct trades, inequality of wealth through inequality of pay is not lineal. Capital accumulation advantage increases or decreases exponentially with the differential in pay for equally-productive labor. Follow this example carefully as you calculate how long the low-paid nation must work to buy one unit of wealth from the high-paid nation and **how many units of wealth the high paid nation can purchase from the low-paid nation while working the same number of hours**: The equally-productive worker in the poorly-paid developing world produces a unique widget, is paid $1 an hour, and is producing one widget an hour. The equally-productive worker in the developed world produces another unique widget, is paid $10 an hour, and produces one widget per hour. Each equally-productive nation likes, and purchases, the other's widgets. All true costs are labor costs so we ignore monopoly capital costs, which go to the developed world and only increases the advantage anyway, and calculate the cost of those widgets at the labor cost of production, $1 an hour and $10 an hour. The $1 an hour equally-productive nation must work 10 hours to buy one of the widgets of the $10 an hour nation but, with the money earned in the same 10 hours, the equally-productive $10 an hour nation can buy 100 of the widgets of the $1 an hour nation. While in a homogenized market (a mixture of high-paid and low-paid equally-productive labor) there is a 10-times differential in buying power. At that 10-times wage differential in a non-homogenized market (this direct trade example) *there is an exponential 100 times differential in capital accumulation power or buying power.*
>
> The wealth accumulation advantage of the higher-paid nation over the lower-paid nation is equal to the high pay divided by the low pay squared: $(Wr/Wp)^2 = A$ (Wr is the wages paid to equally-productive labor in the rich country [$10 earned for every 1-hour time unit of production]; Wp is the wages paid to equally-productive labor in the poor country [$1 earned for every 1-hour time unit of production]; A is the capital accumulation advantage of the well-paid nation [100- to-1 in this example]).[a]

---

[a] We invite all with a talent for econometric formulas to expand upon this simple math to prove the errors in neo-liberal formulas. We would be pleased to publish quality books through this cooperative capitalism project. If you do not publish your own

In direct trades between countries, wealth accumulation advantage compounds in step with the pay differential for equally-productive labor. If the pay differential is five, the difference in wealth accumulation advantage is 25-to-1. If the pay differential is 10, the wealth accumulation advantage is 100-to-1. If the pay differential is 20, the wealth accumulation advantage is 400-to-1. If the pay differential is 40, the wealth accumulation advantage is 1,600-to-1. If the pay differential is 60 (the pay differential between Russia and the victorious America [23-cents an hour against $14 an hour]), the wealth accumulation advantage is 3,600-to-1. And if the pay differential is 100, the pay differential between the collapsed Russia and the victorious Germany, the wealth accumulation advantage is 10,000-to-1. Place a trader between those two unequally paid nations to claim all surplus value both through outright underpaying in hard currency or through paying in soft currency and selling in hard currency, capitalize those profits by 10 to 20 times, and you have accumulated capital through capitalized value.

This math is only in trade between nations with a wage differential for equally-productive labor. It does not represent trade within a homogenized market of both high-paid and low-paid equally-productive workers. It does, however, point the way towards correcting today's neo-liberal economic formulas built from faulty assumptions. Anyone who uses this insight to correct those neo-liberal formulas, we would like to publish your work along with ours.[1]

All wealth is processed from natural resources, most of those resources are in the weak, impoverished world, and both that natural wealth and processed wealth are transferred to the *powerful imperial-centers-of-capital* through unequal pay for equal work, as per this formula. In our previous work from which this quote came, we have thoroughly documented that average wage rates in the developing world for equally-productive labor were 20% that of the developing world and since the currency collapses on the periphery of empire may have dropped to 10%.

Through unequal currency values, thus unequal pay for equally-productive work creating *invisible borders* guiding the world's wealth to *imperial-centers-of-capital*, Europe is able to consume possibly 14 times the natural resources as are within its borders. Equalize currency values to equally-productive labor values, those capital accumulation advantages disappear, developing world deficits become large surpluses, and the wealth produced from the world's resources, are more equally shared.

The Origin of *Plunder-by-Trade*

In their classics, Henri Pirenne, Eli F. Heckscher, and Immanuel Wallerstein describe the origin of the modern market economy through the monopolization of the tools of production and proto-mercantilist trade imposed and controlled through violence:

---

book, we would be pleased to place formulas created at the end of key chapters with full acknowledgment.

> Up to and during the course of the fifteenth century the towns were the sole centers of commerce and industry to such an extent that none of it was allowed to escape into the open country.... The struggle against rural trading and against rural handicrafts lasted at least seven or eight hundred years.... The severity of these measures increased with the growth of 'democratic government.'... All through the fourteenth century regular armed expeditions were sent out against all the villages in the neighborhood and looms and fulling-vats were broken or carried away.[2] The problem of the towns collectively was to control their own markets, that is, be able to reduce the cost of items purchased from the countryside and to minimize the role of stranger merchants. Two techniques were used. On the one hand, towns sought to obtain not only legal rights to tax market operations but also the right to regulate the trading operation (who should trade, when it should take place, what should be traded). Furthermore, they sought to restrict the possibilities of their countryside engaging in trade other than via their town. Over time, these various mechanisms shifted their terms of trade in favor of the townsmen, in favor thus of the urban commercial classes against both the landowning and peasant classes.[3]

With primitive industrial capital—looms, fulling vats, leather making tools, forges, et al.—the city could produce cheaply and trade those commodities to the countryside for wool, food, timber, et al. But it did not take the countryside long to copy those simple technologies and produce their own cloth, leather, and metal products.

The comparative advantage of the countryside of having both the raw materials and the technology meant impoverishment for any city that formerly produced those consumer products. Superior military force eliminated the comparative advantages of the outlying villages and enforced their dependency upon the city. Through monopolizing the *wealth-producing-process* by superior military power, the city laid claim to both the natural wealth of the countryside and the wealth produced by technology. From that obscure beginning, throughout history, the powerful and crafty continually restructured property rights to transfer all wealth (above production costs) produced on, or with, that property to themselves.

The powerful face the same problem today. To maintain the standard of living of their citizens and their wealth and power, powerful nations lay claim to the wealth of weak nations through inequalities in world trade. One becomes a popular leader by protecting and increasing the well being of ones followers. But any sincere economic proposal to better the lot of impoverished nations would instantly and correctly be seen by all in an *imperial-center-of-capital* as an immediate loss to themselves. (This is true only under the current subtle-monopoly structure but not under *democratic-cooperative-capitalism*.)

Thus for a leader to propose a sincere economic policy for the periphery is rare. Reality requires leaders to take care of their own even as millions—no billions—of people on the periphery are impoverished by economic, financial, covert, and overt warfare due to *grand strategies* containing any economic consolidation that would compete for world resources and control of the *wealth-producing-process*.[4] Lewis Mumford provides a historical analysis of this process:

> The leading mercantile cities [of Europe] resorted to armed force in order to destroy rival economic power in other cities and to establish a [more complete] economic monopoly. These conflicts were more costly, destructive, and ultimately even more futile than those between the merchant classes and the feudal orders. Cities like Florence, which wantonly attacked other prosperous communities like Lucca and Siena, undermined both their productivity and their own relative freedom from such atrocious attacks. When capitalism spread overseas, its agents treated the natives they encountered in the same savage fashion that it treated their own nearer rivals.[5]

This policy is still in full force yet today. Title to industrial capital (the tools of production) and control of trade are today the primary mechanisms for claiming the wealth of the weak on the periphery of empire, the countryside, just as it has for the past millennium. Plunder-by-raids has been transformed into *plunder-by-trade*.

Although unacknowledged, the destruction of capital on the periphery of empire today protects the control of the *wealth-producing-process* by the imperial centers yet today. Witness the violent devastation of the industry of Yugoslavia and Iraq and the containment of Iran, Libya, North Korea Nicaragua, Chile, and Cuba, all of whom are denied control of their destinies.

Never did a Nation Develop under Adam Smith Free Trade

> Trade was felt to be the bloodstream of British prosperity. To an island nation it represented the wealth of the world, the factor that made the difference between rich and poor nations. The economic philosophy of the time (later to be termed mercantilism) held that the colonial role in trade was to serve as the source of raw materials and the market for British manufacture, and *never* to usurp the manufacturing function.[6] (Emphasis added)

Adam Smith's own words exposes free trade as only a cover for the same past mercantilist policies:

> The ultimate object ... is always the same, to enrich the country by an advantageous balance of trade. It discourages the exportation of the materials of manufacture [tools and raw material], and the instruments of trade, in order to give our own workmen an advantage, and to enable them to undersell those of other nations in all foreign markets: and by restraining, in this manner, the exportation of a few commodities of no great price, it proposes to occasion a much greater and more valuable exportation of others. It encourages the importation of the materials of manufacture, in order that our own people may be enabled to work them up more cheaply, and thereby

prevent a greater and more valuable importation of the manufactured commodities.[7]

In her early development, Britain structured her laws to protect her industry and commerce. The British Enclosure Acts of the 15th, 16th, and 17th centuries were sparked by the labor shortage created by the Black Death and the need for sheep farming to produce for the wool market created by the Hanseatic traders.

As opposed to today's industry fleeing from high-priced skilled labor and moving to cheap labor, skilled artisans of almost every product in world commerce were brought to England from all over the world to train British labor in those skills. Bounties were given to promote exports of manufactures. And custom duties were enacted to protect those new industries.

Dutch commerce was undercut by the Navigation Acts requiring British products to be transported in British ships. English warships attacked Dutch shipping and English exports and imports rapidly increased. The Methuen treaty of 1703 with Portugal shut the Dutch off from trade with the Portuguese Empire.

The suddenly idled Dutch capital and skilled labor emigrated to the *protective* trade structure of England. The trade and commerce of France and Spain were overwhelmed by similar strategies. Every one of these policies under which Britain developed were the yet-unwritten philosophies of Friedrich List. None were the yet-unwritten philosophies of Adam Smith.[8] And Adam Smith himself knew this well. Note his last statement in this quote:

> A small quantity of manufactured produce purchases a great quantity of rude produce. A trading and manufacturing country, therefore, naturally purchases with a small part of its manufactured produce a great part of the rude produce of other countries; while, on the contrary, a country without trade and manufactures is generally obliged to purchase, at the expense of a great part of its rude produce, a very small part of the manufactured produce of other countries. The one exports what can subsist and accommodate but a very few, and imports the subsistence and accommodation of a great number. The other exports the accommodation and subsistence of a great number, and imports that of a very few only. The inhabitants of the one must always enjoy a much greater quantity of subsistence than what their own lands, in the actual state of their cultivation, could afford. The inhabitants of the other must always enjoy a much smaller quantity.... Few countries ... produce much more rude produce than what is sufficient for the subsistence of their own inhabitants. To send abroad any great quantity of it, therefore, would be to send abroad a part of the necessary subsistence of the people. It is otherwise with the exportation of manufactures. The maintenance of the people employed in them is kept at home, and only the surplus part of their work is exported.... The commodities of Europe were almost all new to America, and many of those of America were new to Europe. A new set of exchanges, therefore, began to take place which had never been thought of before, and

which should naturally have proved as advantageous to the new, as it certainly did to the old continent. The savage injustice of the Europeans rendered an event, which ought to have been beneficial to all, ruinous and destructive to several [most] of those unfortunate countries.[9]

All Successful Nations Developed under Friedrich List's Principles of Protection of Tender Industries and Markets

Friedrich List describes the protectionist maxims under which Britain developed:[a]

[1] Always to favour the importation of productive power, in preference to the importation of goods.
[2] Carefully to cherish and to protect the development of productive power.
[3] To import only raw materials and agricultural products, and to export nothing but manufactured goods.
[4] To direct any surplus of productive power to colonization, and to the subjection of barbarous nations.
[5] To reserve exclusively to the mother country the supply of the colonies and subject countries with manufactured goods, but in return to receive on preferential terms their raw materials and especially their colonial produce.
[6] To devote especial care to the coast navigation; to the trade between the mother country and the colonies; to encourage sea fisheries by means of bounties; and to take as active a part as possible in international navigation.
[7] By these means to found a naval supremacy, and by means of it to extend foreign commerce, and continually increase her colonial possessions.
[8] To grant freedom in trade with the colonies and in navigation only so far as she can gain more by it than she loses.
[9] To grant reciprocal navigation privileges only if the advantage is on the side of England, or if foreign nations can by that means be restrained from introducing restrictions on navigation in their favor.
[10] To grant concessions to foreign independent nations in respect of the import of agricultural products, only in case concessions in respect of her manufactured products can be gained thereby.
[11] In cases where such concessions cannot be obtained by treaty, to attain the object of them by means of contraband trade.
[12] To make wars and to contract alliances with exclusive regard to her manufacturing, commercial, maritime, and colonial interests. To gain by these alike from friends and foes; from the latter by interrupting their commerce at sea; from the former by ruining their manufactures through subsidies which are paid in the shape of English manufactured goods.[10]

---

[a] Lets not forget simple luck as to why Britain became the first industrial nation. Britain's rich coal fields and iron mines were only 15 miles apart and British industries had access to cheap water transportation for both internal and world commerce. The same advantage of rich coal and iron mines and cheap water transportation favored America. It was from those initial natural advantages that Britain expanded by advantageous trade agreements and America is now expanding by structural adjustments imposed upon weak nations that are advantageous to powerful nations.

Napoleon knew all this well:

> Under the existing circumstances ... any state which adopted the principles of free trade must come to the ground .... [and] a nation which combines in itself the power of manufacturers with that of agriculture is an immeasurably more perfect and more wealthy nation than a purely agriculture one."[11]

The Wealth of Nations does not consider the industrial development of the periphery of empire: "Adam Smith and J.B. Say had laid it down that ... nature herself had singled out the people of the United States [and most of the rest of the world] exclusively for agriculture." And Friedrich List, who challenged the philosophy of Adam Smith because his native Germany could not develop under a philosophy designed to maintain the supremacy of Britain, was criticized by his staunchest supporters for considering developing only Europe and America.[12]

William Pitt, British Prime Minister, studied Adam Smith's *Wealth of Nations* closely and saw the opportunity to solidify Britain's control of World trade. If the world could be convinced to follow Adam Smith, he reasoned that no other nation could compete with British industry even if the 12 protectionist policies addressed above were dropped. The British State Department, British intelligence and British industry funded correspondents, columnists, writers, lecturers, and think-tanks mounted a crusade to impose Adam Smith's free-trade philosophy, as they interpreted it, on the world.[13]

So long as the undeveloped world could be made to believe this philosophy, they would hand their wealth to Britain of their own free will and it would not require an army:

> Such arguments did not obtain currency for very long [in France]. England's free trade wrought such havoc amongst the manufacturing industries, which had prospered and grown strong under the Continental blockade system, that a prohibitive *règime* was speedily resorted to under the protecting aegis of which, according to Dupin's testimony, the producing power of French manufactories was doubled between the years 1815 and 1827.[14]

As Napoleon understood, unless it is also equal trade, one country's free trade is another country's impoverishment. Friedrich List, from whose classic much of this part of our story comes, observed the devastation that British free trade created in France, observed France's rapid recovery when she protected herself against predatory British industry, and he also observed firsthand the rapid development of the newly-free United States when they ignored Britain's promotion of Adam Smith free trade as interpreted by British mercantilists.[15]

All True Freedom, is based on Economic Freedom

As the revolution approached, America's founding fathers analyzed that "consumption of foreign luxuries, [and] manufactured stuffs, was one of the chief causes of [the colonies'] economic distress":[16]

> In the harbor of New York there are now 60 ships of which 55 are British. The produce of South Carolina was shipped in 170 ships of which 150 were British.... Surely there is not any American who regards the interest of his country but must see the immediate necessity of an efficient federal government; without it the Northern states will soon be depopulated and dwindle into poverty, while the Southern ones will become silk worms to toil and labour for Europe.... In the present state of disunion the profits of trade are snatched from us; our commerce languishes; and poverty threatens to overspread a country which might outrival the world in riches.[17]

An unequal treaty (Peace of Versailles) was forced on the American colonies in 1783 that "permitted only the smallest American vessels to call at the island ports and prohibited all American vessels from carrying molasses, sugar, coffee, cocoa, and cotton to any port in the world outside the continental United States."[18] Not even a horseshoe nail was to be produced in America, export of manufactured products were forbidden to any port within Britain's trade empire, and the British navy was there to enforce that treaty.

> [America] could import only goods produced in England or goods sent to the colonies by way of England. They were not allowed to export wool, yarn, and woolen cloth from one colony to another, "or to any place whatsoever," nor could they export hats and iron products. They could not erect slitting or rolling mills or forges and furnaces. After 1763, they were forbidden to settle west of the Appalachian Mountains. By the Currency Act of 1764, they were deprived of the right to use legal tender paper money and to establish colonial mints and land banks.[19]

U.S. statesman Henry Clay quotes a British leader as saying: "[N]ations knew, as well as [ourselves], what we meant by 'free trade' was nothing more nor less than, by means of the great advantage we enjoyed, to get a monopoly of all their markets for our manufactures, and to prevent them, one and all, from ever becoming manufacturing nations."[20] England's Lord Brougham "thought it '"well worthwhile to incur a loss upon the first exportation [of English manufactures], in order, by the glut, TO STIFLE IN THE CRADLE THOSE RISING MANUFACTURES IN THE UNITED STATES.'" Britain's efforts to contain America forced the new nation to establish the Naval War College and a powerful navy.[21]

Political freedom gives one the right of the vote, free speech, and choice of religion. But political rights without economic rights can leave one cold, impoverished, and starving to death. Thirty-six years after their revolution, with Britain busy battling Napoleon on the Continent, America won the War of 1812 and it was from winning that struggle that Americans truly gained their independence. America was now both politically and economically free. Except for Canada and Australia, no other colony gained both their political and economic freedom prior to WWII.[a] After that war, many gained their nominal political freedom but only those required for allies to stop fast expanding socialism (Japan, Taiwan, South Korea, Indonesia, and Malaysia) gained their economic freedom.

America chose to ally with its Cultural and Religious Cousins

World Wars I and II, as with most wars throughout history, were battles over control of the world's resources and markets and thus control over the *wealth-producing-process*. The old imperial nations of Europe broke themselves

---

[a] The following books lead you to primary sources on nations, especially America, successfully developing protecting their industries and markets. Though some—because they were needed as allies—developed under others' protection, there are no nations which successfully developed without protection for their industries and markets. Friedrich List, *The National System of Political Economy* (Fairfield, NJ: Augustus M. Kelley, 1977); Clarence Walworth Alvord, *The Mississippi Valley in British Politics: A Study of Trade, Land Speculation, and Experiments in Imperialism Culminating in the American Revolution* (New York: Russell & Russell, 1959); Bairoch, *Economics and World History;* Correli Barnett, *The Collapse of British Power* (New York: Morrow, 1971); Oscar Theodore Barck, Jr. and Hugh Talmage Lefler, *Colonial America*, 2nd ed. (New York: Macmillan, 1968); Samuel Crowther, *America Self-Contained* (Garden City, N.Y.: Doubleday, Doran & Co., 1933); John M . Dobson, *Two Centuries of Tariffs: The Background and Emergence of the U.S. International Trade Commission* (Washington DC: U.S. International Trade Commission, 1976); Alfred E. Eckes, Jr., *Opening America's Markets: U.S. Foreign Trade Policy Since 1776* (Chapel Hill: University of North Carolina Press, 1995); James Thomas Flexner, *George Washington: The Forge of Experience* (Boston: Little Brown and Co., 1965); William J. Gill, *Trade Wars Against America: A History of United States Trade and Monetary Policy* (New York: Praeger, 1990); John Steele Gordon, *Hamilton's Blessing: The Extraordinary Life and Times of Our National Debt* (New York: Walker and Co., 1997); Irwin, *Against the Tide*; Emory R. Johnson, *History of Domestic and Foreign Commerce of the United States* (Washington DC: Carnegie Institute of Washington, 1915); Richard M. Ketchum, ed., *The American Heritage Book of the Revolution* (New York: American Heritage Publishing, 1971); Michael Kraus, *The United States to 1865* (Ann Arbor: University of Michigan Press, 1959); John A. Logan, *The Great Conspiracy: Its Origin and History, 1732-1775* (New York: A.R Hart & Co., 1886); William MacDonald, ed., *Documentary Source Book of American History, 1606-1926,* 3rd ed. (New York: MacMillan, 1926); John C. Miller, *Origins of the American Revolution* (Boston: Little Brown and Co., 1943); Samuel Eliot Morison and Henry Steele Commanger, *Growth of the American Republic*, 5th ed. (New York: W.W. Norton, 1959); Sir Lewis Namier and John Brooke, *Charles Townsend* (New York: St. Martin's Press, 1964); Gus Stelzer, *The Nightmare of Camelot: An Expose of the Free Trade Trojan Horse* (Seattle, Wash.: PB publishing, 1994); Peter D.J. Thomas, *The Townshend Duties Crisis: The Second Phase of the American Revolution, 1776-1773* (Oxford: Clarendon Press, 1987); Arthur Hendrick Vandenberg, *The Greatest American* (New York: G.P. Putman's and Sons, 1921).

in those struggles battling over the world's wealth and no longer had the power to maintain control of the world. The entire former colonial world saw their chance for freedom and most looked to America as the model for their future.

Control of the *wealth-producing-process* was what produced the prosperity of the *imperial-centers-of-capital*. America had enough natural resources to maintain its standard of living and could have chosen to support the world's break for freedom. But the cultural and religious loyalties outweighed the moral option. The powerbrokers of the old imperial nations of Europe handed the baton to America's powerbrokers to suppress the world's break for freedom. The wholesale terrorism addressed in Chapters 4 through 6, even as emerging nations attempted to emulate America's break for freedom, is that story.

Suppression of most nations required bringing key nations within the wealth-producing, wealth-distribution, process. To stop fast expanding socialism required giving key countries (Japan, Taiwan, and South Korea) on the borders of that ideology access to technology, capital, and markets. This, of course, is Friedrich List protectionism, not Adam Smith free trade, even though free trade was preached in every university classroom and every lecture as the governing philosophy. Other Southeast Asian countries, and then finally China, moved in under that Friedrich List protection masquerading as Adam Smith free trade. Their success under that protection and their collapse when that protection was partially removed once the Soviet Union collapsed, prove the soundness of Friedrich List's protection philosophy.

That protection was removed through forced structural adjustments requiring unimpeded access to those markets. Deputy Secretaries of the Treasury Robert Rubin and Larry Summers, and "their henchmen at the International Monetary Fund ... admitted they had made hard choices, and they will even cop to some mistakes."[22] The "hard choices" faced by these "usual suspects"—as described by Professor Stephen Gill, Professor of Political Science at York University in Toronto[23]—can only be letting others take care of themselves whenever an economic collapse is imminent. Professor Peter Gowan of the University of North London explains that Greenspan, Summers, and Rubin were not worried:

> As the crisis spread across the region, the US Treasury and the Federal Reserve were serene about its global consequences. They knew from a wealth of past experience that financial blow-outs in countries of the South provided a welcome boost for the US financial markets and through them the US domestic economy. Huge funds could be expected to flood into the US financial markets, cheapening the cost of credit there, boosting the stock market and boosting domestic growth. And there would be a rich harvest of assets to be reaped in East Asia when these countries fell to their knees before the IMF.[24]

Removing protection from former allies was little more than turning loose the dogs of speculation through structural adjustments requiring access to Asian markets for speculative capital. The steadily declining commodity prices worldwide proved there was plenty of room to print money—better, more equal, and safer yet, permit other regions and other nations to print their own money for industrial and infrastructure development—and expand the world economy. So the decision to shrink the world economy to provide more for the *imperial-centers-of-capital* was a very conscious one:

> [I]f a society spends $100 to manufacture a product within its borders, the money that is used to pay for materials, labor and, other costs moves through the economy as each recipient spends it. Due to this multiplier effect, $100 worth of primary production can add several hundred dollars to the Gross National Product (GNP) of that country. If money is spent in another country, circulation of that money is within the exporting country. This is the reason *an industrialized product-exporting/commodity-importing country is wealthy and an undeveloped product-importing/commodity-exporting country is poor.* Developed countries grow rich by selling capital-intensive (thus cheap) products for a high price and buying labor-intensive (thus expensive) products for a low price. This imbalance of trade expands the gap between rich and poor. The wealthy sell products to be consumed, not tools to produce. This maintains the monopolization of the tools of production, and assures a continued market for the product.[25]

That the periphery would face a meltdown if protection was removed was well understood. In *False Dawn,* Professor John Gray of the London School of Economics points out that free trade and true democracy are incompatible:

> In any long and broad historical perspective the free market is a rare and short-lived aberration. Regulated markets are the norm, arising spontaneously in the life of every society.... The idea that free markets and minimum governments go together ... is an inversion of the truth.... The normal concomitant of free markets is not stable democratic government. It is the volatile politics of economic insecurity.... Since the natural tendency of society is to curb markets, free markets can only be created by the power of a centralized state ... .A global free market is not an iron law of historical development but a political project.... Free markets are the creatures of government and cannot exist without them.... Democracy and free markets are competitors rather than partners .... [just as the disastrous British free market 100 years ago which culminated into two world wars, the current] global free market is an American project.... In the absence of reform, the world economy will fragment, as its imbalances become insupportable.... The world economy will fracture into blocs, each driven by struggles for regional hegemony.[26]

In short, global capital, backed by the American military, is attempting to deny every undeveloped nation the right to protect its resources, industry, markets, and citizens. This outlines the lock that global capital has upon the world. If any nation attempts to protect itself, capital will flee and create even greater poverty. Not only are those countries doubly endangered, with an example of how to plunder the treasury of a powerful country like

Britain, Professor Gowan explains how hedge funds are used to plunder the treasuries of both weak and powerful nations:

> The speculator takes out huge forward contracts to sell pounds for French francs at 9.50 to the pound in one month's time: say forward contracts totaling £10-billion. For these he must pay a fee to a bank. Then he waits until the month is nearly up. Then suddenly he starts buying pounds again in very large volumes and throws them against the exchange rate through selling them. So big is his first sale of pounds that the currency falls, say 3 percent against the franc. At this point other, smaller players see the pound going down and join the trend he has started, driving it down another 3 percent. Overnight he borrows another vast chunk of pounds and sells into francs again, and meanwhile the word is going around the market that none other than the master speculator is in action, so everyone joins the trend and the pound drops another ten percent. And on the day when the forward contract falls due for him to sell pounds for francs at 9.50 the pound in the spot market is down at 5 francs. He takes up his huge forward contract and makes a huge profit. Meanwhile there is a sterling crisis, etc. etc.[27]

Although Americans are currently (2002) riding high as free trade profits flow from the South to the North:

> [A] global free market ... no more works in the interests of the American economy than of any other. Indeed, in a large dislocation of the world markets the America economy would be more exposed than many others.... In this feverish atmosphere a soft landing is a near impossibility. Hubris is not corrected by twenty percent.... Economic collapse and another change of regime in Russia; further deflation and weakening of the financial system in Japan, compelling a repatriation of Japanese holdings of US government bonds; financial crisis in Brazil or Argentina; a Wall Street crash – any or all of these events, together with others that are unforeseeable, may in present circumstances act as the trigger of a global economic dislocation. If any of them come to pass, one of the first consequences will be a swift increase of protectionist sentiment in the United States, starting in Congress.[28]

History Validates Friedrich List

The enormous industrial successes of Britain, America, Bismarck, the Third Reich, the Soviet Union, pre-WWII Japan, post-WWII Europe and Japan, the Asian tigers, and now China—all industrialized following Friedrich List's precepts, and no nation in the world ever developing under Adam Smith free trade (the rhetoric that they did, and are, notwithstanding)—prove the sound logic of List's philosophy of protection for tender new industries and markets.

This is only a very short summary. Almost every chapter of this author's *Economic Democracy*, updated and expanded 3rd edition, addresses some aspect of needed protection for world trade. But the appropriation of the wealth of the weak is not confined to world trade and we address in depth in previous work and in the just released volume, *Cooperative*

Capitalism: A Blueprint for Global Peace and Prosperity, the high need for protection of the weak within domestic economies.[29]

Protection is the norm for all wealthy nations both for their internal economies and in their trades with the world. Although a requirement under structural adjustment rules for weak nations on the periphery of empire, no powerful nation would ever leave its citizens to the predatory whim of global capital. If they did, their citizens would vote them right out of office.

Conscientious citizens would never tolerate their standard of living being maintained through arbitrarily laying claim to the wealth of others let alone the utilization of wholesale terrorism to accomplish those goals. So foreign policy of powerful nations must be kept secret. We next turn to how that was accomplished through establishing the greatest propaganda system the world has ever known to promote the free trade philosophy addressed above that was protecting the claims of powerful nations on the wealth of weak nations.

The exponential expansion or contraction of a nation's potential for accumulation of capital due to inequality of pay for equally-productive labor, the origins of *plunder-by-trade*, and the fact that Adam Smith free trade was an extension of *plunder-by-trade* is missing in both classical and neo-liberal economics. Only by building from a base of true economic history can one write realistic theories of economic development. That true economic history provides its own solutions.

Notes

[1] J.W. Smith, *Economic Democracy: The Political Struggle of the Twenty-First Century*, updated and expanded 3rd edition (www.ied.info/cc.html: The Institute for Economic Democracy, 2003), Chapter 1, for labor rates, citing, Doug Henwood, "Clinton and the Austerity - p. 628. Colin Hines and Tim Lang (Jerry Mander and Edward Goldsmith eds.) in *The Case Against the Global Economy and for A Turn Toward the Local* (San Francisco: Sierra Club, 1996), p. 487 say $24.90 an hour for the Germany and $16.40 for the U.S. When benefits are included German manufacturing wages rise to $30 and hour, America to $20 and hour and Britain to $15 (Richard C. Longworth, *Global Squeeze: The Coming Crisis of First-World Nations* (Chicago: Contemporary Books, 1999), p. 177. Russian wages will increase even greater when benefits are factored in. That increase would have to be factored into prices before it will change the wealth appropriation ratio.

[2] Karl Polanyi, *The Great Transformation* (Boston: Beacon Press, 1957), p. 277. Quoting the classics: Henri Pirenne, *Economic and Social History of Medieval Europe*. (New York: Harcourt, Brace, 1937) and Eli F. Heckscher's *Mercantilism*, 2 vol. (New York: The Macmillan Company, 1955).

[3] Immanuel Wallerstein, *The Origin of The Modern World System*, vol. 1 (New York: Academic Press, 1974), pp. 119-20. See also Paul Bairoch's, *Cities and Economic Development From the Dawn of History to the Present* (Chicago: University of Chicago Press, 1988).
For "plunder-by-trade," see William H. McNeill, *The Pursuit of Power* (Chicago: University of Chicago Press, 1982).

[4] Christopher Layne, "Rethinking American Grand Strategy," *World Policy Journal*, (Summer 1998), pp. 8-28.

5 Lewis Mumford, Technics and Human Development (New York: Harcourt Brace Jovanovich, 1967), p. 279; Kropotkin, Mutual Aid, Chapters 6 and 7; George Renard, Guilds of the Middle Ages (New York: Augustus M. Kelly, 1968), p. 35; Petr Kropotkin, The State (London: Freedom Press, 1987), p. 41; Dan Nadudere, The Political Economy of Imperialism (London: Zed Books, 1977), p. 186.

6 Barbara Tuchman, *The March of Folly* (New York: Alfred A. Knopf, 1984), pp. 130-31. For early mercantilist theory see Douglas A. Irwin, *Against the Tide: An Intellectual History of Free Trade* (Princeton, N.J.: Princeton University Press, 1996).

7 Adam Smith, *The Wealth of Nations* (New York: Random House, 1965), p. 607.

8 Friedrich List, *The National System of Political Economy* (Fairfield, NJ: Auguatus M.Kelley, 1977), pp. 9-33, 40-45, 56, 71-79, 345, Chapters 26, 27.

9 Smith, *The Wealth of Nations,* pp. 413, 426, 642. For free trade philosophy before Adam Smith, see Michael Perelman, *The Invention of Capitalism: Classical Political Economy and the Secret History of Primitive Accumulation* (London: Duke University Press, 2000) and Irwin, *Against the Tide*, Chapter 3.

10 List, *National System*, pp. 366-370.

11 Ibid, p. 73. Earlier theorists on protection against mercantilists were: Alexander Hamilton, 1791; Adam Muller, 1809; Jean-Antoine Chaptal, 1819 and Charles Dupin, 1827, see Paul Bairoch, *Economics and World History: Myths and Paradoxes* (Chicago: University of Chicago Press,

12 Ibid, p. 99.

13 Ibid, pp. xxvii-xxviii, 368-69.

14 Ibid, pp. 73-75.

15 Ibid, p. xxv.

16 Charles A. Beard, *An Economic Interpretation of the Constitution* (New York: Macmillan Publishing Co., 1941), p. 46. See also Michael Barratt Brown, *Fair Trade* (London: Zed Books, 1993), p. 20.

17 Beard, *Economic Interpretation*, pp. 46-47, 171, 173.

18 Richard Barnet, *The Rockets' Red Glare: War, Politics and American Presidency* (New York: Simon and Schuster, 1983), p. 40.

19 Philip S. Foner, *From Colonial Times to the Founding of the American Federation of Labor* (New York: International Publishers, 1982), p. 32; Smith, *Wealth of Nations*, pp. 548-49, Book IV, Chapters VII, VIII; William Appleman Williams, *Contours of American History* (New York: W.W. Norton & Company, 1988), pp. 105-17; Frederic F. Clairmont, *The Rise and Fall of Economic Liberalism* (Goa India: The Other India Press, 1996), p. 100; James Fallows, "How the World Works," *The Atlantic Monthly*. December 1993, p. 42.

20 Williams, Contours of American History, p. 221.

21 Williams, *Contours of American History*, pp. 192-97, 339-40; List, *National System*, especially pp. 59-65, 71-89, 92, 342, 421-22; Chapter XI; Herbert Aptheker, *The Colonial Era*, 2nd ed. (New York: International Publishers, 1966), pp. 23-24; Barnet, *The Rockets' Red Glare*, pp. 40, 60, 68. 21 34Dean Acheson, *Present at the Creation* (New York: W.W. Norton & Company, 1987), p. 7.

22 "The Three Marketeers," *Time*. February 15, 1999, pp. 34-42.

23 Stephen Gill, "The Geopolitics of the Asian Crisis," *Monthly Review* (March, 1999), pp. 1-9.

24 Peter Gowan, *The Global Gamble: Washington's Faustian Bid for World Dominance* (New York: verso, 1999), pp. 104-05.

25 J.W. Smith, *The World's Wasted Wealth 2*, (www.ied.info/cc.html: The Institute for Economic Democracy, 1994), pp. 244-45.

26 John Gray, *False Dawn* (New York: The Free Press, 1998), pp. 210-13, 217-18; see also p. 199.

27 Gowan, *The Global Gamble*, p. 96, see also pp. 95-138 and Richard C. Longworth, *Global Squeeze: The Coming Crisis of First-World Nations* (Chicago: Contemporary Books, 1999), pp. 225, 243.

28 Gray, *False Dawn*, pp. 217, 224-25.

29 Smith, *Economic Democracy*, updated and expanded 3rd edition.

3. The CIA Establishes the Greatest Propaganda Machine in History

> The great masses of the people in the very bottom of their hearts tend to be corrupted rather than purposely or consciously evil ... therefore ... they more easily fall a victim to a big lie than to a little one, since they themselves lie in little things, but would be ashamed of lies that were too big   -Adolph Hitler from *Mein Kampf*

Study a map of the world. Note the large areas where most of the world's resources are located, which is undeveloped and impoverished, and which consumes only 14% of the world's resources. Then note the small area of the world taken up by the *imperial-centers-of-capital* which has few resources—which is developed, wealthy and powerful—and which consumes 86% of the world's resources.[1] Obviously the major share of the wealth of the world is being claimed by a small, but powerful, group of nations.

Most violence around the world is over who will control those resources and thus who will control the *wealth-producing-process*. Because people are taught to be good, are good, and would not tolerate dishonesty and violence in their name, hiding this theft of others wealth is why governments of powerful nations must lie to its people.

After WWII, a shattered Europe no longer had the wealth and power to control its colonies that provided the resources to be transformed into Europe's wealth. If those colonies had broken free and gained control of their destiny, their resources would be converted into products and wealth for those emerging nations. They would have become wealthy while Europe, without natural resources, would have become impoverished. Thus independence was a serious threat to what all powerful nations termed their "national security."

After that war, most of the world's industrial and financial wealth was in America. Instead of championing the freedom of their sister colonies, the powerful and wealthy in America chose to support their war-shattered ethnic and religious cousins in Europe by suppressing the world's break for freedom. That suppression required the use of massive superior military power that killed very large numbers of people and impoverished many more. From the perspective of the people of the developing world, those suppressions of their freedom were very terrifying. The same practices against the "free" world by any nation or any group would have been labeled "terrorism."

Although most emerging nations were looking to America as their political model and for support in their break for freedom, they would soon recognize their expected protector was instead suppressing their freedom and they looked elsewhere for support. Any successful coalition outside the Western political and economic system would be a beacon to the emerging world. Thus, if the colonial world's break for freedom was to be suppressed, the rapidly developing Soviet Union had to be contained.

If a small country like Cuba gained its freedom and its living standards rose, the rest of the world would observe it. They would understand that it was their dependency which maintained their poverty and they would demand their freedom. Hence the otherwise incomprehensible destruction by the world's most powerful nations of small weak nations such as Korea, Vietnam, Chile, Nicaragua, El Salvador, Angola, Mozambique, the Congo, and Yugoslavia who all came close to gaining their freedom (Chapters 4, 5, and 6). The drumbeat of the West being under imminent threat of attack by these nations was a *strategy-of-tension* so that the citizens of these powerful nations would support the extremely violent and terrorizing suppression of those countries break for freedom

Few in the West realize the true dimension of covert violence and intrigue that has gone into controlling their own and others' "free" societies. Thus many will not believe that the covert and overt violent events we enumerate resulted from the national security policies of the "free" world. Therefore, we first provide a brief outline of how the image of a dangerous world was created (propaganda) so citizens, trained in the belief in their nation's goodness would remain unaware of, ignore, or accept, those covert activities.

The deeper history we are addressing—economic, financial, covert, and overt—is hidden only from citizens in the West. Having experienced it, the alert within societies that were the targets of covert and overt wholesale terrorism by the so-called "free" West are very aware. When the imperial centers are targeted at a much lower level of violence, it is rightly called terrorism.

Inoculating America, and much of the World, against philosophies of Full and Equal Rights

Americans have heard of their freedom, rights, and free press all their lives and to believe America had, and has, a propaganda system far more extensive than any empire in history is hard to accept. But, if our thoughts are to be totally free, we must go with the facts and understand the process of protecting wealth and power.

Peter Coleman describes how the Congress for Cultural Freedom, a worldwide writers' support group that had been covertly established and funded by the Central Intelligence Agency (CIA), created the belief within

Western populations that they were about to lose their freedom to terrorist totalitarian dictators:

> Five years after their victory in 1945, the Western democracies were about to lose the battle for Europe, but this time to Stalinist totalitarianism instead of Nazis. To combat this prospect, an intellectual guerrilla group was formed: over 100 European and American writers and intellectuals met in Berlin to establish the Congress for Cultural Freedom to resist the Kremlin's sustained assault on Western and liberal values. During the 1950s the Congress spread throughout the world, creating a network of affiliated national committees, a worldwide community of liberal intellectuals fiercely committed to democratic governance, but supported by grants which, unknown to *most* of them, originated in the Central Intelligence Agency. Through the Congress's influential publications, conferences, and international protests, it kept the issues of Soviet totalitarianism and liberal anti-Communism alive in a largely hostile environment.... It was finally dissolved in 1967 amid the revelations of its funding by the CIA.[2]

Frances Stoner Saunders, in *The Cultural Cold War: The CIA and the World of Arts and Letters*, tells us how every aspect of culture was covertly orchestrated to inoculate the so-called free world against any thoughts which might lead to a restructuring of the philosophical or legal base that was the foundation of current wealth and power:

> Whether they liked it or not, whether they knew it or not, there were few writers, poets, artists, historians, scientists or critics in post-war Europe whose names were not in some way linked to this covert enterprise.... Defining the Cold War as a 'battle for men's' minds' it stockpiled a vast arsenal of cultural weapons: journals, books, conferences, seminars, art exhibitions, concerts, awards.... Endorsed and subsidized by powerful institutions, this non-Communist group became as much a cartel in the intellectual life of the West as Communism had been a few years earlier (and [since it was the intellectual left that was being targeted for control through the establishment of a Non-Communist left] it included many of the same people).... It spied on tens of thousands of Americans, harassed democratically elected governments abroad, plotted assassinations, denied these activities to Congress, and, in the process, elevated the art of lying to new heights.[3]

All will deny it but, according to Frances Stoner Saunders and others cited, leading columnists, reporters, and politicians (Stewart Alsop, Walter Lippman, Averell Harriman, the Bundy brothers, and others) were social friends of CIA leaders, such as William Colby and Frank Wisner, and were in on the *Grand Strategy* of misinforming the public to prepare them for the Cold War. Frequently reporters were given news scoops for publishing CIA wordsmiths' distortions of reality. The Pike and Church Committee hearings of 1975 and 1976 exposed over 400 reporters as being on the CIA payroll. At $200 a month, they were cheaper than Prostitutes. Other reporters would follow up on those creations of reality and government agencies were all primed to support the story. With the CIA's listening posts all over the world, these propagandists' (how else would one describe reporters consciously misinforming a nation) reputations grew ever larger.

The CIA's *strategy-of-tension* to create fear so citizens would support the militarization of America was for their wordsmiths to create thousands of editorials to be sent to newspapers around the world for the editors to restructure and use as their own. Think-tanks and institutes were created, some associated with universities and some independent; which were funded and staffed with ideologically pure editors to further polarize Americans with fear. All this was done in the name of protecting peace, freedom, justice, and human rights.

The propaganda budget to create this fictitious reality absorbed most of the CIA's billions in funding. Those costs were greater than the budgets of AP, Reuters, and UPI even as those news agencies were the primary carriers of their creations. Over 170 foundations (many created by the CIA), the American Federation of Labor, and the Marshall Plan, funneled propaganda money all over the world.

The writings of Peter Coleman (his exposure of the Congress for Cultural Freedom cited above), Henry Luce, Isaih Berlin, Arthur Koestler, Sidney Hook, Reinhold Neibuhr, Robert Conquest, Bertrand Russell, Arthur Schlesinger, and many more, actually thousands more, were covertly coordinated to spread the same fear. Some of their books were bought by the tens of thousands by the CIA and spread around the world. "A central feature of this program was to advance the claim that it [propaganda] did not exist."[4]

Radio Free Europe, Radio Liberty, and the Voice of America, with 100 transmitters each, and stations beaming to Asia, the Middle East, and Latin America were CIA creations. As they were being run by occupation armies, news of political importance disseminated within Japan and Germany, including comic books, was primarily that of CIA wordsmiths.[5] The largest news agency in Germany and major media (radio stations, magazines, newspapers) in many countries were established by the CIA and staffed with ideologically pure editors. Wire services and publishing companies were covertly established, funded, and controlled to further spread the Cold War fear of imminent attack by dictatorial nations.

Dissident voices had to be silenced. Over 300 Hollywood stars and writers were blacklisted and their careers were destroyed. This was pointed out during the March 21, 1999, Academy Awards when the recipient of an Oscar was acknowledged by all major media as having testified against his friends to the House Un-American Activities Committee.

Professors were under greater assault than actors. The careers of thousands of professors and intellectuals were destroyed or badly damaged. Columbia University fired every professor accused under McCarthyism. Meanwhile the careers of those using the fabrications of CIA wordsmiths as factual history blossomed. Sincere professors researched this fraudulent history, wrote syntheses, and then referenced each other as reliable sources. In the created climate of fear, opposing views were unsaleable, thus unwritten. Over time, the CIA version became the only history inside or outside the university classroom.

Corporate-Funded Think-Tanks reinforce the CIA's *Mighty Wurlitzer*

Attorney William Schapp says the CIA

> alone—not to mention its counterparts in the rest of the American intelligence community—owned or controlled some 2,500 media entities all over the world. In addition, it has people ranging from stringers to highly visible journalists and editors in virtually every major media organization.[6] [To that we must add those controlled by the intelligence services of other nations.]

The process of controlling what is thought and what is written is now controlled by conservative foundations by selective funding and, with the belief of enemies lurking in every corner of the world firmly established, is even more effective than when controlled primarily by intelligence services:

> Spearheading the assault has been a core group of 12 conservative foundations: the Lynde and Harry Bradley Foundation, the Carthage Foundation, the Charles G. Koch, David H. Koch and Claude R. Lambe charitable foundations, the Phillip M. McKenna Foundation, The JM Foundation, The John M. Olin Foundation, the Henry Salvatori Foundation, the Sarah Scaife Foundation, and the Smith Richardson Foundation.... From 1992-94, they awarded $300-million in grants, and targeted $210-million to support a wide array of projects and institutions.... The 12 have mounted an impressively coherent and concerted effort to shape public policy by undermining—and ultimately redirecting—what they regard as the institutional strongholds of modern American liberalism: academia, Congress, the judiciary, executive branch agencies, major media, religious institutions, and philanthropy itself. They channeled some $80-million to right-wing policy institutions actively promoting an anti-government unregulated market agenda. Another $80-million supported conservative scholars and academic programs, with $27-million targeted to recruit and train the next generation of right-wing leaders in conservative legal principles, free-market economics, political journalism and policy analysis. And $41.5-million was invested to build a conservative media apparatus, support pro-market legal organizations, fund state-level think-tanks and advocacy organizations, and mobilize new philanthropic resources for conservative policy change.... Conservative foundations also provided $2,734,263 to right-of-center magazines between 1990 and 1993, including *The National Interest, The Public Interest, The New Criterion*, and *The American Spectator*.[7]

"With millions of dollars in funding, conservative institutions have taken" the political offensive on key social, economic, and regulatory policy issues.... These institutions have effectively repositioned the boundaries of national policy discussion, redefining key concepts, molding public opinion, and pushing for a variety of specific policy reforms.... These groups flood the media with hundreds of opinion editorials. Their top staff appears as political pundits and policy experts on dozens of television and radio shows across the country. And their lobbyists work the legislative arenas, distributing policy proposals, briefing papers, and position statements.... [The American Enterprise Institute has] ghost writers for scholars to produce op-ed articles that are sent to the one hundred and one cooperating newspapers—three pieces every two weeks.'... The Hoover Institution's public affairs office ... links to 900 media centers across the U.S. and abroad. The Reason Foundation ... had 359 television and radio appearances in 1995 and more than 1,500 citations in national newspapers and magazines. The Manhattan Institute has held more than 600 forums or briefings for journalists and policy makers on multiple public policy issues and concerns, from tort reform to federal welfare policy.... The Free Congress Foundation, in addition to its National Empowerment Television, is publishing *NetNewsNow*, a broadcast fax letter sent around the country to more than 400 radio producers and news editors.[8]

Although this book is focusing on foreign policy, it must be emphasized that corporations established and funded think-tanks to control both domestic policy and foreign policy.[9] Karen Rothmyer expands on Sally Covington's research:

'Layer upon layer of seminars, studies, conferences, and interviews [can] do much to push along, if not create, the issues, which then become the national agenda of debate.... By multiplying the authorities to whom the media are prepared to give friendly hearing, [conservative donors] have helped to create an illusion of diversity where none exists. The result could be an increasing number of one-sided debates in which the challengers are far outnumbered, if indeed they are heard at all.'.... [The Heartland Institute] introduced *Policy Fax* ... a revolutionary public policy fax-on-demand research service that enables you to receive, by fax, the full text of thousands of documents from more than one hundred of the nation's leading think-tanks, publications, and trade associations. *Policy Fax* is easy to use and it's free for elected officials and journalists.... The American Legislative Exchange Council and the newer State Policy Network provide technical assistance, develop model legislation, and report about communications activities and conferences. ALEC, well funded by private foundations and corporate contributors, is a powerful and growing membership organization, with almost 26,000 state legislators—more than one-third of the nation's total. The organization, which has a staff of 30, responds to 700 information requests each month, and has developed more than 150 pieces of model legislation ranging from education to tax policy. It maintains legislative task forces on every important state policy issue, including education, health care, tax and fiscal policy, and criminal justice.[10] [a]

---

[a] In "A Hostile Takeover" (*The American Prospect*, Spring 2003, pp. A16-A18) Martin Garbus explains how The Federalist Society for Law and Public Policy was highly successful in its purpose: packing the federal courts. We were able to condense how

Corporations buy up newspapers, TV stations, radio stations, and fund a massive array of think-tanks to feed the media. When these conglomerates are sold, ownership only moves to another center of power with the same security interests of protection of wealth and power.

True exposés of monopolies, such as Henry George's *Progress and Poverty,* have a very limited market while heavily funded schools of thought become a society's economic religion; all other beliefs are crowded to the margins. But powerbrokers know that progressive thoughts are out there. Today's neo-liberal philosophy was put in place specifically to suppress the fast expanding belief in Henry George's very sensible philosophy suggesting society collect the landrent (Chapter 8). That philosophy was suppressd through eliminating land as one of the three primary elements of production (land [natural resources], labor, and industrial capital). Land was lumped with industrial capital. Economic philosophy as now taught only requires labor and "capital". Both land and industrial capital disappeared into "capital".[11]

When revolution threatened Czarist Russia in 1917, Kerensky's caretaker government offered to convert the economy to the philosophy of Henry George. So most of the powerful know philosophies which provide for full rights to all people are available; which of course means they know their governments do not provide full rights. The revolutionists, following their own philosophy, overthrew the provisional government, and took over. No matter which philosophy Russia had adopted, communism or that of Henry George, it would have been a threat to capitalist nations, would have been tagged as a dictatorship, and it would have been contained.

In late February 2002, the establishment within the Pentagon of an Office of Strategic Influence (office of disinformation) to plant fraudulent and distorted news in the world press to control Muslim opinion worldwide was exposed. The media took the tack that this was something new. But it is not new. Every intelligence service (the U.S. has at least 14 such services, most nations have several) and state department of major countries practices it, and corporations and politicians practice it to control who will be elected and what laws will be written. To protect wealth and power, control of public opinion requires massive funds to be spent on intelligence services of "democratic" societies.

Very few corporations are directly involved in covertly controlling thoughts of others (locking society between *permitted-parameters-of-debate*) but there is a hard core that is. Trace the covert and overt foreign policy violence to its source and you arrive at that hard core. Trace the funding of the think-tanks which pour out the books and articles and the lobbyists

---

the beliefs of legislators, academia, and the media were controlled to protect wealth and power. The serious researcher can study Garbus's article for how the courts are similarly controlled.

who essentially write our laws and one arrives at the door of the same hard core. David Korten's book title, *When Corporations rule the World,* is quite accurate.

McCarthyism yet stills many Minds in Academia and the Media

The restoration of their reputation after the Cold War of those persecuted under McCarthyism is proof that the very people sworn to provide the nation with an honest education knew they were teaching a fabricated and fraudulent reality. University managers provided leaves of absence to professors to go to Washington and set up mind-controlling black-ops and accepted them back when they returned. As it was a creation of beliefs instead of descriptions of reality, all who knew and failed to inform others became propagandists just as surely as those that had taken leave of the university to set up this propaganda system.[12]

Enough films were produced by the CIA to "rival Hollywood studios."[13] Thousands of propaganda newsreels were produced and provided free to movie theatres for the public to watch. Older American citizens will remember those newsreels. Think-tanks were created, funded, and staffed by ideologues. These think-tanks and professors were coached and subsidized by intelligence agencies of several countries to write thousands of books. Tens of thousands of partly fraudulent to totally fraudulent articles were created by CIA wordsmiths and planted all over the world (700 articles were planted worldwide to control the world's view on the overthrow and assassination of Allende in Chile). Reporters became leading columnists through being provided news scoops in exchange for publication of this nonsense passed off as current history.

Thousands of books were written by sincere academics built from and citing that fraudulent literature. As that is where the market was, novels and movies by authors with no connection to governments were written and that deepened further the beliefs and hysteria of the propagandized audience. These books, articles, and movies became reality to Western citizens. Believing they were under imminent threat of attack by dictatorial, violent, and powerful communists, the propagandized masses, including the media and academia (with the exception of a few on the fringes and we want to remember that forcing alert professors out is what silenced the rest), gave their full support to the Cold War.[14]

All major Western governments of the *allied imperial-centers-of-capital* were busy creating the same *social-control-paradigms* (beliefs which society functions under) through writing the same distorted history. Social scientists are still using those fraudulent books and articles as the foundation of their research as they write today's textbooks. Sincere academics sued for the titles of those fraudulent books to be released. But the Supreme Court ruled that this would endanger the national security. Academia has never refuted the false history they created and those beliefs rule yet today.

History books teach us that, with the exception of communist nations, all countries were free after WWII. This was never true. We will be documenting thoroughly that most in the colonial world were unable to break free.

Buzzwords are the foundations of *social-control paradigms* (belief systems). Through the CIA's *Mighty Wurlitzer*, reality was reversed: buzzword labels of bad people were placed upon targeted emerging democracies attempting to provide their citizens with even more equality and rights than Western "democracies." While defending themselves from subversion, governments as democratic as America—many more democratic—were labeled *communist dictators, tyrants, subversives*, and *extremists* while the nations destabilizing them labeled themselves with the buzzwords of *peace, freedom, democracy, justice, equal rights*, and *majority rule*. Puppet dictators placed in power after those destabilizations, many who—with the support of the imperial centers—imposed extreme violence upon their citizens, had their images softened with the buzzword *"authoritarian."* The media faithfully parroted those buzzwords.

The reader will recognize those, and other, buzzwords in use yet today. McCarthyism has abated but has not disappeared. The enemies created during the Cold War by those buzzwords to retain the loyalty of the masses for these worldwide suppressions remain in our history, are parroted in our daily news as reality, and thus have immense impact on the way a citizenry views the world.

Eliminating the Washingtons, Jeffersons, Madisons, Lenins, Gandhis, and Martin Luther Kings of Emerging Nations

In nations fighting for their freedom, dictators were heavily funded, reactionary newspapers were established and funded, but still it appeared those countries might break free. Rising politicians who could not be controlled and were gaining popularity in those countries might be elected to higher offices so they had to be eliminated.

For years people have been organizing protests against the School of the Americas (nicknamed the School of Assassins and School of Coups) established in Panama in 1946. Note that this was one year before the CIA was established to support *policies-of-state* already in place. This training camp for death squad and coup leaders was booted out of Panama in 1984, moved to Fort Benning Georgia, and renamed the Western Hemisphere Institute for Security Operations. The name, of course, was only a cover for its real purpose; destabilizing progressive governments throughout Latin America.

As this is written 86 nuns, priests, veterans, students, grandmothers, and grandfathers are being sentenced for protesting at the gates of that death squad training (terrorist training) center operating in America. This is an annual event essentially unreported in the American media and, until it is shut down, there will be more in each of the coming years. The defendants were denied the right to use an international law defense but these courageous people would not be silenced and spoke forcefully on the atrocities committed worldwide by graduates of this terrorist training center.

Talking to ex-CIA agent Ralph McGehee I said, "America established and orchestrated those death squads." His instant response was, "Of course we did." On December 3, 2001—President Vicente Fox of Mexico admitted that Mexico kidnapped, tortured, and murdered, hundreds of "leftists" during the 1960s and 1970s. Leftists in any country, of course, are any other than the established right to hard right political powers who may gain a political following.

Feisal Mansoor of Sri Lanka informs us that "idealistic youths were being murdered by the SL state in 1987-1992, the elite did not move until one of their own (Richard De Zoysa, journalist and doyen of Colombo society) was taken away from his home at night and found the next morning shot through the head on a beach South of Colombo." Like the Inquisitions of the Middle Ages, the tortures and deaths abated when they reached into the ruling classes. Obviously orchestrated death squads have been, and are, operating in many countries we have not addressed (see below).

Due to indoctrination through the *Mighty Wurlitzer*, idealistic and honest people—such as you and I but who had not looked deeper into what was happening—thus established and orchestrated death squads which assassinated thousands of teachers, professors, labor leaders, cooperative leaders, and church leaders, the budding Washingtons, Jeffersons, Madisons, Lenins, Gandhis, and Martin Luther Kings of those countries. These totally non-violent people were the courageous few who, knowing their names would go on a terrorist death squad list, still stood up to lead. The purpose of propaganda is to hide truth so the CIA's *Mighty Wurlitzer* recorded many of these brave souls in history as the world's most evil people.

Imposing Beliefs upon Citizens Having Free Speech and a Free Press

To position themselves to be the first to obtain breaking news, major media personalities socialize with the major movers and shakers of government. These columnists, editors, and media owners dare not repeat any of the nation's secrets they learn from such social friends. To do so, would be to immediately be excluded from those social circles and their most precious resource, access to breaking news, would be lost. There was not much danger anyway; the *managers-of-state* designing this Cold War functioned just as you and I would. Most, if not all, allowed within the inner circles of power were already ideologically on the same wavelength.

As discussed above, many media personalities allowed within the inner circle of *managers-of-state* knew the plan was to misinform the public so as to gain support for the planned Cold War. These media giants then knowingly planted those created realities (*Soviet aggression, missile gaps, under imminent threat of attack, potential loss of your freedom,* et al.) designed to place fear in the hearts of the Western world.

Reporters assigned to the highest levels of government instinctively knew their accreditation would be withdrawn if they challenged the official view. When briefed, those reporters would dash for the phone to be the first to get the news out. This sensationalized news becomes lead articles in all media. In one day, whatever the government wants the people to believe is firmly implanted in the public mind. Only a few on the fringes would dare challenge what has now become accepted reality by an entire nation and much of the world.

Once the belief that the West was under imminent threat was firmly in place, the careers of any mainstream reporter who dared a serious exposé of the propaganda system would have been at high risk. Any media that dared publish a serious exposé would face a massive loss of both readers and advertising. No media or reporter will choose obvious suicide over survival by going with the flow.

Thus, once the desired fear was established in the public mind, maintaining that tension (*strategies-of-tension*) was not only easy, finding opposing views in the media of record ranged from difficult to impossible. Multiply these carefully crafted versions of world events by thousands of times and one arrives at today's view of the world. Only on the margins of society can one find media personalities and writers addressing the terrors endured by people (thousands tortured and millions killed) facing the direct actions of security policies of *imperial-centers-of-capital*.

While the Western world was bathed in a view of their generosity and efforts for world peace, the worldwide covert destabilizations were frightening (terrorizing) to those facing the brunt of America's and other *imperial-centers-of-capital's* national security policies. The overt wars, the real reasons (control of resources and the *wealth-producing-process*) also hidden by the massive propaganda of Western generosity and others' violence, were far more violent and terrifying.[15]

Access to Resources and Control of the *Wealth-Producing-Process* was threatened

When China won its revolution in 1949, loss of control of the world's resources and the *wealth-producing-process* seemed imminent. To retain that control, National Security Council Directive 68 (NSC-68) was signed by President Truman on April 12, 1950. That master plan (actually only an affirmation and expansion of the top secret policies of 1947; NSC-4, NSC-4A and NSC-10/2) officially became America's secret policy of covert and overt financial, economic, political, and military, warfare.[16]

This directive called for increasing the U.S. arms budget from $13.5-billion to $46.5-billion (350%). Allowing for inflation, that is the same $300-billion annual budget (1990 dollars) with which America suppressed the world's break for freedom.

Dean Acheson's memoir, *Present at the Creation,* unwittingly exposes NSC-68 as a *Grand Strategy* for increasing the military budget of the United States by 350% to wage covert and overt wars (addressed in the next chapter) to suppress the colonial world's break for freedom:

> Western Europe ... shattered by its civil war, was disintegrating politically, economically, socially, and psychologically. Every effort to bestir itself was paralyzed by two devastating winters and the overshadowing fear of the Soviet Union no longer contained by the stoppers on the east, west, and south—Japan, Germany, and British India.... It was in this period [the first 3 years after the beginning of the Cold War] that we awakened fully to the facts of the surrounding world and to the scope and kind of action required by the interests of the United States; the second period, that of President Truman's second administration, became the time for full action upon those conclusions and for meeting the whole gamut of reactions—favorable, hostile, and merely recalcitrant foreign and domestic—that they produced. In the first period, the main lines of policy were set and begun; in the second, they were put into full effect amid the smoke and confusion of battle.... *The purpose of NSC-68 [the master plan for the Cold War] was to so bludgeon the mass mind of "top government" that not only could the president make a decision but that the decision could be carried out.*[17] (Emphasis added.)

Career CIA agent Ralph McGehee concluded:

> "The CIA is not now nor has it ever been a central intelligence agency. It is the covert action arm of the President's foreign policy advisers. In that capacity it overthrows or supports foreign governments while reporting "intelligence" justifying those activities. It shapes its intelligence ... to support presidential policy. Disinformation is a large part of its covert action responsibility, and the American people are the primary target of its lies."[18]

To retain the support of the citizenry through misinformation, Congress (even those with security clearances), academia, and the media must also be fed a fictitious view of the world. McGehee, whose job was in part testifying to congressional committees, claimed that "he has never once seen a CIA official tell the truth to Congress. Instead there is a steady stream of lies."[19] Thus good people in government are misinformed and unwittingly impose violence on innocent people.

There are just and necessary covert operations such as those by the Office of Strategic Studies (OSS) during WWII. However OSS officers, the primary designers of post-WWII covert actions, and other Western intelligence services had been carrying out major covert operations to suppress the freedom of colonial nations well before the CIA was officially established.

These operations do not have the moral justification of those carried out in the Great War (Greece, thousands of patriots who had kept two-thirds of Greece out of German hands were slaughtered. The French in Vietnam: 20,000 killed in Haiphong Harbor alone and another million killed before America took over to slaughter another 3-million. The Dutch reclaiming Indonesia: 150,000 died. Britain reclaiming Malaysia: thousands killed. Ninety Thousand killed in one bombardment alone in Madagascar's suppression of its bid for freedom.) Powerful nations do not admit mistakes or aggressions. These and the destabilizations described in the next three chapters are wholesale state terrorisms that simply cannot be admitted or discussed.

China, one-fifth of the world's people, gained their freedom in 1949. This created consternation among American *managers-of-state*. They knew well they stood to lose control of the world's resources and the *wealth-producing-process* if those breaks for freedom succeeded. The State Department studied hard through the fall and winter and the learning experiences of suppressing insurgencies since 1945 were codified on April 12, 1950 into NSC-68.

But the world was at peace and the *managers-of-state* admitted that neither the American Congress nor the American people would accept an increase of even $1-billion a year for military purposes and NSC-68 called for an additional $33-billion per year ($300-billion in 2003 dollars).[20]

Immediate action was required and NSC-68 signed in 1950 was the marching order. Within two months of the finalization of master plan for the Cold War, the Congress for Cultural Freedom—to control the beliefs of the imperial centers—was established; McCarthyism—to suppress dissenters in academia, the media, and the government—surfaced; and the Korean War—proving communists were bent on world conquest—broke loose.[21] These were not accidental events, they were part of the *Grand Strategies* to create fear and tension (*strategies-of-tension*) so as to obtain the backing of the Western world's citizens for covert and overt wars the plans' designers knew were going to cost a lot in lives and wealth.

People are moral and good. The fact that America and Europe were embarking on a very violent foreign policy had to be hidden from their own citizens. Their success can be measured by this policy being unknown to most citizens in those parts of the world upon which that violence was imposed.

The CIA's *Mighty Wurlitzer* and McCarthyism, which painted any dissenting opinion as communist, meant anyone courageous enough to be objective and intellectually balanced faced political, social, and career suicide. Even today the political spectrum of discourse in the *imperial-centers-of-capital* remains narrow.

Controlling Elections Worldwide

The potential loss of the imperial centers by the vote required controlling elections, especially in France and Italy. Though financing another nation's election is illegal in America and every other nation, massive funds were spent for that control and it required more than money.

Many leaders of partisans who had fought against Hitler and Mussolini were communist and these heroes would easily win elections. To prevent the only effective political force left in Italy from ruling, Mafia leaders were released from Mussolini's prisons, armed, and placed in charge of the cities as the allies marched up the Italian peninsula.[22]

America's CIA funded programs for discrediting Italian labor politicians while supplying election money to hard-right politicians. Operation Gladio, practicing a terrorist *strategy-of-tension* through planting bombs and blaming it on the "Reds" was a CIA operation. When uncovered, this covert operation was found to have 139 buried caches of explosives and weapons. The bombing of the Bologna railway station, killing 84 people, was one of hundreds of Gladio bombings that killed several hundred people and injured many more.[23]

Operation Statewatch oversaw Operation Gladio and numbered from a high of 2,000 operatives in Italy to a low of 400 in Belgium. It operated worldwide using the same *strategies-of-tension* to discredit socialist elements throughout Europe and Japan and other nations.[24] As virtually no one in the upper echelons of government thought the Soviet Union was going to invade the West or anyone else, even though this is what their citizens were being told, these were not stay-behind-forces to overthrow an invasion as claimed when exposed. These covert forces were to control elections and take back governments by force if they were lost by the vote.

These are not isolated events. *Strategies-of-tension*, blaming the opposition for mayhem (right by CIA training manuals), is standard operating procedure for many governments.[25] Italy's *managers-of-state* decided in secret to place Mussolini in power. The famed march of the black shirts three days later was the *strategy-of-tension* which provided the cover for that transfer of power. Germany's famous Reichstag fire which polarized support for laws establishing the powerbrokers' planned fascist dictatorship was an event several months *after* Hitler had been given power in a secret January meeting of German powerbrokers. President George Bush's Patriot Act put in place after 9/11/2001 is copied from Hitler's Enabling Act put in place after the Reichstag fire and hundreds of thousands of innocent people were imprisoned and some thousands were executed. The taking away of rights under that act defined Fascism. Just as in foreign policy, these internal suppressions of rights were made possible by the Reichstag fire and similar *strategies-of-tension.*

Strategies-of-tension to gain the loyalty of the citizenry in elections or wars is an old political trick. We will be addressing later how the Korean war, where this author spent his military service, was a *strategy-of-tension* so voters would accept the massive expenditures and loss of life required to suppress the world's break for freedom as laid out in the master plan for the Cold War, NSC-68, drafted by President Truman's State Department only two months earlier. The loss of life for this state-sponsored terrorism (wholesale terrorism) was between 12-million and 15-million. Hundreds of millions more died from starvation and disease due to destruction of their economies.[a] These were "terrifying" events for those targeted

The ease with which poverty can be eliminated through *democratic-cooperative-capitalism,* as will be demonstrated in the concluding chapters, proves that this control of resources and the *wealth-producing-process* through military power is the direct cause of the world's poverty.

Destabilizing Internal Political Groups

Preventing other political voices from being heard required destabilizing progressive internal political groups in all allied countries:

> The House Un-American Activities Committee and McCarthyism and the FBI's Operation COINTELPRO were replays of the post-WWI shattering of the forming solid labor front (the destruction of the Wobblies [International Workers of the World, IWW]). CHAOS, Cable Splicer, and Garden Plot were American internal destabilizations by military intelligence services carried out in cooperation with the FBI. This synchronized efforts of political police became urgent when over 500 periodicals critical of the Vietnam War, with a peak circulation of 7-million, sprang up. Through *agent provocateurs, counterfeited letters, planted narcotics, false arrests, poison-pen letters, malicious articles planted in the press, blacklisting from jobs, harassment, electronic surveillance, burglary, mail tampering,* and *other internal strategies of terrorist tension,* hundreds of budding political groupings were destabilized. In March 1998, the Socialist Workers Party (SWP) and Young Socialist Alliance (YSA) won a 15-year legal battle against the FBI for decades of spying, harassment, and disruptions as just described. During that trial, these two groups—out of hundreds that were spied upon and/or destabilized—proved that the FBI had conducted 20,000 days of wiretaps and 12,000 days of listening "bugs" between 1943 and 1963 as well as

---

[a] The official tally of war dead during that timespan is 21-million. Perhaps more than the 12-million to 15-million were also victims of the Cold War but the covert actions were buried so deep they have not been detected.

208 burglaries of offices and homes of their members with the photographing or theft of 9,864 private documents. This is only two groups out of hundreds and only the events that were proven. The American government was ordered to pay Fred Hampton's family $3-million when it was proven in court that his December 4, 1969 death in Chicago was a political assassination resulting from these suppressions. After 27 years in a California prison, Geronimo Pratt was ordered released and he collected $4.5-million when, though other excuses were used by the courts, he essentially proved that his arraignment and conviction for murder was a conspiracy between the FBI and the Los Angeles District Attorney's Office. The FBI had him under surveillance and knew he was 400 miles away at the time of the murder and the prosecutor knew that his witnesses were government informers with no credibility. Proving these conspiracies required some of the longest court cases in American History. As few such targeted people had either resources or determined people behind them, many more innocent people had their lives destroyed by what can only properly be called America's political police, surely some of those totally innocent political prisoners died there and others are still there.[26]

Serious dissident political groups within an *imperial-center-of-capital* cannot be permitted. Once they gain substantial followers, they will be elected to local, state, and national office, their independent voices will be on local and national media, and that will challenge and weaken the *social-control-paradigms* put in place to protect wealth and power.

Dissident voices over the mass media would seriously impede the ability of *managers-of-state* to suppress either internal dissent or the periphery's break for freedom. Thus, for exercising their democratic rights, innocent people have been systematically monitored, systematically destabilized, some were sent to prison, and their voices were silenced.

Opposing philosophies were not permitted by either Cold War bloc. Alternative thoughts were taught negatively and as dictatorial, impractical, and violent. Loyalty oaths and the threat of job loss, as well as peer pressure, assured the weeding out of professors with independent thought.

These gross fabrications are not only a major part of Western literature and history; *they are Western literature and history*. After the Cold War, major universities officially restored the good name of those whose careers had been destroyed (most were dead by then), proving their innocence was known from the beginning.

One would think the organs of social power (academia, politics, and the media) would now be recovering from that suppression of free speech and free thought. But the parroting of the creations of intelligence service wordsmiths by all media during the destabilization and shattering of Yugoslavia, Afghanistan, and Iraq addressed below, and especially in the hysteria of the 9/11/2001 terrorist attacks on the World Trade Center and the Pentagon, give no indication that either true free speech or true free thought will be permitted.

America having a propaganda system far more extensive than most empires in history is hard to accept. But, after reading this book, read Mark Lane's *Plausible Denial: Was the CIA Involved in the Assassination of JFK*; L. Fletcher Prouty's *JFK: The CIA, Vietnam And The Plot to Kill Kennedy*; William Pepper's *An Act of State: The Execution of Martin Luther King*, and Philip Willan's *Puppet Masters: The Political Use of Terrorism in Italy*.

In Prouty's authoritative books (he was 1-of-3 who wrote the how-to book on U.S. covert actions) one will learn how staged violence (a *strategy-of-tension*) is used worldwide to control the beliefs of voters and thus control elections both on the periphery of empire and within the imperial centers. When a *strategy-of-tension* fails and a power-structure is faced with loss of power, actual violence is used—including assassinations of leaders of nations.

Public knowledge of each violent event is controlled through carefully crafted press releases before, during, and following those implementations of *policies-of-state*. Lee Harvey Oswald was effectively fingered as the culprit even though the FBI had quickly ascertained the identities of President Kennedy's actual CIA assassins (see below). Because the plotters obviously reached high into government circles and the entire government would come crashing down, they did not dare move on this information.[a]

Members of the House Select Committee on Assassinations sat on this same information when they learned those same names from the same sources in 1978; but America's vaunted institutions—the Justice Department, the media, the universities, and its political leaders—failed to

---

[a] Even though in charge of governments or departments of governments, these are just mortal men. Not even President Franklin D Roosevelt dared do anything when General Smedley Butler exposed that an organization composed of some of the wealthiest people in the United States had approached him to lead an overthrow of the American government and set up a fascist government as was being done all over Europe at the time. Besides there were a lot more skeletons in the U.S. government's closet than President Kennedy's assassination. If that assassination had been truly investigated, many powerful people would have been destroyed. Those people knew where the skeletons of any who dared attack them were. It is unlikely these people would go down without taking their attackers with them and America's Fascist covert violence all over the world and control of the media worldwide would likely have come to the surface. Both the CIA and the FBI knew all about each others' illegal activities addressed above. So not only was there already an unwritten agreement that neither would expose the other but each must cooperate to suppress any evidence of the other's illegal activities. That suppression of evidence and placing all blame elsewhere was the order of the day for all—the FBI, the CIA, the Warren Commission, the House Select Committee on Assassinations, and the entire U.S. government. Against such a phalanx of power, the media dutifully fell in line. Though the American people had accepted without question many false realities imposed upon them, to their credit, the majority believed the assassination was a conspiracy. But the propaganda apparatus had accomplished its purpose, through the mechanisms of collective denial citizens looked everywhere for those conspirators except where they were, right in the top leadership of the American government, the U.S. military, and the CIA.

inform the public even when everything the FBI and the House Select Committee knew was proven in a court of law when one of the assassins sued the *Spotlight* for publishing his name as one of those professional killers.)

Those assassins were named in the courtroom of Judge James W. Kehoe (verdict February 5, 1985), United States District Court, Miami, Florida, case number 80-1121-civ-JWK, E Howard Hunt [of Watergate fame], plaintiff, versus Liberty Lobby, defendant.

It was actually CIA agent E Howard Hunt's lawyers who irretrievably damaged their own client by asking specifically who these assassins were and what the witness knew of their activities and whereabouts as they organized and carried out the assassination. Claudia Furiati came up with the same names as the assassins when she was allowed access to Cuban intelligence files to write her book, *ZR Rifle: The Plot to Kill Kennedy and Castro*.

Part of the CIA's plans to overthrow the Cuban government included control of information reaching the people as that overthrow unfolded and all was in place for history to be written that this externally coached and financed invasion was an internal Cuban revolution.

When the Cuban overthrow collapsed at the Bay of Pigs and President Kennedy refused to rescue this covert operation with American air power, the Cubans of Miami and their CIA handlers were furious. To them President Kennedy was a traitor to what they viewed was a fight for the survival of the world as they knew it.

Being hardened to orchestrating death squad activity worldwide, these angry agents, certainly under orders from leaders very high in the American government, assassinated President Kennedy just as they had orchestrated the assassination of thousands of other independent thinkers and a few leaders worldwide so the imperial nations would not lose control of the world. The same propaganda machinery that was in place to control the world's belief in the fiction of how the intended overthrow of the Cuban government was an internal event was turned to controlling the world's belief in who assassinated President Kennedy.

We address the suppression of the truth of this assassination in some depth because the very idea that such *social-control-paradigms* are in place in an acclaimed "free country" is so hard to believe even when solidly proven in a court of law. By reading this book and the above listed books one can understand how and why the so-called "free press" failed to inform its readers and listeners. Mark Lane explains how, when the above trial concluded, the jury foreman, Leslie Armstrong, "simply, eloquently, and painstakingly" explained to waiting print, radio, and television reporters that

> the evidence was clear ... the CIA had killed President Kennedy, Hunt had been a part of it, and the evidence, so painstakingly presented, should now be examined by

the relevant institutions of the United States Government so that those responsible for the assassinations might be brought to justice.[27]

Then Lane points out that the a local Miami television station that evening reported only that Hunt had lost a libel case and had ignored the jury foreman's eloquent description of the historic importance of this case. She challenged that station on their reporting. Her words were then accurately reported by that one station but were ignored by all other media, local and national. In contrast, Hunt's winning of the first trial where none of this explosive testimony was given and which was of no historic importance to anyone was widely reported.

William F. Pepper's *An Act of State: The Execution of Martin Luther King* was released just before this manuscript went to the printer. Here too we learn that, in a suit brought by the King family against one of the assassins and others unnamed, it had been proven in Judge Swearingen's Courtroom in Memphis, Tennessee, between November 15, 1999 and March 2000, that Martin Luther King had been assassinated by elements of the Memphis police and the Tennessee State Police with the entire operation overseen by Army Intelligence.[28]

King's assassination was a part of the now well-known Operation COINTELPRO which was established specifically to destabilize rising political groups. William F. Pepper was the King family's lawyer and we encourage the reader to read the story of the 70-plus witnesses bringing the assassination to light. One can only conclude that aristocracy's violent suppression of any who threaten their wealth and power is alive and well in Western democracies.

After Mark Lane's exposure of the CIA being behind President Kennedy's assassination I dismissed the other cited theorists. But the dynamite testimony of President Johnson's mistress (never used so as to avoid the taint of conspiracy theorists) makes it clear most of those private citizens were each tracing a part of the many threads of power directly involved in that assassination. Some of those same powerbrokers were also behind King's assassination. According to her testimony to Mark Lane (unused), those movers and shakers met to plan King's demise less then a month after the threat of President Kennedy shutting down their war plans was eliminated.[29] The media was just as silent on this exposure of assassination of African-American leaders by their own government as they had been about the real assassins of John F. Kennedy.

We will learn below that assassinations of up and coming leaders in periphery countries by death squads is standard practice. Now we have learned that this is also standard practice within the imperial centers. Units within the intelligence communities are specially trained for these jobs, the relevant government structures stand ready to cover it up (plausible denial, the title of Lane's book, but better explained in Pepper's), and the media, local and regional police, and the judicial system are, just as you or I would be, too cowed to expose what they know.

Bobby Kennedy was loved by Americans as much as John F. Kennedy. If he was elected president (and he had just won the California primary the evening he was assassinated) he would have had the will, the knowledge, and the power to expose the true assassins of his brother. That could not be permitted.[30]

We understand why it is so hard to believe that a free media does not inform the public. But that they do not is reality. In *The Best Democracy that Money can Buy* (2003), Greg Palast provides many examples with solid evidence of massive corruption that would have ended the careers of important politicians if exposed but were glossed over and ignored. Through his efforts these stories get on British television but do not get on Americas TV. Any American who wishes to stay fully informed in his or her own country should study his website, www.gregpalast.com.

How and why the true assassins got away with this can be summed up in two sentences: In *Economic Democracy: The political struggle of the 21st-Century*, we learned that anyone who exposed that Japan was running a pure mercantilist controlled economy and their company would be totally ostracized and destroyed. In the same way in America if anyone in the media or academia were ever a threat to exposing the system they would immediately face the full force of the system and be ostracized to the margins of society or (as we see by the Kennedy and King assassinations) worse.

By studying the above books and this author's books one will begin to understand how *social-control-beliefs* are imposed upon an acclaimed "free press" and academia who then, largely unwittingly, impose it upon a population whose government, educational institutions, and press claim to be honest recorders of history.[a]

---

[a] For clear illumination as to who killed President Kennedy, first read the solidly authoritative Mark Lane, *Plausible Denial: Was the CIA Involved in the Assassination of JFK?* (New York: Thunder Mouth Press, 1991); William F. Pepper, *An Act of State: The Execution of Martin Luther King* (New York: Verso, 2003), p. 127 and Claudia Furiati, *ZR Rifle: The Plot to Kill Kennedy and Castro* (Melbourne: Ocean Press, 1994). For further information read Mathew Smith, *Say Goodbye to America: The Sensational and untold Story of the Assassination of John F. Kennedy* (London: Mainstream Publishing, 2001); L. Fletcher Prouty, *JFK: The CIA, Vietnam, And the Plot to Kill Kennedy* (New York: Carol Publishing, 1992); For a view of how the CIA used terrorism and assassinations all over the world, including Europe, to protect the old imperial-centers-of-capital, read Philip Willan's *Puppet Masters: The Political Use of Terrorism in Italy*. After reading those four books, one can spot the solid evidence in the following books, pass over where they go down wrong trails, and track how the powerful accomplished the massive cover-up of Kennedy's true killers: Jim Garrison, *On the Trail of the Assassins* (New York: Sheridan Square Press, 1988); Walt Brown, *Treachery in Dallas* (New York: Carroll & Graf, 1995); Harrison Edward Livingston, *Killing the Truth: Deceit and Deception in the JFK Case* (New

Most Professors and Intellectuals are locked into Protecting Empire

During the Cold War, dissident professors were silenced.[31] Due to peer pressure, desire for advancement, and even job insecurity, most progressive professors in the university will, understandably, not challenge the official line. They are conscientious and sincere. But if anyone has any doubts about residual McCarthyism and peer pressure control consider the statement of an assistant professor who was approached by another professor to help research this history: "It would be suicidal to research such concepts."

French economic graduate students understood that economic theory as taught had no relation to reality. In the fall of 2000 they revolted and academic administrators agreed to address what heretofore had been "controversial" subjects. Twenty-seven Ph.D. economic students at the University of Cambridge, UK, signed a similar, but milder, letter of protest in 2001.

Before the 9/11/2001 terrorist attack on the World Trade Center and the Pentagon, alternative thoughts were surfacing. However those stirring thoughts were only a whisper against the thunder of *social-control paradigms* that have been carefully cultivated by the *managers-of-state* of powerful nations for 50 years, no for centuries. The terror unleashed by that bombing may regress society back to the intellectual silence of the Cold War.

York: Carroll & Graf, 1993); Jim Marrs, *Crossfire: The Plot that Killed Kennedy* (New York: Carroll & Graf, 1989); Anthony Summers, *Conspiracy* (New York: Paragon House, 1989). Those books and a documentary, "The Men Who Killed Kennedy," made in Britain for release on the twenty-fifth anniversary of Kennedy's assassination (but self-censored by the American media) was not shown in the U.S. until 11 years later, leave little doubt it was a political assassination (New Video Group, 250 Park Ave. S., NY, NY 10010, 212-532-3392, catalog number AAE-21201 through 21206, or A&E Home Video, Box Hv1, 233 E. 45th St, NY, NY 10017). See also Oliver Stone's outstanding move JFK, Prouty is the man X in that movie which would have been better yet, actually complete and unchallengeable, with the information of Mark Lane and Claudia Furiati. As we have pointed out, the American government would have fallen if the major media had alerted its citizens that key leaders of the American government, the U.S. military, and the CIA assassinated their president. Perhaps not even Oliver Stone had the courage to alert the masses that the true Assassins of President Kennedy were known and had been named in a court of law. We now understand a little better how a society's deepest secrets are kept from the masses. Knowledge of such truths mean revolutions and a revolution may destroy society as we know it.

Protecting Wealth and Power through Creation of Enemies

Every society has its enemies and its friends. The belief in an enemy is consistently strengthened by the use of demeaning buzzwords—infidels, savages, the red peril, dictators, terrorists, et al. This functions as a social-survival-mechanism. Many, actually almost all, gentle cultures that did not follow those rules of defense of their culture do not exist today. They were displaced by violent cultures. Looking at it from a Darwinian point of view, it is survival of the meanest, not necessarily the fittest.

Also crucial for survival of a society are gentle, kind, and proud words to describe one's friends and compatriots. From each society's perspective, they are right and they are good. But, from the other society's perspective, it is your society which is bad and theirs is good. The common belief is that these differences are religious, cultural, and ideological. But our books have thoroughly shown that the causes are really economics, wealth, and power addressed through *policies-of-state*.

The Inquisitions

The terrors of the Inquisitions during the Middle Ages were created by the *Mighty Wurlitzer* of the church. Roman emperors Constantine and Theodosius I, in the 4th-Century AD, made the Catholic Church the Roman State religion. Over time, about 700 years, all high offices of the church, bishops, cardinals, and the Pope, were taken over by aristocracy. The First and Second Estates had become one. Through that alliance of aristocratic and religious powers, the practice of purchasing one's way out of purgatory became rampant.

In the 11th and 12th centuries, returning Crusaders brought back with them branches of Christianity that did not require the purchase of one's salvation. The Church stood to shrink rapidly when other Christian churches offered free salvation. The enormous wealth and power of the Roman church was at stake.

The largest of these Christian churches were the Cathars and Waldensians (similar to today's Protestants). Isolated burning at the stake of heretics coalesced in the 12th-Century into the founding of the Franciscan and Dominican Mendicant Orders to preach against heresy. In the 13th-Century, the Lantern Council listed "clause by clause" heretical interpretations of the faith and the formal Inquisition was born.

Heresy was primarily targeted at subjects who believed in those threatening competing Christian sects. Under the cries of *infidels, heretics,* and more, many were killed in battles to take over their property (remember, it was an alliance of Church and state). Over 500,000 were burned at the stake. The Cathars disappeared and only a few Waldensians were left. Jews survived modestly and the Muslims grew strong but only outside the borders of Christianity. "Only the fear of losing power acquired over a period of a thousand years can satisfactorily explain such violent reactions."[32]

The Eradication of the Knights Templar

The Knights Templars formed in 1119 to protect pilgrims to the Holy Land. No group could claim more loyalty to the Church. Over time, they became very powerful and immense wealth was bestowed upon them by the Church and secular powers. Later kings and nobles became jealous of these commoners wealth and power. In 1305, King Philip IV of France and other nobles gained the backing of the Pope for the destruction of the Templars. They spread vicious rumors and

> on the night of the 13th of October, [1307], all the Templars in the French dominions were simultaneously arrested.... They were accused of worshipping an idol covered with an old skin, embalmed, having the appearance of a piece of polished oil-cloth. "In this idol," we are assured, "there were two carbuncles for eyes, bright as the brightness of heaven, and it is certain that all hope of the Templars was placed in it: it was their sovereign god, and they trusted in it with all their heart." They are accused of burning the bodies of the deceased brethren, and making the ashes into a powder, which they administered to the younger brethren in their food and drink, to make them hold fast their faith and idolatry; of cooking and roasting infants, and anointing their idols with the fat; of celebrating hidden rites and mysteries, to which the young and tender virgins were introduced, and of a variety of abominations too absurd and horrible to be named.[33]

Few citizens will stand up to the power of Church and government. Through being portrayed as an enemy, and over 2,000 confessing under torture, the powerful and beloved Templars were destroyed in only 9 years. Just as with the elimination of Cathars and Waldensians, the creators of these vicious falsehoods then owned those valuable properties.

The Inquisitorial Suppression of the Illuminati

In 1776, the year of the American Revolution, Professor Adam Weishaupt of the University of Ingolstadt in Bavaria (Germany) established the Bavarian Illuminati ("enlightened ones"). Rather than a terrorist group threatening one's peace, the Illuminati were attempting to expand the rights of the people just as was the American Revolution. In 1789, the French Revolution portended even far greater gains in rights for the masses.

As a gain in rights for the masses meant a lowering of the excessive rights (and wealth) of the church and aristocracy, the church and allied secular powers again faced a crisis. The war cry went out: "Look out for the Illuminati! Look out for the Illuminati! They want to take over your country! Your church! The world!" Of course, all who lived through WWII and the Cold War will recognize that the Germans heard the same words against different enemies and that the "free" West heard the same words against Germans and later against the Soviet Union.[34]

To lay claim to their wealth and gain the loyalty of the masses, the Czarist Secret Police demonized the Jews. This was only the umpteenth time a power-structure had done that. But it was they who created the fraudulent *Protocols of the Learned Elders of Zion*, outlining the Jewish plan to rule the world, which extremists still use today to demonize the Jews.[35]

Of course, every major threat is demonized as wanting to rule the world. Napoleon was demonized as such by aristocracy and the Church and that is how he is recorded in history today. But who ruled the world? Aristocracy and the Church of course.[a] When Britain ruled much of the world Germany was demonized as wanting to rule the world. Though now allied together, during the fist half the 20th-Century those *imperial-centers-of-capital* were demonizing each other as wanting to rule the world. The second half of that century those now allied imperial centers were demonizing the embattled Soviet Union as wanting to rule the world.

One need not give any more examples. It is virtually the history of the world. Every nation or allied group of nations gains the loyalty of their people by portraying a targeted nation as an implacable enemy. Though many do fight for their freedom and rights, almost universally, the party thundering the loudest is not really being threatened by anyone. It is they who are suppressing others, almost always it is they who are laying claim to someone else's wealth, and that thunder of an enemy is only to maintain the loyalty of the masses to protect that wealth appropriation process. It is the loss of control of the *wealth-producing-process* and the gaining of others of their share of that wealth that is the real threat.

The alert among the suppressed masses understand this. As a group they have no hope of attaining a quality life, know they have no power, and a few get very angry. In desperation, hopelessness, anger, and having nothing to lose, they turn to terror to protect not themselves but their people.

Through equal rights providing the opportunities for a quality life style that anger can be contained and dissipated. *Democratic-cooperative-capitalism*, as this book is proposing, increases economic efficiency equal to the invention of money, the printing press, and electricity. That efficiency can provide the necessary improvement in quality of life.

---

[a] As proof that the fear was of an expansion of rights for the people, not the fear that Napoleon wanted to rule the world, the Napoleonic Codes spread throughout Europe triggered the slow collapse of Feudalism. Those democratic codes are the foundation laws of over 30 countries today. Aristocracy's fear of increased rights for the masses proved right. The masses still do not have full rights and powerbrokers are just as afraid of the common people attaining full rights as aristocracy was 200 years ago.

That capitalism, as structured, is efficient is only a belief imposed through the educational system for centuries to protect wealth and power. Since the wealth and power of university trustees and that of financially supportive alumni are at stake, almost all professorial rewards go to those who protect the system and the sanctions are heavy against those who would take an opposing stand. Thus this protection of wealth and power is unwittingly provided by the university system yet today.

With the passage of America's Patriot Act, knowledge of how propaganda works in the world's so-called "free" press is sobering. That post 9-11 act is a recreation of Germany's post Reichstag fire Enabling Act under which Hitler took all rights away from, and jailed and executed, targeted people. The parallels are apparent. Entire ethnic groups are targeted in both cases, databases of potential enemies are created, those enemies are watched by a newly reorganized or newly created internal intelligence service, neighbors are asked to report on neighbors, people have disappeared with—as of this writing—no rights to lawyers, torture of suspects is openly discussed even as it is obviously practiced but not admitted. It is estimated that in the War on Terrorism America has over 3,000 people from various countries so held (January 2003).

If that does not seem like many people we must remember that the overwhelming masses of the German people were not targeted. Instead they were told that it was they who were under threat. It was not until Fascism was defeated that the excesses and abuses of so many people were exposed. We now turn to the Inquisitions of the Cold War

Notes

[1] *United Nations Human Development Report*, 1998.

[2] Peter Coleman, *Liberal Conspiracy* (London: Collier Macmillan Publishers), check dustjacket; Frances Stoner Saunders, *The Cultural Cold War: The CIA and the World of Arts and Letters* (New York: The Free Press, 1999). Run a Google Internet search.

[3] Saunders, *The Cultural Cold War*, pp. 1-3, 197.

[4] Saunders, *The Cultural Cold War*, pp. 1-3, 37, 60-63, 68, 71, 91, 101-39, 142, 150-51, 166, 201, 206, 245, 294-99, 353-58, 382, 402-403, 409-411, 420, check the dustjacket for names; Angus MacKenzie, *Secrets: The CIA's War at Home* (Berkeley: University of California Press, 1997), pp. 2, 29, 40, 61-72, 185; See also, Coleman, *Liberal Conspiracy*.

[5] Ibid, David Kaplan and Michael Schaffer, "Losing the Psywar," *U.S. News & World Report* (October 8, 2001), p. 46.

[6] William F. Pepper, *An Act of State: The Execution of Martin Luther King* (NY: Verso, 2003), p. 135.

[7] Sally Covington, "Right Thinking, Big Grants, and Long Term Strategy: How Conservative Philanthropies and Think Tanks Transform U.S. Policy," *CovertAction Quarterly* (Winter 1998), pp. 6-16; see also Saunders, *The Cultural Cold War*, pp. 116, 135, 138-39, 142, 353-58, 409.

[8] Ibid. Run a Google Internet search using many combinations of keywords on thee pages.

[9] Alex Carey, *Taking the Risk Out Of Democracy: Corporate Propaganda Versus Freedom and Liberty* (Champaign ILL: University of Illinois Press, 1995).

[10] Sally Covington, "Right Thinking, pp. 6-16; Saunders, *The Cultural Cold War*, pp. 116, 135, 138-39, 142, 353-58, 409. Run a Google Internet search.

[11] Mason Gaffney, Fred Harrison, *The Corruption of Economics* (London: Shepheard-Walwyn, 1994).

[12] Robin W. Winks, *Cloak and Gown: Scholars in the Secret War*, 1939-1961 (New York: Quill, 1987); Saunders, *The Cultural Cold War*.

[13] Kaplan and Schaffer, "Losing the Psywar," p. 46. Run a Google Internet search.

[14] Coleman's *Liberal Conspiracy*, especially Appendix D, lists almost 200 of these thought control books; Saunders, The Cultural Cold War, pp. 60, 63, 111, 140, 294-96, 105-106; see endnote 15.

[15] Run a Google Internet search using many different combinations of keywords and these authors. The history of America's state terrorism worldwide is deeply hidden and most records have been destroyed. (Witness Bamford's exposure on how General Lemnitzer destroyed the records on the Pentagon's plans for staging an attack on America, which included American deaths, to create an excuse to overthrow Fidel Castro of Cuba.) The following books provide a good view of that history: Austin Murphy, *The Triumph of Evil: The Reality of the USA's Cold War Victory* (Italy: European Press Academic Publishing, 2000); James Bamford, *Body of Secrets: Anatomy of the Ultra-Secret National Security Agency* (New York: Doubleday, 2001), especially pp. 70-75; John Quigley, *The Ruses for War: American Interventionism Since World War II* (Buffalo: Prometheus Books, 1992); L. Fletcher Prouty, *The Secret Team* (Englewood Cliffs, NJ: Prentice-Hall, 1973); Ralph McGehee, CIABASE (12-megabyte database on this history), http://come.to/CIABASE/, Box 5022, Herndon, VA 22070 (Caution: Run an Internet search for Ralph McGehee. The CIA is harassing him and may be sabotaging his database.); Coleman, *Liberal Conspiracy*, Michael T. Klare, *Resource Wars: The New Landscape of Global Conflict* (New York: Henry Holt and Company, 2001); Michel Chossudovsky, *The Globalization of Poverty: Impacts of IMF and World Bank Reforms* (London: Zed Books, 1997); William Blum, *Rogue State: A Guide to the World's Only Super Power* (Monroe, ME: Common Courage Press, 2000), *Killing Hope: U.S. Military Interventions Since World War II* (Monroe, ME: Common Courage Press, 1995), and *The CIA: A Forgotten History* (London: Zed Press, 1986), pp. 127-28, 131, 185; Chalmers Johnson, *Blowback: The Cost and Consequences of American Empire* (New York: Henry Holt & Company, 2000), p. 117; John Prados, *The Presidents' Secret Wars* (New York: William Morrow, 1986) and *The President' Secret Wars: CIA and Pentagon Covert Operations From World War II Through the Persian Gulf War* Warwick: Elephant Paperbacks, 1996); John Stockwell, *The Praetorian Guard* (Boston: South End Press, 1991), pp. 100-101; Ted Gup, *The Book of Honor: Covert Lives and Classified Deaths at the CIA* (New York: Doubleday, 2,000); Dan Jacobs, *The Brutality of Nations* (New York: Alfred A. Knopf, 1987); P.V. Parakal, *Secret Wars of the CIA* (New Delhi: Sterling Publishers, 1984); K. Nair, *Devil and His Dart: How the CIA is Plotting in the Third World* (New Delhi: Sterling, 1986); I.F. Stone, *The Hidden History of the Korean War* (Boston: Little Brown and Company, 1952); Victor Marchetti and John D. Marks, *The CIA and the Cult of Intelligence* (New York: Dell, 1980), Chapter 6, especially pp. 152-56, also pp. 53-54, 62-63, 541-42; Ralph W. McGehee, *Deadly Deceits* (New York: Sheridan Square Press, 1983), especially pp. 30, 58, 62, 189; Philip Agee and Louis Wolf, *Dirty Work* (London: Zed Press, 1978), especially p. 262; Loch .K. Johnson, *America's Secret Power* (New York: Oxford University Press, 1989); David Wise, Thomas B. Ross, *The Espionage Establishment* (New York: Bantam Books, 1978), pp. 256, 257; H.B. Westerfield, *Inside CIA's Private World: Declassified Articles from the Agency's Internal Journal 1955-1992* (New Haven, CT. Yale University Press, 1995); Frank J. Donner, *The Age of Surveillance: The Aims and Methods of America's Political Intelligence System* (New York: Random House, 1981); John Prados, *Keepers of the Keys: A History of the National Security Council from Truman to Bush* (New York: William Morrow, 1991); C.D. Ameringer, *U.S. Foreign Intelligence* (Lexington, MA: Lexington Books, 1990); J. Adams, *Secret Armies* (New York: Atlantic Monthly Press, 1987); T. Powers, *The Man Who Kept the Secrets*

(New York: Alfred A. Knopf, 1979); Christopher Simpson, *Blowback* (New York: Weidenfeld & Nicolson, 1988); Ernest Volkman, Blaine Baggett, *Secret Intelligence* (New York: Doubleday, 1989); John Ranelagh, *The Agency: The Rise and Decline of the CIA* (New York: Simon & Schuster, 1987); Darrell Garwood, *Under Cover: Thirty-Five Years of CIA Deception* (New York: Grove Press Inc., 1985); Philip Agee, *Inside the Company: CIA Diary* (New York: Bantam Books, 1975); B. Hersh, *The Old Boys: The American Elite and the Origins of the CIA* (New York: Charles Scribner's Sons, 1992); H. Rositzke, *The CIA's Secret Operations* (New York: Thomas Y. Crowell Company, 1977); E. Thomas, *The Very Best Men Four Who Dared: The Early Years of the CIA* (New York: Simon & Schuster, 1995); D.S. Blaufarb, *The Counterinsurgency Era: U.S. Doctrine and Performance 1950 to Present* (New York: The Free Press, 1977); Michael T. Klare and P. Kornbluh, *Low Intensity Warfare* (New York: Pantheon Books, 1988); Alexander Cockburn and Jeffrey St. Clair, *Whiteout: The CIA, Drugs and the Press* (New York: Verso, 1998); S.E. Ambrose, *Ike's Spies* (Garden City, New York: Doubleday & Company, 1981); Susanne Jonas, *The Battle for Guatemala: Rebels, Death Squads, and U.S. Power* (San Francisco: Westview Press, 1991); C. Andrew, *For the President's Eyes Only: Secret Intelligence and the American Presidency from Washington to Bush* (New York: HarperCollins Publishers 1995); H. Frazier, ed., *Uncloaking the CIA* (New York: The Free Press, 1978); *Covert Action Information Bulletin*, all issues; *Counterspy*, all issues. See also, Wendell Minnick, *Spies and Provocateurs: A Worldwide Encyclopedia of Persons Conducting Espionage and Covert Action, 1946-1991* (Jefferson, North Carolina: McFarland & Company,1992); John Loftus, *The Belarus Secret* (New York: Alfred A. Knopf, 1982); Robin W. Winks, *Cloak & Gown*; D.F. Fleming, *The Cold War and Its Origins* (New York: Doubleday & Company, 1961); Milton Mayer, *They Thought They Were Free* (Chicago: University of Chicago Press, 1955).

To understand financial and economic warfare, read Peter Gowan, *The Global Gamble: Washington's Faustian Bid for World Dominance* (New York: verso, 1999); John Gray, *False Dawn* (New York: The Free Press, 1998); Robert A. Pastor, Ed., *A Century's Journey: How the Great Powers Shape the World* (New York: Basic Books, 1999); Anders Stephanson, Kennan and the Art of Foreign Policy (Cambridge: Harvard University Press, 1989); David Mayers, *George Kennan and the Dilemmas of US Foreign Policy* (New York: Oxford University Press, 1988); John R. Commons, *Legal Foundations of Capitalism* (New Brunswick/London: Transaction Publishers, 1995); John R. Commons, *Institutional Economics* (New Brunswick/London: Transaction Publishers, 1995); Carey B. Joynt and Percy E. Corbett, *Theory and Reality in World Politics* (Pittsburgh: University of Pittsburgh Press, 1978); Richard L. Rubenstein, *The Age of Triage* (Boston: Beacon Press, 1983); Peter Rodman, *More Precious than Peace* (New York: Charles Scribner & Sons, 1994); Angelo Codevilla, *Informing Statecraft* (New York: The Free Press, 1992); Arie E. David, *The Strategy of Treaty Termination* (New Haven: Yale University Press, 1975); Francis Neilson, *How Diplomats Make War* (San Francisco: Cobden Press); Jerry Fresia, *Toward an American Revolution: Exposing the Constitution and Other Illusions* (Boston, South End Press), 1988.

For an understanding that internal assassinations are carried out and for a view of self-censorship by the media on national security issues, as described in this chapter, read Mark Lane, *Plausible Denial: Was the CIA Involved in the Assassination of JFK?* (New York: Thunder Mouth Press, 1991) and Claudia Furiati, *ZR Rifle: The Plot to Kill Kennedy And Castro*.(Melbourne: Ocean Press, 1994). For how the purpose of Western intelligence services are to control the belief systems of its citizens, and how much of the violence are covert operations to maintain this control, read L. Fletcher Prouty, *JFK: The CIA, Vietnam, And the Plot to Kill Kennedy* (New York: Carol Publishing, 1992) and Philip. Willan, *Puppetmasters: The Political Use of Terrorism in Italy* (London: Constable, 1991), provides a short description of how strategies-of-tension are used worldwide to control beliefs and thus control elections. Alex Carey's *Taking the Risk out of Democracy; Corporate Propaganda versus Freedom and Liberty* (Chicago: University of Illinois Press, 1995) is an in-depth analysis of corporate propaganda pushed through the government, media, and academia throughout the 20th century.

[16] Dean Acheson, *Present at the Creation* (New York: W.W. Norton & Company, 1987), pp. 373-379; the complete NSC-68 document can be found in Thomas H. Etzold and John Lewis Gaddis, *Containment: Documents on American Policy and Strategy*, 1945-50, (New York: Columbia University Press, 1978), Chapter 7. See endnote 15.

[17] Acheson, *Present at the Creation* p. 377; Etzold and Gaddis, Containment, Chapter 7.

[18] Ralph McGehee, *Deadly Deceit*. (New York: Sheridan Square Press, 1983), p. 192.

[19] McGehee, http://come.to/CIABASE/, check Wade Frazier's review of McGehee's *Deadly Deceits*..

[20] Acheson, Present at the Creation, p. 377. See also Stone, *Hidden History*, and Etzold and Gaddis, *Containment*.

[21] Stone, *Hidden History*; Coleman, *Liberal Conspiracy*; Saunders, *The Cultural Cold War*; Ellen Schrecker, No Ivory Tower: *McCarthyism in the Universities*. New York: Oxford University Press, 1986; Etzold and Gaddis, *Containment*, Chapter 7. Run a Google Internet search.

[22] See endnote 15 and run that Google Internet search.

[23] William Blum, *Rogue State*, Chapter 4; Willan, *Puppetmasters*, Chapters 1-3, pp. 146-159; Thomas, Very Best Men, pp. 65-66; David A. Yallop, *In God's Name* (New York: Bantam Books, 1984); Saunders, *The Cultural Cold War*, p. 143; See endnote 15. See also Prouty, *JFK*, Chapter Three and Blum, *Rogue State*, Chapters Four and Sixteen.

[24] Chalmers Johnson, *Blowback*, p. 117.

[25] See endnote 15, especially Prouty, JFK, Chapter Three and Blum, *Rogue State*, Chapter Four.

[26] Smith, *Economic Democracy*, Chapter 6. See MacKenzie, Secrets, pp. 2, 4-6, 27, 29-41; Michael Parenti, *History as Mystery* (San Francisco: City Lights Books, 2000), pp. 178, 183-89; Holly Sklar, *Washington's War on Nicaragua* (Boston: South End Press, 1988), p. 359; Rositzke, *CIA's Secret Operations*, pp. 218-20; Powers, *Man Who Kept the Secrets*, pp. 246-70, 364; Angus MacKenzie and David Weir, *Secrets: The CIA's War at Home* (University of California Press, 1997); M. Wesley Swearingen, *FBI Secrets: An Agent's Exposé* (Boston: South End Press, 1995); Ward Churchhill, *Cointelpro Papers: Documents from the FBI's Secret Wars Against Domestic Dissent* (South End Press, 1990); Nelson Blackstock, *Cointelpro: The FBI's Secret War on Political Freedom* (New York: Anchor Foundation, 1988); Margaret Jayko, *FBI on Trial: The Victory of the Socialist Workers Party Suit Against Government Spying* (New York: Pathfinder Press, 1989): Ward Churchhill, *Agents of Repression : The FBI's Secret Wars Against the Black Panther Party and the American Indian Movement* (Boston South End Press, 1989); Martin Luther King Jr, Philip S. Foner, editor, *The Black Panthers Speak* (New York: Da Capo Press, 1995); Hugh Pearson, *The Shadow of the Panther: Huey Newton and the Price of Black Power in America* (Readings, MA: Perseus Press, 1995); Blum, *Rogue State*, Chapter 4 and pp. 258-59. The full story of Post World War II suppression of dissent in America has not been written yet. Stephen M. Kohn, *American Political Prisoners: Prosecution under the Espionage and Sedition Acts* (Westport: Praeger Publishers, 1994), covers that history before and after WWI. also see above endnote.

[27] Lane, Plausible Denial, pp. 239-323, especially 320-22.

[28] William F. Pepper, An Act of State: *The Execution of Martin Luther King* (New York: Verso, 2003), pp. 11, 15, 65, 76, 107.

[29] Ibid, p. 127.

[30] Run a Google Internet search.

[31] Ellen Schrecker, *No Ivory Tower* (New York: Oxford University Press, 1986).

[32] J.W. Smith, *Economic Democracy: The Political Struggle of the Twenty-First Century*, updated and expanded 3rd edition (www.ied.info/cc.html: *The Institute for Economic Democracy*, 2003), Chapter 9, citing Edward Burman, *The Inquisition: Hammer of Heresy* (New York: Dorset Press, 1992); Henry Charles Lea, *The Inquisition of the Middle Ages* (New York: Citadel Press, 1954), a condensation of his 1887 three-volume monumental work, *A History of the Inquisition of the Middle Ages*.

[33] Charles G. Addison, *The Knights Templar* (London: Longman, Brown, Green, and Longman, 1842), pp. 194-203, especially p. 203. See also Burman, *Inquisition*, pp. 95-99; James Burnes, *The Knights Templar* (London: Paybe and Foss, 1840), pp. 12-14; and Stephen Howarth's *Knights Templar* (New York: Dorset Press, 1982).

[34] David Caute, *The Great Fear* (New York: Simon and Schuster, 1978), pp. 18-19; Heiko Oberman, *The Roots of Anti-Semitism* (Philadelphia: Fortress Press, 1984); Barnet Litvinoff, *The Burning Bush* (New York: E.P. Dutton, 1988); Arkon Daraul, *A History of Secret Societies* (Secaucus, NJ: Citadel Press, 1961); Richard Hofstadter, *The Paranoid Style in American Politics* (Chicago: University of Chicago Press, 1979), pp. 10-11; James and Suzanne Pool, *Who Financed Hitler?* (New York: Dial Press, 1978); David H. Bennet, *The Party of Fear* (London: University of North Carolina Press, 1988), pp. 23-26, 205-06.

[35] David Fromkin, *A Peace to End all Peace* (New York: Avon Books, 1989), pp. 468-69; Michael Kettle, *The Allies and the Russian Collapse* (Minneapolis, University of Minnesota Press, 1981), p. 17. F.L. Carsten, *The Rise of Fascism* (Berkeley: University of California Press, 1982), pp. 24, 29, 118. 184; Pool and Pool, *Who Financed Hitler*, pp. 3, 23, Chapter 3.

4. Destabilizing Emerging Democracies Worldwide

Destabilizing a Newly-Free Iran

In 1951, Dr. Mohammed Mossadeq took the reins of power in Iran from its British-backed ruler, the Shah. Like Vietnamese leaders who wished to copy the U.S. constitution but ended up fighting the United States for their independence, this progressive leader, and most literate Iranians, viewed

> America as a land of wonderful opportunities and wonderful people.... [Mossadeq] never became anti-American and continued to believe that the United States was still the only major power capable of making a positive contribution to the reshaping of the world in favor of those nations which had long suffered from European imperialism.[1]

But European imperialists had destroyed each other's wealth in WWII battling over the world's resources and the *wealth-producing-process* and, unknown to Middle Eastern societies (or to the American people), U.S. foreign policy was designed to protect the wealth of the West through denying independence to any nation that might ally with the East or whose independence might trigger other breaks for freedom.[a]

For two years Mossadeq held out, while Western oil interests pulled government strings to embargo Iran's oil and deny that country funds. During this time, and even with the loss of 100,000 jobs in the oil industry due to that embargo, there was a "slight improvement in employment, overall economic production, and balance of trade." In its effort to break the West's embargo, Iran threatened to start trading with the Soviet bloc.[2]

That was a fatal mistake. The fear that an independent Iran might someday join forces with their Soviet neighbor guided the West's Middle

---

[a]This policy was undertaken under National Security Council Directive 68 (NSC-68) only one year before Iran became free. The CIA admitted in the Church Committee hearings in 1975-76 that under this policy they had orchestrated 50 major covert operations, and thousands of minor ones. In cases like Iran, Chile, Brazil, Indonesia, Nicaragua, et al., where local governments were attempting to reclaim control of their destiny. Under the Cold War master plan, NSC-68, the CIA overthrew those popular, democratically elected, governments and regained control of that wealth for foreign corporations.

East policies. Instead of using its influence and power to break the chains of British and French colonialism by supporting the budding democracy, the United States joined hands with Britain in the 1953 covert intervention (Operation Ajax, with Gulf Oil's future Vice President, Kermit Roosevelt, in charge) that placed the feudal Shah back in power. America gained 40% of Iranian oil rights, Britain claimed the rest. A few thousand Iranians were tortured and a few hundred were killed to re-impose feudalism in Iran.[3] Even though this was largely a British MI6 operation, the Americans, in a burst of self-congratulation, openly took credit for it.

The CIA's *Mighty Wurlitzer* cranked out massive misinformation and a docile press passed these fraudulent stories to the gentle masses of the idealistic free world with never a whisper that the terrorism within Iran was being carried out with the support of their governments. When Iranians eventually overthrew the Shah, the same *Mighty Wurlitzer* cranked out the rhetoric of an enemy and, knowing it was the leaders of the "free" world who overthrew their democracy, Iranians now were a true enemy.

Remember, Iran was America's very good friend, planning to emulate its freedom and democratic structure. Iranians had the resources and were looking forward to the same quality of life. To maintain control of his people, the Shah and his secret police (Savak) instituted a reign of terror, torture, and atrocities that lasted for 25 years. Obviously the values of rights, justice, and freedom that Americans cherish so deeply had been set aside when it applied to others and replaced by an agenda of the world's powerbrokers for protecting and expanding their wealth and power.

With an immediate payment of $45-million (part of an eventual $21-billion), the wealthy nations then removed their economic blockade, renewed their aid, and went on to make Iran their Middle East surrogate and regional military power.[4] Of course, the billions of dollars' worth of military hardware were bought with Iran's oil. That was not by chance. Later, when OPEC was formed, oil prices started rising and money started moving outside the control of the old powerbrokers. Just as when Iran declared its independence, the neo-mercantile monopolization was broken and President Nixon's national security advisor, Henry Kissinger, recommended "massive arms sales to Middle East oil states as a way of recycling the petrodollars that were rapidly flowing out of the United States."[5]

Note how Iran's oil wealth was returned to the centers of capital through arms sales, both when their surrogate, the Shah, was in power and again when the Middle East was temporarily outside their control. This is a crucial aspect of foreign policies of *imperial-centers-of-capital*. In spite of the rhetoric of compassion and aid for the world's impoverished, we must remember how—except when allies are needed in balance of power struggles—the owners of capital have always tried to prevent the accumulation of competing capital.ª The oil money in the Middle East had to be soaked up and returned to the *old centers-of-capital* or it would have become *another center-of-capital* that could build industry and take over resources and markets.6

As oil sources are limited, the developed world did not have the option of excluding the entire Middle East from world markets as they had done with Iran and as they did with Iraq (1991-2003). If used for both fuel and raw material, the industrial nations' refineries and chemical complexes could never compete with the cheap oil in the Middle East. The developed world was in the position identical to that of the free cities of Europe centuries ago who stood to lose their industry and trade to the countryside (Chapter 2). If permitted capital, the comparative advantage of the Middle East's raw material and fuel (oil almost free flowing) would eliminate the current centers of capital as refiners and marketers of the finished products.

Meanwhile, having tasted freedom, such repressive measures against their sovereignty converted the friendly Iranians, who once looked to America for guidance and support, into deadly enemies. The Ayatollah Khomeini and his Islamic followers overthrew the Shah in 1979 and Muslim extremists gained full control. It was the loss of those oil resources and the potential loss of refineries and markets that dictated Iran be depicted as an enemy to the citizens of "free" nations. If this had been reversed, the justice of the battle to control one's own wealth would have been obvious to us all—that is to all except the citizens of the empirical

---

ªInstead of buying developed world industrial technology or building industry (capital) for all Arabs, much of this money was deposited in U.S. and European banks and lent to the developing world. If the Arabs had built industry, their cheaper raw material, fuel, and labor would have assured the capture of much of the current market and destroyed other industry that once serviced that segment of the market. Iran, Libya, and Iraq became free from direct control, were taking control of their resources and destiny as just described, and thus became pariah rogue states and efforts to embargo them from world trade are on-going yet today.

Though other excuses have been given or created, this almost certainly would, and did, precipitate an attack to protect the current owners of capital: the Persian Gulf War. Iraq had ambitious development plans and with the control of Kuwaiti oil might have been strong enough to have federated and developed the entire Arab bloc.

The control of the price of oil by the West since the formation of OPEC has been highly successful. The price of gas in 1950 was about 22-cents a gallon. Allowing for inflation, a comparable price when the Persian Gulf crisis arose was officially acknowledged to be two dollars. As it was around $1.24 a gallon both before and after the Persian Gulf crisis, this demonstrates a lowering of the price about 38% and the risk of that loss of control was certainly a major factor in the Persian Gulf War. (History is repeating itself in 2003 as the imperial centers gain control of Iraqi oil.)

As the East was now defeated, bringing weapons of mass destruction—nuclear, chemical, and biological—under control was also a very high priority for that war. We can anticipate that this control of military potential will expand to other emerging nations.

society who would have heard resounding rhetoric portraying Americans, the insurgents struggling for their freedom, as enemies.

While the media were giving the American public massive exposure on how barbaric Iranians were holding innocent American's hostage, not a word was heard that the Iranian democracy had been overthrown and the dictator Shah put in power by the CIA. Nor did the Americans hear about the thousands of Iranians tortured and many killed by the Shah's secret service, Savak, established and trained by the CIA. Who were those tortured and killed? They were no less than patriots battling for democracy and freedom for Iranians; the Churchills, George Washingtons, Thomas Jeffersons, Gandhis, and Martin Luther Kings of Iran.

How angry would Americans be if a powerful nation overthrew their government and placed Britain back in power? Is it not a certainty that America's greatest heroes would be those that continued that fight for freedom? Is it not a high possibility that many of these very angry people of other societies are what we view as terrorists today? Would American's view as terrorists any who continued the fight for their freedom if Britain had overthrown their democracy and their wealth was still being drained to that imperial center?

All the Middle East is logically one country and is considered so by many Arabs. After all, where would America's wealth be if Mexico set up and controlled governments in Texas and Oklahoma, Japan controlled California, England the northeast, Spain the south, and the rest of the country was divided into small emirates with an elite power-structure under external control?

Containing Iraq

After overthrowing "democracy's" puppet government in Iran, on November 4, 1979 zealous Muslims overran the American Embassy, and held 52 Americans hostage for 444 days.[7] Until the World Trade Center/Pentagon terrorist bombings, this was the greatest peacetime tweak of America's nose in its history. To think that America would peacefully take that nose tweaking and the loss of control of Iranian oil is an exercise in extreme denial.

Here we can observe the importance of propaganda. One's own society is portrayed as *"peaceful* and *democratic"* even as it controls other societies through military power and terror. Meantime the societies whose freedom and rights are being suppressed are labeled *dictators* and *terrorists*.

The Iran-Iraq War started while those hostages were being held. The CIA's *Mighty Wurlitzer* was telling the American people the Soviet Union was backing Iraq. But when the Iraqis gassed their own Kurdish population (actually Iran did that, run a Google search) a U.S. senator angrily fumed on national news, "We have $800-million of arms in the pipeline to Iraq and we should cancel it all."

Any imperial nation would pursue every option to damage a nation that was holding its citizens hostage and Iraq was surely coached into that invasion with the promise of backing for their claim to the oil fields right across its borders. With the entire "free" world behind the Iraqis and Iran in turmoil, Iraq would have felt assured of success.

Even though they were arming Iraq, Americans wanted neither side to win. To maintain a stalemate, satellite intelligence was provided to whichever side was threatened with losing territory. In its nine years, that war cost between 500,000 and 1-million dead, possibly 1.5-million wounded, and 2.5-million refugees.

Before the early 20th-Century subdivision of the Middle East as described in Chapter 1, Kuwait was a province of Iraq. Badly bruised from the Iran/Iraq war, upset about Kuwait's horizontal, cross-border, drilling stealing oil from Iraq, and feeling America was now their friend after their immense support providing arms for that war, Iraq moved to bring her lost province back into the fold.[a] This led to the 1991 Gulf War which cost Iraq 200,000 killed, destruction of her industry and infrastructure, a 12-year embargo in which over a million Iraqis died for lack of food and medicine, and the 1993 2nd Gulf War. The Al-Qaeda, along with thousands of extremist Muslims worldwide, know this history as well as the many other slaughters and suppressions of freedom addressed in the next chapter.

The price of oil at $30 a barrel or more threatens the economies of the *imperial-centers-of-capital* which appear to be stalling. Powerbrokers feel that oil priced under $20 a barrel and possibly under $10 will give the world economy a boost. America will overthrow Saddam Hussein and install a puppet government and it will gain control of Iraq's oil fields.[8] Any who fail to support that overthrow will be excluded and America will gain control of the pricing of all OPEC oil. Running a Google Internet search using the keywords "Defense Planning Guide, Cheney, Wolfowitz, 1992" will alert one that the Iraq war in 2003 was planned over 11 years earlier by the very people who promoted and conducted that war.

A meeting of President George W. Bush's advisors was held within days after his election in 2000 in which the decision to depose Saddam Hussein was made. U.S. Intelligence would have known that Iraq Venezuela and Iran were considering switching to euros as their reserve currency which could crash the American economy.[9]

As America's Middle East outpost there will be substantial incentive to destroy all hostile powers bordering Israel. Witness the release of pressure with the threat of Hussein removed; especially if Iraqi oil is piped to Israel.

As soon as the war was over the Economic and Social Commission for Western Asia (ESCWA,) met and concluded that the first Gulf War cost

---

[a] Most destabilizations were of progressive governments. Saddam Hussein's wars against his neighbors and suppressions internally mark him as a leader justifiably deposed.

them $600 billion and anticipated this 2nd Gulf war will cost them $1 trillion. All the destabilizations and overthrows of governments we are addressing were because of the potential for success if those countries gained or retained their freedom. There is no reason to doubt that the same reason applies to this war (search for ESCWA, $600 million, 1,000 billion).

The war is on to install a "democratic" government in Iraq and the overwhelming force means it will obviously succeed. But we must remember that democratic in this context means a government subservient to the West. Regime changes by empires is as old as history. But installing a "democratic" Muslim government to rule against the best interests of Muslims is a contradiction in terms. (For by far the best analysis on American foreign policy read Michel Chossudovsky, *War and Globalization: The Truth behind September 11.*)

Thus it is easy to understand why activist Muslims are very upset, withdraw into the protection of their religion, and use their CIA terrorist training to blow up American emblems worldwide, reaching right into the heart of America to hijack planes and flying those now flying jet-fuel bombs into the most visible emblems of American Imperialism—New York's World Trade Center and the Pentagon—killing 266 passengers and crew and almost 3,000 on the ground. Indeed, one of the greatest private terrorist acts in history but very small when laid against state terrorism as the *imperial-centers-of-capital* fought to suppress freedom breaking out all over the world.[a] Even mainstream Muslims are upset over this Iraq war.

Containing Indonesia

The overthrow of Sukarno in 1965 is a blatant example of how state terrorism is used to prevent freedom of choice on the periphery of empire. Indonesians had enormous natural resources and when they broke free after WWII they were bursting with idealism and confidence. As 25% of their population believed in communism, that political group was to be allotted 25% of the government seats.

---

[a] Run a Google Internet search. CIA Director William Casey suggested to the Muslim terrorists they were training that, after overthrowing the Afghanistan government, the U.S. would support their terrorizing/destabilizing the Muslim provinces of the Soviet Union. Though the claim is made that this was never carried out, we must remember that virtually every CIA covert action must be plausibly denied. Those terrorists did move into those provinces just as suggested by Casey and the slaughter in the Russian provinces of Chechnya and Georgia as Russia attempts to suppress the breaking away of those Muslim states is likely only the start of many years of strife throughout the region. Just as Christian missionaries seem unstoppable, those zealous Muslims will not stop there. They will simultaneously attempt to break the rest of the Muslim world away from the West. The World Trade Center/Pentagon terrorist bombing is surely a major move to create that fissure and now even moderate Muslims are becoming zealous.

This attempt at full democracy was not to be permitted by America which claimed democracy under a system of two almost identical political parties, both subservient to corporate powers. (Smaller reformist political groups become marginalized to obscurity.[a]) On its second attempt the CIA overthrew Sukarno, installed Suharto, a list of over 4,000 political leaders and activists to be executed was provided, and soon—with CIA coaching and by that intelligence agency's own estimate—800,000 Indonesians were slaughtered.[10]

This wholesale terror was for no more reason than Indonesians were going to establish a full democracy and its assured success, if not thwarted, would be a beacon to other regions of the world that contained resources and markets crucial to entrenched capitalists.

Containing Libya

We hear of rogue states. All the buzz word "rogue states" means is that these countries are bent on taking control of their own destiny. Most of the battles against such efforts for self development are only efforts to regain control of those countries, rhetoric otherwise notwithstanding. If Libya, Iran, or Iraq were permitted control of their own destiny, their resources, oil, pumped out of the ground for pennies per barrel could far undersell Western products (fuel, medicines, plastics, synthetic fibers, et al.) produced with oil costing the industrialized world anywhere from $15 to $40 a barrel.

After Libya declared its freedom, several efforts by Britain to covertly overthrow the Libyan government failed, Libya responded by supporting elements actively battling imperial elements in their countries. After attacks by American warplanes, one of which killed President Muammar Khadaffi's adopted daughter, Libya abandoned such supports. At this time there is no evidence that the embargo against Libya will be lifted.

Containing Vietnam

While the Vietnam War was raging, the majority of Americans were deeply patriotic and supportive. Yet not many today believe America had any honest reason for that war. Three million Vietnamese, Laotians, and Cambodians died fighting for the same reason Americans fought their Revolutionary War, freedom. Four million died when one counts those killed by the French before the U.S. took over that suppression of freedom. Four times the bombs (6.3-million tons) were dropped on tiny Vietnam (a country slightly larger than New York State) as were dropped during WWII.

---

[a] Under this system of the majority take all and, since a dissident vote rarely has any impact, minorities are essentially unrepresented. At the very best, they are far underrepresented. As America's Democratic Party and Republican Party are financed by the same wealthy interests, they are essentially one party. So America has a one-party government masquerading as a democracy.

Millions of acres were devastated by Agent Orange, causing tens of thousands of deformed Vietnamese babies. This was massive state terror by any measure. Though America lost that battle they won the war, Vietnamese resources are available to the West and their economy is now open for penetration by Western capital.[11]

Containing Nigeria

From 1966 to 1971 relief efforts were actively interfered with as possibly 2-million Biafrans, mostly children starved in Nigeria as British attempted to control Nigerian oil. After long research, Dan Jacobs turned to an American National Security Council Staff person and said, "The British did this." The response, "Oh, of course, the British orchestrated the whole thing."[12]

Destabilizing Guatemala

With several truly independent political parties, of which the communists were one of the smallest, the newly elected Jacobo Arbenz proceeded to turn Guatemalan resources to the benefit of Guatemalans. United Fruit was not even using the land the Guatemalan government was reclaiming with bonds which were valued at the same rate as the land was assessed for taxes.

That is pretty fair considering United Fruit obtained that land for even less money when they essentially owned the Guatemalan Government. Under the *Mighty Wurlitzer's* battle cry of a communist dictatorship, hundreds of propaganda articles were planted throughout South America along with tens of thousands of pamphlets and cartoon posters. Three propaganda movies were created.

With transmitters overriding Guatemalan radio, CIA planes strafed Guatemala City, smoke bombs made it appear like a 20-times larger attack, and the Guatemalan government fell. The Guatemalan Truth Commission concluded that 93% of the 200,000 slaughtered in Guatemala's battle to regain their freedom were killed by U.S. supported military and CIA orchestrated terrorist death squads. Fifty-eight Guatemalan leaders were on a CIA assassination list when that government was overthrown. One can safely assume those on that list are among the many thousands killed by CIA established and orchestrated death squads.[13]

Destabilizing Chile

Managers of the American State went into shock in 1972 when Salvadore Allende's communist party won the election in Chile. Plans for his overthrow were quickly drawn up and implemented (including his assassination) and General Pinochet was placed in power. Among the 3,197 innocents officially acknowledged as killed (a huge undercount) by Pinochet's forces were Americans, Spanish, and a few other nationalities. A Spanish judge charged Pinochet with killing 300 Spanish citizens. So far he has both avoided extradition and evaded Chilean justice but the acknowledgment of most countries of the legality of extradition to stand trial for other even more heinous crimes has curbed the travels of many powerful people, including some Americans.[14] The concept that leaders of powerful nations can be tried for their actions is spreading. On February 13, 2003, a Belgian court ruled that President Ariel Sharon of Israel may be tried for war crimes for his involvement in the Sabra and Shatilla massacre of 800 Palestinians in Lebanon in 1982. An International Criminal Court not under the control of the imperial nations as is the International Criminal Tribunal (ICTY), is, as this is being written, being established in the Hague. Countries with lots to hide and not wanting to face an honest court are taking measures to not be subject to their jurisdiction.

Destabilizing El Salvador

El Salvador never did break free but fought hard to do so from 1980 through 1992. As in Guatemala, the US-backed elite's desperation to prevent democracy from functioning was brutal. When several tortured bodies showed up each week in the El Salvador dump with their thumbs wired behind their back (the trademark of the death squads) and there was no attempt by officials to find their killers, one can be sure the El Salvador government was behind their murders. There were over 70,000 deaths from security forces armed and advised by the U.S. military and another 7,000 killed by death squads orchestrated by the same advisors.[15]

Destabilizing Nicaragua

The newly free Nicaraguan government of July 19, 1979 immediately implemented programs that started improving their citizens' education, health, and standard of living. Again the danger of a successful example of freedom was imminent and these heroic people came under immediate attack by Nicaraguan defectors trained, funded, and coached by the CIA. Only a few thousand Nicaraguans were killed but the economy was devastated. Nicaragua accommodated America with another election. With U.S. desired candidates heavily subsidized by the very nation assaulting them, the government slipped back into U.S. acceptable political hands. Billions were available to overthrow the popular government but, as always, little or no money was available to rebuild what had been destroyed. One in nine Nicaraguan children now face serious malnutrition (BBC news used the word starving), and Nicaragua is again a country going nowhere.[16] They cannot be an example for other restless colonies who wish to gain control of their destinies. Their resources effectively remain under the control of the imperial nations which is what the struggles are all about.

Angola, Mozambique and other Frontline States

The CIA officer in charge of the Angola desk, John Stockwell, said that American, and South African, support of National Union for Total Independence (UNITA) was wrong. He recognized that Angolans wanted the Popular Movement for the Liberation of Angola (MPLA) and that this group was, "best qualified to run Angola; nor [were they] hostile to the United States." Obviously the political and economic shattering of Angola was the purpose of supporting Savimbi, not the establishment of a functional friendly government.[17]

Newly free Mozambique endured a massive terror campaign orchestrated by the apartheid South African government. The frontline states of Zambia, Namibia, Zimbabwe, and Botswana faced smaller, but similar destabilizations.[18]

The Congo was immensely rich in minerals. There was no way to prevent the popular Patrice Lumumba from being their elected leader so he was assassinated. Still the Congo could not be controlled so the province of Zaire, with most the mineral wealth, was carved off and Joseph Mobutu was installed as the Belgian/American puppet where he proceeded to send billions of dollars out of the country to his private bank accounts.[19] Of course for every billion dollars Mobutu stole from the Congo many tens of billions of dollars of mineral wealth was transferred to the *imperial-centers-of-capital*.

The destabilization of these immensely resource-wealthy emerging nations left between 1.5-million and 2-million dead, left the entire region impoverished, and that battle to control the immense wealth of Africa with huge loss of life is ongoing yet today.

Containing Cuba

Fidel Castro's 1959 overthrow of the American puppet General Batista created a crisis for American *managers-of-state*. Castro was not communist but he was free to guide the destiny of Cuba and that is always a problem for an imperial nation. Embargoes were immediately put in place and this forced Castro to turn to the Soviet Union for support. Cuba's economy grew rapidly and soon its education equaled America's and its average education level now leads the world. Of course, this only heightened the crisis. A successful emerging nation not under the control of the imperial center would alert all dependent nations to take control of their governments, their resources, and their destiny.

A total embargo was imposed and no corporation from any nation which did business with Cuba could do business with America. Any ship which docked at a Cuban port was denied rights to dock at any American port. Cane fields were both infected with fungus and burned, tobacco was infected with mildew, potatoes were infected with Thrips-palmi, 500,000 pigs infected with African swine fever had to be destroyed, Cubans were infected with dengue fever and 158 died, and a Cuban airliner with Cuba's champion fencing team was downed over the ocean.[a]

There have been enough Cuban dissidents admitting to this sabotage that few will challenge this record. This author watched a news broadcast interviewing one of the saboteurs. He bragged about over 50 forays into Cuba, one in which he sabotaged a train on a trestle and watched it go into the ravine like in the movies.

The reader should note that, until the terrorist attack on the World Trade Center and anthrax spread through the mail, no one was blowing up American or European trains and refineries, no one was burning American or European grain fields, no one poisoned 7000 American dairy cattle such as was done to East Germany, and no one was practicing germ and crop

---

[a] Newly released CIA documents alerted researchers that crop warfare was practiced against a number of impoverished countries. James Bamford, *Body of Secrets: Anatomy of the Ultra-Secret National Security Agency* (New York: Doubleday, 2001), pp. 70-75, especially p. 82, describes how several plans for faking a Cuban attack on Americans to justify an invasion of Cuba. Several of these plans meant the death of American citizens. President John F. Kennedy would not approve any of those plans. Shortly later General Lyman Lemnitzer was transferred to Europe, a major demotion from Chairman of the Joints Chief of staff. Shortly after that, CIA director Allen Dulles was fired. Soon after, Kennedy was assassinated. More on biological warfare in: Blum, *Rogue State*, Chapters 3 through 10; Stephen Endicott and Edward Hagerman, *The United States and Biological Warfare: Secrets from the Early Cold War and Korea*. Bloomington, IN: Indiana University Press, 1998; Minnick, *Spies and Provocateurs*, especially p. 262; R. Ridenour, *Back Fire: The CIA's Biggest Burn* (Havana, Cuba: Jose Marti Publishing House, 1991), especially pp. 73, 77-78, 145-49; Garwood, *Under Cover*, especially p. 92; P.V. Parakal, *Secret Wars of the CIA* (New Delhi: Sterling Publishers, 1984); Prados, *Presidents Secret Wars*, 1996 ed., pp. 333, 337, 349; Prados, *Keepers of the Keys*, especially pp. 142-44, 203-317; D. Corn, *Blond Ghost: Ted Shackley and the CIA's Crusades* (New York: Simon & Schuster, 1994); J.T. Richelson, *The U.S. Intelligence Community* (Cambridge, MA: Ballinger Publishing Company, 1985), especially p. 231; R. S. Cline, *Secrets, Spies, and Scholars* (Washington, DC: Acropolis Books, 1976), especially p. 195; P. Wyden, *Bay of Pigs, the Untold Story* (New York: Simon and Schuster, 1979); D. Martin, *Wilderness of Mirrors* (New York: Harper & Row, 1980), especially pp. 151-53; Ranelagh, *Agency*, especially pp. 356-60; G. Treverton, *Covert Action, The Limits of Intervention in the Postwar World* (New York, NY: Basic Books, Inc., Publishers, 1987); L.F. Prouty, *The Secret Team* (Englewood Cliffs, NJ: Prentice-Hall, 1973); Borosage and Marks, *CIA File*; Hersh, *Old Boys*; Thomas, *Very Best Men*; Jeffreys-Jones, R., *The CIA & American Democracy* (New Haven: Yale University Press), 1989; B. Watson, S. Watson, and G. Hopple, *United States Intelligence: An Encyclopedia* (New York: Garland Publishing, 1990); *Covert Action Information Bulletin*; *Counterspy*; McGehee's *CIABASE* (Caution: Run an Internet search for Ralph McGehee. The CIA is harassing him and may be sabotaging his database.). Run a Google Internet search.

warfare against the West. (A very short list of a very long history of worldwide terrorism maintaining control of the periphery of empire.)

In short, the truth is exactly apposite of what the CIA's *Mighty Wurlitzer* has propagandized the world to believe. No countries were attempting to overthrow Western nations. It is the rest of the world that was under assault by the West for the purpose of controlling their governments, their resources, and the *wealth-producing-process*.

Due to the CIA's *Mighty Wurlitzer* cranking out the misinformation of dictators and murderers, American people remained blissfully unaware that Cubans had attained a level of education and health care equal to America and had eliminated hunger while the rest of Latin America remained in poverty.

Note how successful these *strategies-of-tension* are for controlling the mindset of a population. Talk to any American on the street. Most will know nothing of Cuba's successes and, even though it is Cuba being terrorized by America and Cuba is not terrorizing anyone, they believe Cuba is a terrorist state in poverty.

Test your peers and bring up the subject of Cuba. You will find they believe Castro is a murderous dictator and Cubans under Castro are incompetent and impoverished. The truth is that those killed by the Cuban government were few and those that were killed were working under the guidance of the CIA to suppress Cuban freedom. That is a capital offense in most countries.

On a positive note, Cuba is slowly recovering from the loss of the Soviet Union as a trading partner (that was a condition imposed on Russia in trade for support money after the 1991 Soviet collapse). She may yet succeed to control her own destiny. Cuban doctors have gone to the poorest regions of the world's poorest countries to provide medical care. Cuba is now providing free medical scholarships to students from poor nations and has even provided 50 free scholarships to poor American students with the understanding that they will practice in the poorer parts of the U.S. which have a shortage of good doctors.[20] So much for Cuban terrorists.

The Korean War: A *Strategy-of-Tension* to gain Citizen Support for Suppressions of Breaks for Freedom

Any power-structure, "democratic" or dictatorship, facing the loss of control on the periphery of empire, will find or create an excuse for war. Because all the records were not destroyed as ordered, it is now known the American Joint Chiefs of Staff urged President Kennedy to create an excuse for a war with Cuba. To create massive anger, and thus support for war, it was planned for innocent Americans to die:

In the name of anticommunism, they proposed launching a secret and bloody war of terrorism against their own country in order to trick the American public into supporting an ill-conceived war they intended to launch against Cuba. Codenamed Operation Northwoods, the plans which had the approval of the Chairman and every member of the Joint Chiefs of Staff, called for innocent Americans to be shot on American streets; for boats carrying refugees from Cuba to be sunk in the high seas; for a wave of violent terrorism to be launched in Washington D.C., Miami, and elsewhere. People would be blamed for bombings they did not commit; planes would be hijacked. Using phony evidence, all of it would be blamed on Castro, thus giving Lemnitzer and his cabal the excuse, as well as the public and international backing, they needed to launch their war.[21] [a]

The Korean War was a similar *strategy-of-tension* putting National Security Council Directive 68, the master plan for the Cold War, into effect. The managers of the American state realized that suppressing the world's break for freedom would require increasing the military budget 350%. Only a long-standing threat to the wealthy world's security could justify such massive remilitarization. The purpose of the Korean War was to prove to the world that the threat of the loss of their liberty (the massive propaganda coming from the CIA's *Mighty Wurlitzer*) was real and imminent.[b]

Even with massive slaughters in South Korea (over 100,000 killed) as its citizens protested against the Syngman Rhee government installed by America, that outpost of empire was already lost. So there was nothing to lose by going to war and there was a whole world to gain through remilitarization to suppress the rest of the world's break for freedom.

As proven by the accidental release to history of a conversation within General Douglas MacArthur's staff, and the fact that it took three days for the North Koreans to push the South Koreans out of Heiju, well above the 38th parallel and into North Korea's territory, it was South Korea that started that war.[22]

The battle was very unequal; 35,000 Americans were killed while 4-million Koreans and Chinese perished. As with the Gulf War, the Yugoslavian destabilization, the overthrow of the Taliban in Afghanistan,

---

[a] Historians should look close the anthrax scare after 9/11/2001. Those anthrax spores were proven to be biologically identical to that produced at the U.S. germ warfare facility at the Dugway Proving Grounds in Utah. John Pilger stated in the *New Statesman,* December 16, 2002, that America's leading powerbrokers spoke of "needing "some catastrophic and catalyzing event—like a new Pearl Harbor"—so as to gain the loyalty of the American people for their violent foreign policy. The source of that anthrax is not in dispute. The probability is very high that propagandists took advantage of the 9/11/2001 terrorist attack to further their *strategies-of-tension* to maintain that loyalty. Run Google Internet searches using the many keywords on this page.
[b] Though we are providing key citations, read this author's *Economic Democracy: The Political Struggle of the Twenty-First Century,* updated and expanded 3rd edition, for the full story.

and the current war against Iraq, there was no risk that America was going to lose that war or even that their casualties would be high. This, of course, is more proof that North Korea did not start that war? Why would they start a war they were unprepared for and when the massive riots in South Korea indicated the two halves of Korea were going to rejoin as a free and independent nation? Peace was far more advantageous to North Korea than war while war was far more advantageous to the *imperial-centers-of-capital* than peace.[a]

Any battle is traumatic and the Americans when pushed out of North Korea by the Chinese did face a capable enemy. However, I.F. Stone, our primary source, explains how many of the early battles in the South were little more than press releases passed out by intelligence service wordsmiths. American troops would make sweeps and were often searching for enemies they could not find. But those sweeps were recorded in the media of record as vicious battles. If you or I had been the reporters, we would have reported the same fictitious battles. Those news reports were taken right off U.S. army daily press releases.

But the relatively small number of Americans killed and the massive numbers of North Koreans and Chinese killed tell the real story. While the poorly equipped North Koreans and Chinese did suffer heavy casualties on the front line, most of the 4-million were killed by America napalming North Korea to the ground. There was hardly a building left standing in the North which, until very late in the war, was totally defenseless against America's air force and navy. There were few war industries to bomb and one wonders at the morality of military commanders ordering the bombing and burning of undefended cities. The napalming of those modest homes accounts for half the 4-million killed being women and children.

The essential story of the Korean War was that peace could not be permitted until the entire Western world was psychologically programmed to accept rearming and to accept the suppressions of breaks for freedom (called insurgencies) all over the world. Each time peace seemed about to break out at the Panmunjom peace negotiations, there would be a massive ground offensive, air raid, naval bombardment, or all three.

Besides press releases distorting the battles, fraudulent history omits slaughters that do occur. The greatest naval and air bombardment in history was in the Korean War and went unreported in the Western Press. The navies of three countries and the American air force bombed, strafed, and shelled three defenseless North Korean cities for 41 straight days and nights, all to tweak the nose of the North Koreans and Chinese so they would not sign a peace agreement.[23]

---

[a] While this author was obtaining his Ph.D., he attended a workshop on a Kentucky army base hosted by that bases history officer. The conclusions of my research were verified when he admitted we suckered the North Koreans into that war.

Any signing under such pressure would have been a total surrender and, with the Chinese now fighting the battle, neither the Chinese nor the North Koreans were about to surrender. A peace agreement was not signed until the West's war machine was rebuilt to a level to successfully suppress the worldwide breaks for freedom.

This is how "*strategies-of-tensions*" work. Powerful nations create a crisis to obtain the loyalty of their citizens for *policies-of-state* that would never be accepted by their own people if the full story were known.

The strategy was successful. The entire Western world rearmed, virtually every break for freedom—except Cuba's and China's—was suppressed, the world's resources remained under the control of the imperial centers, control of the *wealth-producing-process* is secure, and the world's wealth continues to flow to the *imperial-centers-of-capital*.

Though the old imperial nations supported these destabilizations, occasionally very substantially, the suppression of the world's break for freedom was carried out primarily by America. Not even those being bombed and napalmed could believe America was doing this. But some within the targeted nations became aware and they became just as angry as Americans when they were targeted for terrorist attacks on 9/11/2001. For that matter, some Americans who became aware of the immorality of American foreign policy also became angry. But most remained unaware and this foreign policy must be kept secret because few Americans would tolerate it if they knew.

Not only is current history kept secret, the violent and embarrassing aspects of earlier history are also ignored. What must be understood is that early Christians violently destroyed other religions and even other peaceful Christian sects. From a Darwinian view, it has been *survival of the meanest*. In 1099 the first Crusaders sacked Jerusalem and massacred Muslims, Jews, and even Christians. When the Muslim leader Saladin retook Jerusalem in 1187, none were killed when the Christians surrendered and protection was provided for the departing caravans of Christian refugees.[24] Christians destroyed the Library of Alexandria (says Gibbons, challenged by others) and executed virtually every educated Egyptian. Cultural destruction was so thorough that both their written language and their history disappeared.[a] The same policies destroyed Aztec temples and other cultures as Christianity spread across the world. Their history too was erased, and is only now being resurrected. Only heavily populated and advanced societies could absorb the blows of an expanding Christian/Western culture.

---

[a] Gibbons is almost certainly correct. All empires throughout history have covertly weakened those whose power may at some point threaten them just as we are describing is being done today. The destruction of the Library of Alexandria and the alliance of Christians and the Roman Empire both occurred in the 4th century and both powers would have viewed the Egyptians as a threat.

Surviving Eastern and Southern Hemisphere cultures are absorbing those blows from Western culture yet today.[a]

Full rights are based in economics. Under assault and with their natural wealth appropriated by Western societies, other cultures cannot provide rights to their people. Through processing the world's natural wealth into industries and consumer products the aggressive wealthy world is able to provide both economic rights and political rights to their citizens.

With U.S. military forces in over 100 countries around the world 12 years after the Cold War is over, with America spending more on arms than the entire rest of the world, and with most those powers allied with the U.S., it is impossible for America to deny it is an empire or that, with its military and trading allies, it forms an *allied imperial-center-of-capital*. Those covert and overt suppressions of breaks for freedom on the periphery of empire as America protects the wealthy world's access to resources and the *wealth-producing-process*, violently killing millions and destroying entire economies, is *wholesale terrorism*.

Secure control of the world is not possible when a non-allied powerful nation is free to support struggles for freedom on the periphery of empire. We now turn to the necessary containment of the Soviet Union and Eastern Europe to eliminate that threat.

Notes

1. Amir Taheri, *Nest of Spies* (New York: Pantheon Books, 1988), chs. 1-3, esp. pp. 22, 32-40.
2. Darrell Garwood, Under Cover: *Thirty-Five Years of CIA Deception* (New York: Grove Press, 1985), pp. 198-200; William Blum, *The CIA: A Forgotten History* (New Jersey: Zed Books Ltd., 1986), pp. 67-76.
3. Taheri, *Nest of Spies*; Richard Labeviere, *Dollars for Terror: The United States and Iran* (New York: Algora Publishing, 2000), p. 44; Burton Hersh, *The Old Boys: The American Elite and the Origins of the CIA* (New York: Charles Scribner's Sons, 1992), 330-34; Kermit Roosevelt, *Countercoup: The Struggle for the Control of Iran* (New York: McGraw-Hill 1979): C. Andrew, *For the President's Eyes Only: Secret Intelligence and the American Presidency from Washington to Bush* (New York: HarperCollins Publishers, 1995), pp. 203-05; McGehee, *CIABASE*.
4. Garwood, *Under Cover*, p. 200; Stephen Rosskamm Shalom, Imperial *Alibis* (Boston: South End Press, 1993), p. 40.
5. William D. Hartung, "Breaking The Arms-Sales Addiction," *World Policy Journal* (Winter 1990-91): p. 7.
6. Jeremy Rifkin, *Biosphere Politics* (San Francisco: HarperCollins, 1992), p. 125.

---

[a] The lead article in *CovertAction Quarterly*, Fall 2002, is titled "Imperial Wizard: Soros is not just doling out cash—he's fleecing entire countries," by Heather Cottin. This is a must-read for serious researchers on how propaganda works. While being portrayed, and portraying himself as a great philanthropist, George Soros is obviously working closely with the IMF, the World Bank, the National Endowment for Democracy, and many other offshoots of American intelligence to subvert the economies of entire nations. He then picks prime assets for pennies on the dollars. There has to be many others in on that blatant fleecing of the weak impoverished world. Run a Google Internet Search. Use many combinations of key words, names, and countries.

7 Taheri, *Nest of Spies*, pp. 122-126.

8 Neil Mackay, "Bush Planned Iraq 'Regime Change' Before Coming President," *The Sunday Herald* (Scotland), September 15, 2002; Dan Morgan and David B Ottaway, "In Iraqi Oil Scenario, Oil is Key Issue: U.S. Drillers Eye Huge Petroleum Pool," *Washington Post*, September 14, 2002; Scott Peterson, "In War, Some Facts Less Factual," *The Christian Science Monitor* September 6, 2002; Bill Powell, "Iraq We Win, Then What, *Fortune* November 5, 2002, pp. 61-72; Milan Rai, *War Plan Iraq* (London: Verso Press, 2002); William Rivers Pitt, Scott Ritter, *War on Iraq* (New York: Context Books, 2002).

9 Mackay, "Bush Planned Iraq 'Regime Change'"; http://www.ratical.org/ratville/CAH/ RRiraqWar.html; W. Clark, "The Real Reason for the upcoming War with Iraq, http://www.ratical.org/ratville/CAH/ RRiraqWar.html; Anthony Arnove, Editor, *Iraq Under Siege: The Deadly Impact of Sanctions and War* (Boston: South End Press, 2002).

10 Dan Murphy, "Indonesia Confronts Unruly Past" (*The Christian Science Monitor*, November 20, 2000), pp. 1, 10; William Blum, *Rogue State: A Guide to the World's Only Super Power*. Monroe, ME: Common Courage Press, 2000), Chapter Seventeen; Philip Agee, *Inside the Company* (New York: Bantam Books, 1975), p. 9; .Steve Weissman, *The Trojan Horse* (Palo Alto: Ramparts Press, 1975); McT Kahin, *Subversion as Foreign Policy: The Secret Eisenhower and Dulles Debacle in Indonesia* (New York: New Press, 1995); Wendell Minnick, *Spies and Provocateurs: A Worldwide Encyclopedia of Persons Conducting Espionage and Covert Action, 1946-1991* (Jefferson, North Carolina: McFarland, 1992), especially pp. 183-84; S.E. Ambrose, *Ike's Spies* (Garden City, New York: Doubleday, 1981), p. 251; M. Caldwell, Editor, *Ten Years Military Terror Indonesia* (Nottingham: Spokesmen Books, no date); Blum, *The CIA*, especially p. 221; search databases for articles or books by Kathy Kadane, reporter for States News Service; see Chapter 3, endnote 15; McGehee, CIABASE.

11 John Stockwell, *Praetorian Guard* (Boston: South End Press, 1991), p. 78.

12 Dan Jacobs, *The Brutality of Nations* (New York: Alfred A. Knopf, 1987), especially p. 5.

13 Stephen Schlesinger and Stephen Kinzer, *Bitter Fruit* (New York: Anchor Press/Doubleday, 1984); Peter Grose, *Gentleman Spy : The Life of Allen Dulles* (Boston: University of Massachusetts Press, 1996); *United Nations Guatemalan Truth Commission Report* carried on AP wires February 25, 1999; Susanne Jonas, *The Battle for Guatemala: Rebels, Death Squads, and U.S. Power* (San Francisco: Westview Press, 1991); P. Gleijeses, *Shattered Hope: The Guatemalan Revolution and the United States 1944-1954* (Princeton, NJ: Princeton University Press, 1991); Beatriz Manz *Refugees of A Hidden War: The Aftermath of Counterinsurgency in Guatemala* (New York: State University of New York, 1988); D.A, Phillips, The Night Watch (New York: Atheneum 1977); Jean-Marie Simon, *Guatemala: Eternal Spring Eternal Tyranny* (New York: W. W. Norton, 1988); Michael McClintock, *The American Connection: State Terror and Popular Resistance in Guatemala* (London: Zed Books, 1985); B. Cook, The Declassified Eisenhower; Thomas, Very Best Men; T. McCann, *An American Company: The Tragedy of United Fruit* (New York: Crown Publishers, 1976); Andrew, *For the President's Eyes Only; Eduardo Galeano, Guatemala: Occupied Country* (New York: Monthly Review Press, 1969); J. Heidenry, *Theirs Was the Kingdom: Lila and Dewitt Wallace and the Story of the Reader's Digest* (New York: W.W. Norton, 1993), pp. 594-97; *CovertAction Quarterly*; *Counterspy*; run library database searches for anything written by Allen Nairn; Blum, The CIA; William Blum, *Rogue State*, Chapters 3 through 10 and Chapter 17; and his book *Killing Hope: U.S. Military Interventions Since World War II* (Monroe, Me: Common Courage Press, 1995); N. Miller, *Spying for America* (New York: Paragon House, 1989); H.J. Hunt, *Undercover: Memoirs of an American Secret Agent* (New York: Berkeley Publishing, 1974); McGehee, CIABASE.

14 Marc Cooper, Chile and the End of Pinochet," *The Nation* (February 26, 2001), pp. 11-18; P. Gunson, A. Thompson, G. Chamberlain, *The Dictionary of Contemporary Politics of South America* (New York: Routledge, 1989), p. 228; Elton Rayack, *Not so Free to Choose: The Political Economy of Milton Friedman and Ronald Reagan* (Westport, Conn: Praeger, 1986).

15 United Nations Commission on the Truth in El Salvador, *From Madness to Hope: The 12-Year War in El Salvador* (U.N. Security Council, 1993); Charles Kernaghan, "Sweatshop Blues," *Dollars and Sense* (March/April, 1999); Blum, *Rogue State*, Chapter 17 and *Killing Hope*; Michael McClintock, *The American Connection: State Terror and Popular Resistance in El Salvador* (London: Zed Books, 1985); Blum, *The CIA*, pp. 232-43; Dennis Volman, "Salvador Death Squads, a CIA connection?" *The Christian Science Monitor*, May 8, 1984, p. 1; many issues of the *CovertAction Quarterly* and *Counterspy*; Klare & Kornbluh, *Low*

Intensity Warfare; Edward S. Herman, F. Broadhead, *Demonstration Elections: U.S. Staged Elections in the Dominican Republic, Vietnam, and El Salvador* (Boston: South End Press, 1984); Jonathan Kwitny, *Endless Enemies: The Making of an Unfriendly World* (New York: Congdon & Weed, 1984); see Chapter 3, endnote 15 and run a Google search using many combinations of keywords.

[16] Blum, *Rogue State*, Chapter 17 and *Killing Hope*; William I. Robinson, *A Faustian Bargain: U.S. Intervention in the Nicaraguan Elections and American Foreign Policy in the Post-Cold War Era* (Boulder, CO: Westview Press, 1992); Peter Kornbluth, *Nicaragua, The Price of Intervention: Reagan's War Against the Sandinistas* (Washington, DC: Institute for Policy Studies, 1987); Reed Brody, *Contra Terror in Nicaragua: Report of A Fact Finding Mission: September 1984-January 1985* (Boston: South End Press, 1985); Garvin, G., *Everybody Has His Own Gringo: The CIA and the Contras* (New York: Brassey's,1992); *The Rise and Fall of the Nicaraguan Revolution* (New York: New International, 1994); Peter Kornbluth and M. Byrne, *The Iran-Contra Scandal: The Declassified History* (New York: A National Security Archive Documents Reader, The New Press, 1993); *Twentieth Century Fund, The Need to Know: The Report of the Twentieth Century Fund Task Force on Covert Action and American Democracy* (New York: The Twentieth Century Fund Press, 1992); E. Chamorro, "Packaging the Contras: A Case of CIA Disinformation." *Institute for Media Analysis, Inc.* Monograph Series Number 2 (New York, Institute for Media Analysis, Inc, 1987); J. Adams, *Secret Armies* (New York: The Atlantic Monthly Press 1987); Minnick, *Spies and Provocateurs*; John Prados, *Keepers of the Keys: A History of the National Security Council from Truman to Bush* (New York: William Morrow, 1991); Loch .K. Johnson, *America's Secret Power* (New York: Oxford University Press, 1989); C,D. Ameringer, *U.S. Foreign Intelligence* (Lexington, MA: Lexington Books, 1990); H.B. Westerfield, ed., *Inside CIA's Private World: Declassified Articles from the Agency's Internal Journal* 1955-1992 (New Haven, CT. Yale University Press, 1995); Tony Avirgan and M. Honey, eds., Lapenca: *On Trial in Costa Rica* (San Jose, CA: Editorial Porvenir, 1987); J. Marshall, P.D. Scott, and J. Hunter, *The Iran-Contra Connection* (Boston, MA: South End Press, 1987); P.V. Parakal, *Secret Wars of the CIA* (New Delhi: Sterling Publishers, 1984); Christopher Simpson, *Blowback* (New York: Weidenfeld & Nicolson, 1988); *National Endowment for Democracy, Annual Report*; McGehee, CIABASE.

[17] Blum, *Rogue State*, Chapters 3 through 10; John Stockwell, *In Search of Enemies* (New York: W.W. Norton, 1978), especially pp. 43, 63-64, 272; Stockwell, *Praetorian Guard*; Jonathan Kwitny, *The Crimes of Patriots* (New York: W. W. Norton, 1987); S. Gervasi and S. Wong, "The Reagan Doctrine and the Destabilization of Southern Africa" (Unpublished paper from McGehee's CIABASE, April 1990); Clarridge, *A Spy for all Seasons*; H. Rositzke, *The CIA's Secret Operations* (New York: Thomas Y. Crowell Company, 1977); B. Freemantle, *CIA* (New York: Stein and Day, 1983), p. 68.

[18] Blum, *Rogue State*, Chapter 17; Gervasi and Wong, *Reagan Doctrine*, pp. 56-57; W. Minter, *Apartheid's Contras: An Inquiry into the Roots of War in Angola and Mozambique* (London, ZED Books, 1994).

[19] Stockwell, In Search of Enemies, pp. 10, 105, 137, 169, 172, 236-37; Blum, Rogue State, Chapter 17; Sean Kelley, *America's Tyrant: The CIA and Mobutu of Zaire* (Washington DC: American University Press, 1993); D. Gibbs, *The Political Economy of Third World Intervention: Mines, Money and U.S. Policy in the Congo Crisis* (Chicago, IL: University of Chicago Press, 1991); R. L. Borosage, J. Marks, The CIA File (New York: Grossman Publishers, 1976); Gervasi and Wong, Reagan Doctrine; Prados, Presidents Secret Wars; Kwitny, Endless Enemies; Blum, Killing Hope; see Chapter 3, endnote 15;.

[20] Fidel Castro, *Capitalism in Crisis: Globalization and World Politics Today* (New York: Ocean Press, 2000), p. 138; Nadia Marsh, M.D., "U.S. Med Students Arrive in Cuba," *The Workers' World*, April 19, 2001.

[21] James Bamford, *Body of Secrets: Anatomy of the Ultra-Secret National Security Agency* (New York: Doubleday, 2001), pp. 70-91, especially p. 82; Linda Robinson, "What didn't we do to get rid of Castro," *U.S. News & World Report*, October 26, 98, p. 41; Castro, *Capitalism in Crisis*, p. 215-17; John Quigley, *The Ruses for War: American Intervention Since World War II* (Buffalo: Prometheus Books, 1992).

[22] I.F. Stone, *The Hidden History of the Korean War* (Boston: Little Brown and Company, 1952), especially pp. 1-3

[23] Stone, Hidden History, especially pp. 263-64.

[24] Andrew Curry, "The First Holy War," *U.S. News & World Report*, April 8, 2002, pp. 36-42. See also Barry Yeoman, "The Stealth Crusade," *Mother Jones*, May/June 2002. An unrealistic, but well organized, minority of Christians whose goal is to convert Muslims to Christianity.

5. Containing and Destabilizing the Soviet Union and Eastern Europe

Suppression of the periphery of empire to protect wealth and power is as old as history. In fact it is history. The *managers-of-state* of the Western World knew that the Russian Revolution was being watched closely by economic theorists and, though that break for freedom occurred three generations earlier and it took 60 years to bring it down, that huge country was successfully destabilized.

As soon as WWI ended, 14 countries sent in 300,000 troops to overthrow the Russian Revolution and place that nation back under elite control. Because it would be a beacon to the restless masses both on the periphery of empire and within the *imperial-centers-of-capital*, labor successfully governing a large nation could not be permitted.[1]

The West's intervention was partially successful. Finland, Latvia, Lithuania, Estonia (each a part of the old Russian empire for over 100 years), Bessarabia, and the Eastern half of Poland were brought back within the fold of Western Europe.[2] The almost bloodless Russian Revolution turned into the deaths of possibly 15-million from hunger and disease through the Russians being unable to reorganize their economy during the invasion to suppress their break for freedom.[3] Slowing down the reorganization of the Russian economy also bought time for the *imperial-centers-of-capital*. If that newly-free nation had been left alone, it would not have lost its provinces. Without the additional three-year disruption of its economy and without the loss of the more developed provinces its industrial development would have progressed to where it is likely Germany would not have dared attack in 1941. So the successes were substantial.

We will not address the various crises in the Soviet Union point by point. But we will caution the reader that America's *Mighty Wurlitzer* to control the beliefs of a citizenry during the Cold War is nothing new. The problem of the Russian Revolution was not incompetence; it was that they were super competent. If they had been incompetent, there would have been no threat and nothing to worry about. Due to outside intervention, it took Russia 12 years to rebuild to her pre-WWI industrial level (3% that of America). But in the next 12 years Russia's industrial capacity matched

Britain, soared well past France, Japan, and Italy, and rose to 25% the capacity of the United States.⁴

We will leave it to the reader to muse on the fear created in Western capitals at the Soviet Union's rapid industrialization and how much that had to do with the Second World War. Germany's second in command, Rudolf Hess, flying to England 43 days before Germany attacked the Soviet Union can only have been to get plans for the containment and overthrow of the Soviets back on track. When sentenced to life in prison, Hess had a 24 hour-a-day guard preventing him from discussing anything beyond daily events of family life. The secrets of the planned coordinated overthrow of the Soviet Union by an allied West were to die with him.⁵

The Soviet Union's super competency is apparent in any honest study of WWII. Russia moved her industry ahead of the German army, held the Germans at the borders of Moscow for three years, and then attacked with five times the manpower, five times the heavy armor, seven times the artillery, and 17 times the airpower as the Germans.⁶ The Germans were cleared from half the occupied territory in six months. Obviously if the Soviets had just five more years to develop industrially (and remember the Intervention cost them possibly 10 years and some of their most industrialized provinces) they would have been too strong for Germany to dare attack.

After the allies landed at Normandy on June 6, 1944, two German Soldiers out of every three were on the Eastern Front. The allies were in trouble during the Battle of the Bulge and, to take the pressure off, the Soviets launched an all-out attack. The Germans rushed troops from the Western Front to their Eastern Front to stem that offensive and there were now seven German soldiers facing the Soviets for every one facing the West.⁷

Had the Soviets collapsed, there was no foreseeable combination of forces that could have dislodged those Germans from control of Europe and control of Europe meant control of the world. They would have been masters of all of Europe, Eurasia, and—through the colonial connections and their immense military power—most of the world. From those commanding heights, German power would have influenced governments all over the world much as we have been describing America has done from her superior economic, financial, and military power. Instead of it being America who saved the world, the entire Western world and perhaps the entire world, owed the Soviet Union an enormous debt for saving them against Hitler's fascism.

The Costs to the Soviets were Enormous

We are told the Soviets lost 20-million citizens in WWII. That was soon upgraded by the Soviets to 27-million but the true figure, as noted by Stalin in a response to Churchill's 1946 Iron Curtain speech, was 7-million. (The *Mighty Wurlitzers* of all empires creating reality to gain the loyalty of the masses never ceases.) The Russians destroyed infrastructure as they retreated and then the Germans destroyed even more as they retreated, entire cities and villages were burned to the ground and the regions infrastructure (railroads, oil wells, coal mines, dams, et al.) were dynamited.

As the Soviets starved, the Germans hauled 7-million horses, 17-million cattle, 20-million hogs, 27- million sheep and goats and 110-million poultry away to feed Germany.[8] Twenty-five million Soviet citizens were eating sunflower seeds and living in holes in the ground and 7-million were dead while America had only 12.3-million men and women under arms, lost 405,399, its homeland was untouched, and its industrial capacity had increased 50%.[9]

Soviet industrial capacity was again less than 10% of America. But while Industrial capacity can be quickly built, it is the social infrastructure—homes and businesses—that are expensive and time consuming to replace.

U.S. Secretary of State General George C. Marshall made a trip across Western Europe, Eastern Europe, and The Soviet Union in 1947 all the way to Moscow. With 20% the war damage of Eastern Europe and The Soviet Union, laissez-faire Western Europe was prostrate while the shattered communal Eastern Europeans and Soviets were rapidly rebuilding. A competing society's success strikes fear into the heart of every imperialist. Marshall rushed back to Washington to report that capitalism's security interests were seriously at risk:

> "All the way back to Washington," [fellow diplomat] Bohlen wrote, "Marshall talked of the importance of finding some initiative to prevent the complete breakdown of Western Europe.".... [In a speech to the nation, Marshall gave a bleak report.] We cannot ignore the factor of time. The recovery of Europe has been far slower than had been anticipated. Disintegrating forces are becoming evident. The patient is sinking while the doctors deliberate. So I believe that action cannot [a]wait compromise through exhaustion. New issues arise daily. Whatever action is possible to meet these pressing problems must be taken without delay.[10]

The *managers-of-state* in the West immediately abandoned Adam Smith philosophy and embraced Friedrich List's protection principles. The Marshall Plan for American industry to quickly rebuild Europe went into effect in 1948 and Europe was rebuilt in about five years.

With most of their natural resources under permafrost 3,000 miles away, commodity production costs for the Soviets were roughly 1.8 times those of America. Damaged far worse than Western Europe, forced to produce arms to protect against the ring of steel being built around them by the same countries that had attempted to overthrow their revolution, and without a wealthy patron to rebuild their industry, it would take the Soviets and Eastern Europe two generations to rebuild and, of course, they could never equal the West with their highly developed industry and cheap resources all over the world under the firm control of that *allied imperial-center-of-capital*.

This exposes the fiction of the Soviet military threat being the reason for America's huge military. Ten years after the Soviet collapse, there has not only been no serious reduction in Western military forces there has been a steep increase. America alone spends more for arms than the next 15 top military powers and most of those are allied with America as one *imperial-center-of-capital*. The reason for that military was, and still is, to suppress any attempt by any nation on the periphery to take control of their destiny. Freedom is, and always will be, a threat to an empire.

Errors in Soviet Planning

By 1980, in only 60 years, Soviet industrial production approached equality with America. By 1990, Soviet technology was only eight years behind America.[11] But the Soviet economy was becoming distorted, that technology was reaching the military and basic infrastructure but not the civilian economy. Seventy-seven percent of their products were each produced in one giant factory and only 5% of this production was for consumer durables. The rest of the industry was building arms (51.4%) and their enormously expensive infrastructure (43%).[12]

The biggest mistake was not establishing competing smaller factories. Where huge factories initially produce cheaper, retooling is expensive and, with no competition, managers simply will not quickly retool. With competition, a factory will develop new and better products, will retool to produce those higher quality products, will establish distribution systems, will train repair personnel, they will receive feedback from their customers, and that cycle will be continuous. Without that development cycle, the Soviet economy became moribund.

Errors aside, any serious study of economic growth rates will conclude that the Soviet socialist system accumulated capital and industrialized far faster than any capitalist country except those essentially given capital and technology after WWII so as to contain fast expanding socialism (Germany, Japan, Taiwan, and South Korea). One can only wonder what the Soviets would have accomplished if they had not been shattered by WWII and even then if they had not had to arm to offset the ring of steel placed around them.

The Official Enemy was Communism

Senior lecturer in European politics at the University of North London, Peter Gowan, describes early plans to destabilize The Soviet bloc:

> [I]n the closing decades of the Cold War, the Atlantic Alliance had combined a formidable economic blockade against Eastern Europe.... The West possessed two principal means of control. Through the IMF, it exerted political control over international finance and currency matters. Furthermore, it could restrict commercial access to Western markets through bilateral export policy, through the Coordinating Committee for Multilateral Export Controls (Cocom) on high technology, and through import duties—largely imposed by the European Community (EC)—on ECE goods.... It is scarcely an exaggeration, therefore, to say that following the upheaval of 1989 the West had the capacity to shape events in ECE to an extent comparable to that enjoyed by the Soviet government in the region after 1945. In field after field the ability of governments to deliver to their people depended on the intervening decisions of the G7 [the seven leading Western countries]. Employing this power, Western policy makers could shape the destiny of the region according to a very particular, and very political, agenda. The Western powers did not respond to the challenge of 1989 in a piecemeal fashion. Although the form and speed of the collapse took most policy makers by surprise, the G7 had, by the summer of 1989, established new machinery for handling the political transformation of Poland and Hungary and had worked out both the goals and the means of policy. Even before the region's first noncommunist government ... took power in Poland in September 1989, the G7 framework was in place.... Coercive diplomacy, not persuasion, became the tool by which the West established market economies in the East.[13]

Where America granted Western Europe $500-billion (adjusted to year 2000 values) and access to U.S. markets under the Marshall Plan to rebuild from WWII, the Soviet Union was granted $3.5-billion, a small fraction of the wealth fleeing that region each year. To protect Western industries, access to Western markets was severely restricted both by negotiation and by arbitrary tariffs (no such protection of their industries and markets were permitted Russia and other impoverished and embattled nations). When the Soviets collapsed, Western products sold in the now unprotected former Soviet Union bled the entire region dry.

All countries required as allies after WWII to stop fast expanding socialism were permitted to use exchange controls to prevent capital flight as they industrialized. The shattered former Soviet Union however was required to maintain completely open capital markets and finance capital fled Russia at an estimated $10-billion to $15-billion per year (Fidel Castro estimates it 2-to-4 times higher[14]). Eastern European countries closer to, and religiously and culturally tied to, Western Europe received both substantial government funds and private investments from the West and were simultaneously given a roadmap of precise steps they must take to eventually become members of the European Union.[15] Peter Gowan explains further:

> The EC, the G7, and the IMF treated each country separately according to its domestic program, setting off a race among the governments of the region to achieve the closest relations with, and best terms from, the West.... The

economic "liberalization" measures urged upon the new governments of ECE by Western agencies were bound to push these economies into serious recession, a situation only made worse by the disruption of regional economic links and the collapse of the Soviet Union. The result has been less a move to the market than a large-scale market destruction.... G7 experts were well aware that the drive for social system change would thoroughly destabilize ECE economies.[16]

Russian people were not so foolish as to throw away their wealth. But instead of care for all Russians, the powerbrokers were given the opportunity to immediately own the vast natural wealth of that nation. Shock therapy in the former Soviet Union compressed the 70 years of America's robber barons into a few short years. Fifty percent of Russia's GDP came under the control of what became known as the "Russian Mafia."[17]

These thieves sent the money out of Russia as fast as it came into their hands. Thousands of homes were purchased with this money in Spain and thousands more in France, Cyprus, Austria, and many other countries and purchasers of each of these homes had many times those values stashed in overseas bank accounts. Thus, by the estimates of Fidel Castro, $200-billion to $500-billion fled Russia in the decade of the 1990s (2-to-3 times other estimates).[18]

Subversive funds flowed in through the collapsed Russian borders (much of it from the National Endowment for Democracy (NED) and George Soros' *destabilization foundations*[19] to organize political parties and organize and coordinate a media to promote Adam Smith "free trade." Those corrupt oligarchs won enough control to, through heavily funded politicians, pass the necessary laws and gain title to valuable properties. Massive amounts of consumer products produced in the West were sold to Soviet citizens to soak up and return to the *Western imperial-centers-of-capital* even the small amount of money that was created within that defeated nation.

To survive, whether they stay independent or reform as one nation, those former Soviet provinces will have to limit access to both their resources and their consumer markets. The wealth appropriation math addressed in Chapter 2 makes this clear:

> The pay differential between the defeated Russia and the victorious America (23-cents an hour against $14 an hour), was a wealth accumulation potential in favor of America of 3,600-to-1 while Germany's higher wages ($23 per hour) gave her a wealth accumulation advantage of 10,000-to-1.... Obviously the Russian workers' factory is essentially shut down, they are still being paid their 23-cents an hour, nothing is produced, and, on that basis, the formula appears inaccurate. But it is the basis that is inaccurate, not the formula. Before their collapse, the Soviet Union was calculated to be within eight years of equaling the West in technology. With its huge resources and its highly skilled workforce operating factories utilizing the latest technology, and assuming it

had access to markets, Russia could theoretically produce just as efficiently as anyone else. But the billions of dollars poured into Russia since its collapse were not building any *manufacturing* industry at all, let alone modern industries. The problem is not the productivity of labor in the developing world per se. The problem is denial of technology and denial of access to markets. Immense sums flowing into a country or region are meaningless if there is no access to technology and markets.[20]

Simultaneously advocating opposite policies for the collapsed East as that which the booming West operated their economies, as we have been documenting, indicates the economic health of the Soviets was not the concern.

Economist Jeffrey Sachs of the Harvard Institute for International Development oversaw Russia's final destabilization. It is unknown if there is a connection to the hiring of economists by the CIA during the middle and late 1980s, and it is unknown if Sach's institute was established by the CIA. But consider these points:

- The wholesale shutdown of Soviet industry was done following the advice of that institute.
- These same economists would surely not offer the same advice to an allied nation, as the comment on opening Japan's markets destabilizing them demonstrates.
- Any student of mercantilism would have recognized these suggestions would destroy Russia's industry and commerce and create a dependency.
- Any economist could analyze that there was virtually nothing anywhere to replace the industry that was being de-funded and shut down except imports from the West.
- And we know that imposing beliefs to protect an imperial nation's "national interest" (the way Adam Smith free trade was imposed upon the world) is a highly-used tactic of *managers-of-state* of already developed nations.

So, how else can the guided collapse of the Soviet Union be interpreted? As would be expected, the Soviet collapse rapidly worsened as industries were shut down. The Russians figured that out after it was too late and those advisors were expelled from Russia.[21]

After the Soviets collapsed in 1991, consumer imports quickly rose to an unsustainable 39% by 1996 and climbed to an official 50% (estimated 60%) by 1998 with no compensating manufactured exports.

Documentaries and news showing impoverished Russian soldiers begging for food and other soldiers unloading cases of food with American labels on them unwittingly expose the cause of Russia's impoverishment— importing, instead of producing, consumer needs. The second most powerful country in the world, formerly totally self sufficient—except for bananas, coffee and coconuts—is quickly impoverished through massive consumer imports. A country's economic multiplier is its economic health and Russia's economic multiplier collapsed when its operating currency was spent on importing 50% of its consumer needs. There simply was too little money left circulating in Russia to run their economy.

Meanwhile, America has large compensating exports to protect the 30% of consumer products that are imported and still many economists are concerned, including the "Harvard boys" mentioned above. Couple Russia's impoverishing import statistics with the fact that it had a $35-billion-per-year trade surplus even as its industrial production fell 80% and capital investment fell nearly 90% and it is obvious the touted Russian trade surplus success is really an enormous success for the West's *Grand strategy* laying claim to others' wealth through inequalities of trade.[22] That trade surplus can only have come from massive natural resources exported to pay for a small amount of manufactured wealth—this is a mirror image of centuries ago when raiders from the cities of Europe controlled the resources of the countryside to lay claim to their wealth.

Any discussion of the collapse of the Soviet economy is not complete without addressing the collapse of the Russian ruble. Before that collapse, one Ruble equaled $1 in value and within the Soviet Union would buy far more than the dollar. At that time, one ruble would buy breakfast, lunch, and dinner with change left over. After the collapse, 6,000 rubles equaled $1. The Russians traded those old rubles for new ones at the rate of 1,000-to-1, which reduced the exchange rate to six rubles for $1. The value of that new ruble then fell by two-thirds (to 18 rubles for $1). Most Russian savings were wiped out in the first currency collapse and the second collapse took two-thirds of what was left.[23]

A healthy economy requires faith in a nation's currency. Without trust in a nation's banks, money will flee which is exactly what it did in Russia. Worse yet, once a population has lost their money thought safely stored in the bank, trust in a nation's banks cannot be restored for at least 1-to-2-generations. Loss in faith in banks means efficient capitalism cannot be established in Russia for a very long time. This, of course, is the outline of a very successful periphery destabilization policy for *imperial-centers-of-capital*.

And, as the destruction of the ruble demonstrates, this has all the marks of a planned destabilization. Jeffrey Sachs knew that Russian citizens had massive savings in the bank. In any other society, a population with huge savings would be considered a big plus. But Sachs referred to it as that "pesky overhang." A healthy economy must have both industries and buying power. If the ruble had not been arbitrarily made worthless, those private funds would have keep those industries operating throughout the process of building new industries and shutting down old industries. But the goal was to transfer that social wealth both to Russian oligarchs and to the West; the rights and well-being of the masses were of no concern.[24]

Sale of the Century by Chrystia Freeland is a highly recommended masterly study on the collapse of Russia after the breakup of the Soviet Union.[25] However, as a correspondent for the *Financial Times* when doing her research, the author focuses only on finance and politics and ignores basic economics. She also ignores Russia's highly motivated labor ready to make the transition to capitalism, the National Endowment for Democracy's funding and management of Yeltsin's election, the American election specialists orchestrating that election,[a] the Harvard Institute for International Development advising Russia's "young reformers" throughout that collapse, and she ignored how the massive imports of consumer products sucked the wealth out of Russia and collapsed the economic multiplier.

Without the economic multiplier as money from wages circulates, a country essentially has no economy. Yet, while intending to document the full history of the attempt to restructure the Russian economy, that author fails to notice that the "young reformers" paid no attention to primary production in Russia. These neophytes were so immersed in classical Western philosophy that they thought all there was to establishing capitalism was to create rich capitalists by giving title to valuable resources, industries, and banks to a few "oligarchs" who pulled off one of the greatest thefts of social wealth in history.

In the West, preventing the rise to political power of labor is a primary consideration. Thus the highly motivated "golden children" who were ready to restructure Russia's economy were never given the opportunity. Instead, the neophyte agents of capitalism (the "Young Reformers") were intent on the obviously impossible job of telescoping the 70 years of America's robber barons into less than 10 years.

The "golden children" (the children of older leaders) running Russia's economy wanted to restructure to capitalism, and would have understood how to do so successfully. But labor in charge of any part of an economy is anathema to theorists of Western philosophy. So the only people offered a serious opportunity to buy Russia's productive industries for a fraction of its true value were the new "oligarchs" with no experience in running any part of the Russian economy. Without any background on running industries, or much of anything else, these oligarchs were expected to become the leading capitalists of Russia.

No country has ever developed under the principles imposed upon post Soviet Russia. In fact, economic protections for the developed world

---

[a] This was very successful. Through covert black ops and political pressure, even former popular leader Michael Gorbachev was denied access to local reporters, media, or even an audience to speak to, wherever he went. Chrystia Freeland, *Sale of the Century: Russia's Wild Ride From Communism to Capitalism* (New York: Crown Publishers, 2000), Chapter 9.

are all in place and functioning and no wealthy nation would consider subjecting its economies to such harsh economic medicine as was imposed on Russia. To double, triple, and quadruple prices while shutting down industry right and left and destroying consumer savings is a recipe for disaster in any economics class.

A Sensible Restructuring Plan for Russia

The easiest way to understand the failure of the restructuring of the Russian economy is by outlining a sensible plan to restructure to efficient *democratic-cooperative-capitalism* as opposed to subtle-monopoly capitalism:

- Industry and media shares should have been distributed to those workers; after all it was industry already considered as collectively owned by them.[a]
- Modern industries should have been built with financing as per the money subchapter in Chapter 8.
- Until those efficient industries were established and they and the economy competitive, import restrictions should have stayed in force.
- As fast as those modern industries came on stream, Russia's obsolete huge factories would be shut down.
- An inescapable landrent tax as per Chapter 8 should have been placed into law, including royalties on natural resources such as oil, minerals, timber, and communications spectrums.
- Citizens should have received title to their homes through paying the first year's landrent taxes in advance. Remember that "pesky overhang" of enormous Russian savings. This would have been a simple and economically sound move. The landrent taxes each year would have operated the Russian government as opposed to that nation, both citizens and government, being essentially bankrupt today.
- Businesses, farmers, and homeowners should have been given title to their land through landrent bids. Citizen savings (that pesky overhang) were there to buy their homes and the annual landrent would have provided the money to operate the government.
- And locally owned banks should have been put in place to fund consumers, farmers, and producers, and an easily adjustable, inescapable, transaction tax on the circulation of money should have been put in place to cover all government expenses while reforming. This tax would be only if unforeseen capital needs emerged. A landrent tax is far the most efficient economic structure.

---

[a] This was done through vouchers but, as Chrystia Freeland documents, there were many schemes for the oligarchs to buy up those vouchers, not the least being they had to be sold for survival.

With financing available and massive buying power in the hands of the people, retailers would spring up automatically and this would be the ideal moment to establish an efficient distribution system as per Chapter 9. Certainly there are many other factors to consider, some of which we address in the conclusion, but the above would have been the foundation of a workable restructure plan.

Monopolization of technology is the biggest barrier. Virtually any successful restructure plan must provide access to technology, natural resources and markets. That is what the struggles are all about. All Europe is almost devoid of most resources and a part of Russia's massive resources could have been bartered for that technology. Patent licensing could have been imposed by law. This is accepted as legal in international law, was being tested in court with AIDS drugs in South Africa, and the major drug companies capitulated rather than go to trial.

The reason these sensible restructure plans were not a suggestion of Western advisors is obvious; labor would have ended up with enormous wealth and political power. If they had been given the chance, Russia's egalitarian-trained and idealistic "golden children" could have established *democratic-cooperative-capitalism* as opposed to being today a dependency on the periphery of *imperial-centers-of-capital*. If that had happened, the secret that no power-structure in the imperial centers had yet given their citizens full rights would have been exposed and all the world would be demanding their full rights.

Could the Soviet Union have avoided the Cold War?

When Russian President Boris Yeltsin met with President George Bush in 1992, he said, "We may have American Prisoners yet." This created momentary consternation. All was quiet on the subject as reporters started digging and then came this headline: "Yeltsin: POWs 'Summarily Executed.'" But the last line of that front-page article depicting these execution horrors told the real story: "The largest group of Americans imprisoned in the Soviet Union included more than 730 pilots and other airmen who either made forced landings on Soviet territory or were shot down on Cold War spy [and sabotage] flights." There were over 10,000, and possibly over 20,000 sabotage and mapping flights over Soviet territory and the surviving crashed American airmen finished out their lives in Soviet prisons while their families were given a cover story that they had died in another event somewhere else.[26] The threat of war was from the West, not from the Soviet Union.

The Soviets remembered that mapping overflights preceded Germany's invasion in 1941. They remembered the invasion by 14 Western nations attempting to overthrow their revolution (the same nations now overflying their territory). They heard the thunderous rhetoric from some of those same countries that they were evil. They knew of the thousands of times that trained assassins and saboteurs were parachuted or smuggled into their country. And the ring of steel and alliances encircling them and targeting them with nuclear intercontinental bombers and missiles left no doubt that somewhere in the future an excuse for war would be created.

The Soviets were roughly 10 years behind the West developing and installing every new super weapon. But the Soviets built atomic and hydrogen bombs before America could build enough atomic weapons to destroy that ideological menace. Analysts are right when they say the West would not attack the Soviet Union. But that is only because the Soviets developed the atomic bomb too quick. Papers in President Johnson's library tell us that an excuse for war was to be created and a first strike was planned. Study the history of suppressions worldwide we are addressing, study why tiny impoverished Vietnam faced such an assault, study why every offer of the Soviets for mutual disarmament was ignored.

No empire will stand if any nation on the periphery breaks free and proceeds to provide their citizens with a better standard of living. If that happens, all countries would demand the same freedom and the periphery of empire would melt away. The names of the now declassified plans for war against the Soviet Union (Bushwhacker, Broiler, Sizzle, Shakedown, Dropshot, Trojan, Pincher, and Frolic) graphically portray their offensive purpose. Some of those plans addressed the actual occupation of the Soviet Union.[27]

Make no mistake about it, the intention was to destroy the Soviet Union and suppress any other breaks for freedom and both goals were reached. Those destabilizations cost trillions of dollars, 12-million to 15-million lives, and hundreds of millions of deaths from disease and hunger as other nations' economies were destroyed. (Keep in mind, only $40-billion a year properly invested would have eliminated most hunger and provided clean water and health care to the entire world. World development and elimination of poverty have not been the goals of the *imperial-centers-of capital*.)

A key part of Western propaganda has always been that there was a lack of rights in the Soviet Union and that the secret police were everywhere. But America and most of Western Europe could give freedom and rights to their citizens because they were not subject to bombings, assassinations, and threats of invasion; the CIA's *Mighty Wurlitzer* saying otherwise notwithstanding.

Once America itself faced externally organized terrorism, the World Trade Center/Pentagon bombings and the anthrax biological warfare scare, the security practices of the former Soviet Union such as stalking foreigners and asking neighbors to spy on each other (Muslim neighbors in this case) is seen as something Americans must do. One major difference: saboteurs and assassins smuggled into the former Soviet Union were not as easily ethnically identifiable as those currently targeting America. The West's security, through denial of full rights for targeted people, will be much easier.

Afghanistan, the Final Straw that Collapsed the Soviet Union

The CIA's largest covert operation was 1985 National Security Council Directive 166 ordering the destabilization of Afghanistan. That directive was only a massive expansion of what the CIA had already been doing since 1979 under a finding signed by President Carter on July 3, 1979, five months before the Soviet forces were invited into Afghanistan to suppress that destabilization. The CIA, working behind the scenes through Pakistani intelligence, provided massive arms (eventually reaching 65,000-tons a year) and training to Afghanistan's Mujahideen and 35,000 Muslim extremists recruited from over 40 countries.

All support seemed to be coming from Pakistan. Most Muslims would have been unaware that their terrorist operation against Afghanistan and the Soviet Union was a CIA designed, funded, and coordinated operation. America's current leading terrorist enemy, Osama Bin Laden, worked with the CIA in establishing, financing, arming, and training the Mujahideen as well as those recruited from all over the world. Those who returned to their homes became the cells of Al-Qaeda whose goals were the destruction of America.

Afghanistan was not the primary target. The goal was to destabilize the six Eastern Muslim provinces of the Soviet Union both by smuggling in subversive propaganda (books on Soviet atrocities against Muslim people) and sabotage teams (focused especially on assassinating Soviet officers and destroying factories and supply depots). The Mujahideen rebels were based safely in Pakistan from which as many as 11 teams at a time would infiltrate across the borders to attack airports, railroads, fuel depots, electricity pylons, bridges and roads.

Satellite reconnaissance guided the Afghan resistance to Soviet targets and they were equipped with the latest missiles; including hand held stinger missiles, to shoot down Soviet helicopter gunships and other aircraft. A stinger missile electronic simulator was brought to Pakistan to train the Mujahideen. Soviet battle plans were intercepted by spy satellites and this information relayed to the resistance which were supplied with secure communications technology. Massive amounts of propaganda books were distributed to the population.

It worked. The progressive government of Afghanistan, and the Soviet forces supporting them at the request of the freely elected government, were defeated and those Muslim "freedom fighters" went on to destabilize Eastern Soviet provinces. Today's civil war in Russia's Muslim Chechnya and Georgia where America is now training Russian soldiers to root out the Al-Qaeda they trained, now called terrorists because they have turned on America, is a residual of that CIA master plan.

The website www.emperors-clothes.com has chosen the destabilization of Yugoslavia, Afghanistan, and Iraq as the focus of their research and they cite solid sources describing the same American-trained Muslim terrorists in Afghanistan were later destabilizing Kosovo and Macedonia under the funding and guidance of American and German intelligence services (BND). The Kosovo Liberation Army (KLA) eventually reached a strength of 30,000 as they destabilized Kosovo by assassinating policemen and Serb leaders.

Later these same intelligence services were reported to be organizing the Ethnic Albanian insurgency in Macedonia, utilizing some of these same American-trained Muslim terrorists. (This would be MPRI and other supposed private armies under the supervision of the Pentagon's Special Operations Command, SOCOM. Run a Google computer search using those keywords.) The escort to safety of surrounded and trapped Ethnic Albanian insurgents by American troops provides strong support for these reports. For those sources in the media of record the reader will have to check that website and future books by the authors cited.[28]

The Soviets withdrew from Afghanistan in 1989, the government was soon overthrown, and those progressive leaders attempting to build a modern Afghanistan were promptly hanged. All this was made palatable by intelligence agency wordsmiths (that *Mighty Wurlitzer* again) use of terrorist adjectives (butchers) to describe the progressive leaders they had overthrown.

But the CIA and all *managers-of-state* knew better. CIA study-books available in most libraries described that government as freeing women and peasants, establishing clinics and schools with massive literacy programs, returning the land to those who farmed it, canceling the mortgage debts of small farmers, and canceling usurious debts. Sale of brides was prohibited and women were able to choose their own husbands. In fact, Afghanistan was then one of the leading nations in the world for providing women's rights. More women were in universities than men.

Within that region, Afghanistan's new freedom was just as great a revolution as the French Revolution in 1789; arguably history's most important revolution in the world's slow, and still ongoing, escape from feudalism. But, just as the French Revolution was overthrown, by 1996 the Taliban came into power, feudal rule was reestablished, and women could no longer hold jobs or go to school. Nor could they leave the home without being fully covered and accompanied by a male relative.

Afghanistan then went from one of the fastest developing nations in the world with full rights extended to all citizens to one of the most repressive in the world where a woman did not dare show her uncovered face in public, could not go to school, and could not hold a job.

The one aspect of this history that stands out is how these same people are terrorists when they turned on America and had been freedom fighters when, under American financial support and guidance, they were terrorizing and destabilizing America's competitors. This distortion of reality was an enormously effective use of propaganda and control of the media.

The 'Official' Enemy is now Terrorism

While discussing that the 1979 covert U.S. intervention was the reason the USSR sent in troops, Zbigniew Brzezinski, President Carter's National Security Advisor, declared, "That secret operation was an excellent idea, the effect was to draw the Russians into the Afghan trap." Over 35,000 Muslims from all over the world were directly influenced by the Muslim extremist success in Afghanistan and they then scattered all over the world to spread the knowledge on terror and destabilization of countries taught to them by the CIA.[29]

Energized by the CIA designed Jihad to expel Soviet influence from Afghanistan and the Soviet Union's Eastern provinces, the "freedom fighters" then restructured their newly gained knowledge into a Jihad to free all Muslim nations from Western domination. The bombs falling on Afghanistan in late 2001 were blowing apart terrorist training camps built by the CIA in the 1980s to destabilize the Soviet Union. These students of terrorism had turned their deadly skills towards destabilizing the very nation who trained them and America is now searching out and killing terrorists they trained.

Control of discourse and self-censorship by the media is thorough. Although one-sentence statements that America trained those terrorists to attack the Soviet Union are uttered, the immorality, the injustice, and the lawlessness of the West's training of terrorists to destabilize peaceful nations is never discussed.

It was the political and economic shattering of a country rapidly moving towards modernization that Brzezinski thought was such an "excellent idea," Two million Afghans (out of a population of 15-million) were killed, 5-million more became refugees, and, unless America is sincere in establishing a truly democratic government and providing funds to rebuild the country they destroyed under the orders of National Security Council Directive 166 (so far no real development money), there is no end in sight to Afghanistan's impoverishment.

What would happen in America if outside forces supported African-Americans or any other political or religious groups with immense funds, arms, training in sabotage, and the promise of continued support to gain more rights or even to become America's leaders? What would happen in Europe if disaffected groups were funded and armed to sabotage and destabilize their countries? The 9/11/2001 terrorist attack on New York's World Trade Center and the Pentagon provides the answer.

The Taliban of Afghanistan, once sheltering terrorists, are marginalized and many of their leaders are killed or imprisoned. But there are tens of thousands of equally angry supporters and hundreds of thousands of unprotected Western personnel and property scattered all over the world. Even though economic violence, financial violence, and open violence has been practiced against them, this author believes Americans and their property will be in only slightly more danger than before the War on Terrorism. Few societies have the long history of violent destabilization of other societies as the West. It is not in their nature. However, if the poverty on the periphery deepens as the wealth in the imperial centers increases, their options for control of their own destiny will keep getting fewer.

We now take a look at why the imperial nations decided Yugoslavia had to be destroyed.

Notes

[1] Lloyd C. Gardner, *Safe for Democracy* (New York: Oxford University Press, 1984), pp. 197-8; Philip Knightley, *The First Casualty* (New York: Harcourt Brace Jovanovich, Publishers, 1975), Chapter 7; Mikhail Gorbachev, *Perestroika* (New York: Harper and Row, 1987), p. 33, note 2; Edmond Taylor, *The Fall of the Dynasties* (New York: Dorset Press, 1989), p. 359; Ernest Volkman, Blaine Baggett, *Secret Intelligence* (New York: Doubleday, 1989), Chapter 1.

[2] Walter Isaacson, Evan Thomas, *The Wise Men* (New York: Simon and Schuster, 1986), p. 150; Michael Kettle, *The Allies and the Russian Collapse* (Minneapolis, University of Minnesota Press, 1981), p.15; Taylor, *Fall of the Dynasties*, p. 381.

[3] Philip Knightley, *First Casualty*, p. 138; D. F. Fleming, *The Cold War and its Origins* (New York: Doubleday, 1961, 2 vols.), pp. 26, 1038.

[4] Paul Kennedy, *The Rise and Fall of the Great Powers*, (New York: Random House, 1987), pp. 321, 323.

[5] James Douglas-Hamilton, *Motive For a Mission: The Story Behind Rudolf Hess's Flight to Britain*, (New York: Paragon House, 1979).

[6] Vilnis Sipols, *The Road to Great Victory* (Moscow: Progress Publishers, 1985), pp. 109, 132, 179-80; Kennedy, *Rise and Fall*, especially pp. 321, 323, 352, in part quoting J. Erickson, *The Road to Berlin* (London: 1983), p. 447.

[7] Jeffrey Jukes, *Stalingrad at the Turning Point* (New York: Ballantine Books, 1968), p. 154; *National Geographic TV* (August 23, 1987); Fleming, *Cold War and its Origins*, p. 157; Kolko, Politics of War, pp. 19, 351, 372.

[8] Kennedy, *Rise and Fall*, pp. 357-58; David Mayers, *George Kennan* (New York: Oxford University Press, 1988), pp. 190-91; Oleg Rzheshevsky, *World War II: Myths and the Realities* (Moscow, USSR: Progress Publishers, 1984), p. 175.

[9] Sidney Lens, *Permanent War* (New York: Schocken Books, 1987), pp. 20-21; William Appleman Williams, *The Tragedy of American Diplomacy* (New York: W. W. Norton, 1988, pp. 208, 235.

[10] Don Cook, *Forging the Alliance*, (London: Seeker and Warburg, 1989), pp. 78-9.

[11] Rich Thomas, "From Russia, with Chips," *Newsweek*, August 6, 1990.

[12] Lester Thurow, *The Future of Capitalism: How Today's Economic Forces Shape Tomorrow's World* (England: Penguin Books, 1996), p. 56; Lester Thurow, *Head to Head: The Coming Economic Battle Among Japan, Europe, and America* (New York: William Morrow and Company, 1992), pp. 92, 95; Patrick Flaherty, "Behind Shatalinomics: Politics of Privatization," *Guardian*.

October 10, 1990, p. 11; David Kotz, "Russia in Shock: How Capitalist 'Shock Therapy' is Destroying Russia's Economy," *Dollars and Sense*, June 1993, p. 9.

[13] Peter Gowan, "Old Medicine in New Bottles," *World Policy Journal* (Winter 1991-92), pp. 3-5.

[14] Fidel Castro, *Capitalism in Crisis: Globalization and World Politics Today* (New York: Ocean Press, 2000 pp. 42, 104.

[15] Charles William Maynes, "A New Strategy for Old Foes and New Friends" *World Policy Journal*, Summer 2000, pp. 71-72; Castro, *Capitalism in Crisis*, p. 104.

[16] Peter Gowan, "Old Medicine in New Bottles," *World Policy Journal* (Winter 1991-92), pp. 6-8, 13.

[17] John Gray, *False Dawn* (New York: The Free Press, 1998), Chapter Six; Alexander Buzgalin and Andrei Kolganov, *Bloody October in Moscow: Political Repression in the Name of Reform* (New York: Monthly Review Press, 1994); Boris Kagarlitsky, *Square Wheels: How Russian Democracy Got Derailed,* (New York: Monthly Review Press, 1994). The tables of contents of most good magazines, both mainstream and alternative news, will have many good articles on the legal theft of the wealth of the Soviet Union through privatization.

[18] Castro, Capitalism in Crisis, pp. 42, 104.

[19] George Soros, "Imperial Wizard: Master Builder of the New Bribe Sector, Systematically Bilking the World," *CovertAction Quarterly* (November 2002), pp. 1-7.

[20] J.W. Smith, *Economic Democracy: The Political Struggle of the Twenty-First Century*, updated and expanded 3rd edition (www.ied.info/cc.html: The Institute for Economic Democracy, 2003), Chapter 1; Thurow, *The Future of Capitalism*, pp. 35-36 says German wages were $30 an hour in 1996, see also pp. 46 and 168 for wages in Eastern and Central Europe at five percent to ten percent of German wages; Doug Henwood, "Clinton and the Austerity Cops," *The Nation*, November 23, 1992, p. 628. Colin Hines, Tim Lang, Jerry Mander, and Edward Goldsmith, editors, *The Case Against the Global Economy and A Turn Toward the Local* (San Francisco: Sierra Club, 1996), p. 487, say $24.90 an hour for Germany, $16.40 for the U.S.

[21] Janine R. Wedel, "The Harvard Boys Do Russia," *The Nation*. June 1, 1998, pp. 11-16.

[22] Thurow, *The Future of Capitalism*, pp. 43-45; Castro, *Capitalism in Crisis*, pp. 99-104; "Proud Russia on Its Knees," *U.S. News & World Report*, February 8, 1999, pp. 30-36; David R. Francis, "Debt -riddled Russia to Ask for Forgiveness," *The Christian Science Monitor*, April 5, 1999, p. 17; Katrina vanden Heuvel, editorial, *The Nation*, August 10-17, 1998, pp. 4-6. See also Julie Corwin, Douglas Stranglin, Suzanne Possehl, Jeff Trimble, "The Looting of Russia," *U.S. News & World Report*, March 7, 1994; John Feffer, "The Browning of Russia," *CovertAction Quarterly* (Spring 1996).

[23] Castro, *Capitalism in Crisis*, pp. 99-104.

[24] Ann Williamson, "An Inconvenient History," http://www.geocities.com/Athens/7842/wcessay04.htm.

[25] Chrystia Freeland, *Sale of the Century: Russia's Wild Ride From Communism to Capitalism* (New York: Crown Publishers, 2000. See also, Stephen Cohen, *Failed Crusade: America and the Tragedy of Post-Communist Russia.* (New York: W.W. Norton, 2000).

[26] Michael Ross, "Yeltsin: POWs 'Summarily Executed'," *The Spokesman Review* (November 12, 1992), pp. B1, A10; Volkman and Baggett, *Secret Intelligence*, p. 187; John Loftus, *Belarus Secret* (New York: Alfred A. Knopf, 1982), especially Chapters 5-8, pp. 109-10; Blum, *A Forgotten History*, Chapters 6, 7, 8, 15, 17, especially p. 124; *U.S. News & World Report*, March 15, 1993, pp. 30-56; see Chapter 3, endnote 15.

[27] Michio Kaku and Daniel Axelrod, *To Win A Nuclear War*, (Boston: South End Press, 1987), especially p. X.

[28] Linda Robinson, "America's Secret Armies," *U.S. News & World Report* (November 4, 2002), pp. 38-43; Greg Guma, "Cracks in the Covert Iceberg" *Toward Freedom* (May 1998), p. 2;

Ahmed Rashid, *Taliban: Militant Islam, Oil and Fundamentalism in Central Asia* (New York: Yale University Press, 2001); Michael Griffin, *Reaping the Whirlwind: The Taliban Movement in Afghanistan* (Sterling, VA: Pluto Press, 2001); John Cooley, *Unholy Wars: Afghanistan, America, and International Terrorism* (Sterling, VA: Pluto Press, 2000); Yousai Mohammad and M. Adkin, *The Beartrap: Afghanistan's Untold Story* (London, England: Leo Cooper, 1992); William Blum, *Rogue State: A Guide to the World's Only Super Power* (Monroe, ME: Common Courage Press, 2000), Chapter Two; K. Lohbeck, *Holy War, Unholy Victory: Eyewitness to the CIA's Secret War in Afghanistan* (Washington DC: Regnery Gateway, 1993); Alexander and Michael S. Swetnam. *Osama Bin Laden's al-Queda: Profile of a Terrorist Network* (Ardsley NY: Transnational Publishers, 2001); Peter L. Bergen, *Holy War Inc.: Inside the Secret World of Osama Bin Laden* (New York: Simon & Schuster, 2001); M.J. Gohari, *The Taliban: Ascent to Power.* (New York: Oxford University Press, 2000); Larry P. Goodson, *Afghanistan's Endless War: State failure, Regional Politics, and the Rise of the Taliban* (Seattle: University of Washington Press, 2001); Robin Wright, *Sacred Rage: The Wrath of Militant Islam* (New York: Simon & Schuster, 1985).; Michael Griffin, *Reaping the Whirlwind: The Taliban Movement in Afghanistan* (Sterling, VA: Pluto Press, 2001); J. Peterzell, *Reagan's Secret Wars, CNSS Report 108* (Washington, DC: Center for National Security Studies, 1984); T. Weiner, *Blank Check: The Pentagon's Black Budget* (New York: Warners Books, 1990); E.T. Chester, *Covert Network: Progressives, the International Rescue Committee, and the CIA* (New York: M.E. Sharpe, 1995); D. Cordovez, and S.S. Harrison, *Out of Afghanistan: The Inside Story of the Soviet Withdrawal* (New York: Oxford University Press, 1995); S. Emerson, *Secret Warriors* (New York: G.P. Putnam, 1988); Westerfield, Inside CIA's Private World; L.K. Johnson, America's Secret Power; R. Kessler, *Inside the CIA: Revealing the Secrets of the World's Most Powerful Spy Agency* (New York: Pocket Books, 1992); Duane A. Clarridge, *A Spy for all Seasons: My Life in the CIA* (New York: Scribner, 1997). Run a Google Internet search.

[29] Ibid, especially Guma, "Cracks in the Covert Iceberg."

6. It was Yugoslavia's Turn to be destabilized

The destabilizations of most of Eastern Europe discussed above were under America's 1982 National Security Council Directive 54 (NSD-54). All East European countries except Yugoslavia were targeted. Yugoslavia was a special case that had prospered as the West provided them with money and technology in an attempt to wean it away from the Soviet bloc. Yugoslavs had a respectable standard of living; education and medical care were free. Each citizen was guaranteed a job with 30 days paid vacation. This multi-ethnic melting pot organized under communal principals enjoyed secure jobs, cheap transportation, cheap housing, inexpensive utilities, and a relatively high average quality of life.

As they knew it would devastate their economy, Yugoslavia was not about to leave the well-being of its citizens to the vagaries of a fictitious "free market." As with Cuba, Nicaragua, Chile, and other nations which attempted to chart an independent course and protect their citizens, such independence was the one thing not tolerated by international capital. To understand the process, we need only look at the on-going destabilization of the once relatively prosperous Yugoslavia.

IMF demands for currency devaluation and an increase in the Yugoslavian Central Bank's discount rate in 1980-84 were the opening guns of financial warfare for the destabilization of Yugoslavia. As their debt and interest rate increased from that currency devaluation, the Yugoslav economy slowed.

Then the 1984 U.S. National Security Council Directive 133 (NSD-133), labeled "SECRET SENSITIVE" and titled "United States Policy towards Yugoslavia," ordered the final fragmentation of that nation: A freeze was placed on transfer payments to the outlying provinces and the IMF denied Yugoslavia the right to credit (money creation) from its own central bank. They could no longer fund crucial economic and social programs such as industry and health care. (Note the similarity to the same "structural adjustments" imposed throughout the developing world by the IMF/World Bank.)

The results were planned and predictable: A 7.1% growth rate between 1966 and 1979 dropped to 2.8% from 1980-87, zero in 1987-88, and in

1990 it reached an appalling minus 10.6%. This worked so well for the West they ordered another 30% currency devaluation which accelerated a 140% inflation rate to 937% in 1992 and 1,134% a year later, GDP dropped 50% in four years.[a] The result was the destruction of Yugoslav buying power quite similar to what was done to the Soviet Union (as discussed above) under the pretext of establishing capitalism. Basic economics teaches that a prosperous nation must have buying power. No Western nation would ever inflict such a wound on its own economy; destabilizing the Yugoslav economy, not development, was the goal.

Simultaneous with creating the extreme crisis in Yugoslavia, German foreign minister Hans Dietrich Genscher, was promoting independence to his counterpart in the Yugoslav province of Croatia. In an annual event for funding destabilizations, U.S. 1990-91 legislation the "Foreign Operations Appropriations Bill" demanded separate elections for each Yugoslav province with the U.S. State Department approving their conduct and outcome. This aid was to go only to independent republics, none to the central government. Independence meant there would be funding and trade for the provinces while continued federation with Yugoslavia meant continued embargoes and no funds.

All this, along with an eight-year embargo, assured the final breakup of Yugoslavia. Under the 1995 Dayton Accords, a constitution was written for the Bosnian Federation by the U.S. State Department stipulating that the negotiating coalition could appoint a High Representative (HR) with full executive powers to overrule the government. That façade of democracy

---

[a] Acting Secretary of State Lawrence Eagleburger acknowledged this on the *McNeil/Lehrer Report* (May 6, 1993), and many other talk shows and news programs, pointing out that there were those who pushed for the collapse of Yugoslavia, specifically pointing to Germany. Michael Elliot of the respected British publication, *The Economist*, speaking on that same show, agreed. Ramsey Clark, *Hidden Agenda: U.S./NATO Takeover of Yugoslavia* (New York: International action Center, 2002); Michel Collon, *Liars Poker: The Great Powers, Yugoslavia and the Wars of the future* (New York:: International action Center, 2002); Michel Chossudovsky, *The Globalization of Poverty: Impacts of IMF and World Bank Reforms* (London: Zed Books, 1997), Chapter 13; Michel Chossudovsky, "Dismantling Yugoslavia, Colonizing Bosnia," *CovertAction Quarterly* (Spring, 1996), pp. 31-37; Michael Parenti, *To Kill a Nation: The Attack on Yugoslavia* (New York: Verso, 2000), p. 26; William Tabb, *The Amoral Elephant: Globalization and the Struggle for Social Justice in the Twenty-First Century* (New York: Monthly Review Press, 2001), Chapter 6, espec. pp. 149, 153-54; Dusko Doder, Yugoslavia: "New War, Old Hatreds," *Foreign Policy* (Summer 1993), pp. 4, 9-11, 18-19; Thomas Kielinger, Max Otte, "Germany: The Presumed Power," *Foreign Policy* (Summer 1993), p. 55David Lorge Parnas, "Con: Dayton's a Step Back—Way Back," *Peace* (March/April 1996), pp. 17-22; Sean Gervasi, "Germany, U.S., and the Yugoslavian Crisis," *CovertAction Quarterly* (Winter 1992-93), pp. 41-45, 64-66; McClintock, *Instruments of Statecraft*, pp. 71-82; Catherine Samaray, *Yugoslavia Dismembered* (New York: Monthly Review Press, 1995; Charles Lane, Theodore Stanger, Tom Post, "The Ghosts of Serbia," *Newsweek*. April 19, 1993, pp. 30-31. Run a Google Internet Search.

(the Parliamentary Assembly) simply rubber-stamped the decisions of the HR and his expatriate advisors. Those accords stipulated that, "the first governor of the Central Bank of Bosnia and Herzegovina is to be appointed by the IMF and 'shall not be a citizen of Bosnia and Herzegovina or a neighboring state.'" Because he objected to forcibly selling off banks, water, energy, telecommunications, transportation, and metal industries, at firesale prices, the elected president of the Serbian segment of Bosnia was forcibly removed by NATO.[1] All this was done under the flags of "freedom and democracy."

A peaceful relatively prosperous country, with 30% of marriages interethnic, erupted into civil war. Macedonia, Slovenia, Croatia, and Bosnia-Herzegovina were torn away from the Yugoslav federation. Yugoslavia's Serbian population, which had forgiven the Western Christians for the slaughter of possibly one-third of the Eastern Orthodox Serbian men during Hitler's holocaust, was again facing second-class citizenship imposed by Western Christians.

As Serbians fled, ethnic Albanians, 40% of Kosovo at the end of WWII, increased to 80%. American and German intelligence armed and coached the Kosovo Liberation Army (KLA). These mercenaries surfaced in 1997, started assassinating Serbian police officers and ethnic Albanian collaborators (over 1,100 attacks on Serb police and Kosovar Albanian collaborationists, many fatal). The once relatively peaceful Kosovar rebellion had turned violent and the Yugoslav army was called in.[a] Croatian General, Agim Ceku—who had been in command of artillery in the ethnic cleansing of Serbs from the Krajina region of Croatia—took over command of the KLA in February 1998. This was a sure sign that America's CIA, Germany's BND, and the Military Professional Resources (MPRI, retired U.S. generals under Pentagon contract) were still orchestrating this destabilization.[2]

An assembly was convened in Rambouillet, France, a replay of the Dayton Accords, to essentially dictate the carving off of Kosovo. The accords called for 50,000 NATO troops to oversee that autonomous republic and they were to be granted the use of all airports, roads, rail, and ports free of any charges. Not only were they not to be subject to Yugoslav law they were to have supremacy over Yugoslav police and authorities and the right to inspect any part of not just Kosovo but Serbia itself. The Kosovo economy was to be structurally adjusted as per the Bosnia-Herzegovina economy and the Russian economy described above.

---

[a] This is exactly what any other country would have done if outside forces were orchestrating the assassination of their policemen and politicians. Witness America's National Guard called out to protect thousands of facilities nationwide and the mobilization of armed forces worldwide to eradicate Al-Qaeda after the 9/11/2001 terrorist attack on America.

Yugoslavia had only two choices: sign the accords (dictates) or be bombed. Every diplomat of good conscience agreed that these were articles of surrender that no sovereign nation could sign. Those accords were essentially a disguised declaration of war.

The world, of course, heard only the prepared *Mighty Wurlitzer* press releases of an intransigent Yugoslavia as, with the support of the majority of their citizens who patriotically believed what they were told about Serbian atrocities, NATO proceeded to bomb the regional Orthodox Christians back to pre-1940 status.[3]

Taking over the Media of the Defeated Serbia

The destabilization of Yugoslavia gives us a chance to study how propaganda works in democracies with so-called "freedom of the press." Previously, Yugoslavia had opposition radio stations, dissident publications, several major political parties and each party had its own newspapers, radio stations, and TV stations. Milosevic had been elected three times, twice as President of Serbia and later as President of Yugoslavia. The Yugoslav President had a cabinet to discuss and decide policy and an elected coalition parliament which approved all decisions and which included four major political parties and several smaller ones, more than any other country in Europe and they ranged fully from the left political spectrum to the right. This governing process had even been shown, possibly unwittingly, on Western TV.

During the Western orchestrated coup that overthrew Milosevic, armed units seized all major TV, Radio, and newspaper outlets. When the dust settled, there remained essentially only one media. Just as in the West, all papers published the same stories and were written much the same. Just as Americans can see the same news with the same slant on all TV channels, Serbs now found the same news with the same slant on all their TV channels. A nation with a wide choice of views suddenly had only the Western view.

Now on both Yugoslavia news and Western news Milosevic was labeled a *dictator* while Croatian descendants of Hitler's Ustase were simultaneously labeled *democratic*. The Ustase ethnically cleansing Jews, Gypsies, and Serbs during WWII was called the Three-Thirds Doctrine: one-third of the Serbs were to be deported, one-third were forced to become Catholics, and one-third were to be executed. Those Ustase descendants had just imposed a one-party press, and ethnically cleansed several hundred thousand Serbs from Croatia and Bosnia.[a] It is obvious that the *Mighty Wurlitzer* buzzwords which build our images of the world are

---

[a] In Croatia Hitler's mobile death squads were known as Ustase, in Romania as the Iron Guard, and in Latvia as Vanagas. Run a Google Internet Search.

primarily for protection of wealth and power and have only a marginal relation to reality.

Western puppets purged their territory of ethnic minorities even as the West accused Serbia of these atrocities. That besieged nation is in fact the home to 26 ethnic groups, 1-million of whom are refugees ethnically cleansed from former provinces of Yugoslavia, including 350,000 Serbs and others ethnically cleansed from Kosovo after NATO's takeover of that province.[4]

Reality as opposed to the Thunder of the *Mighty Wurlitzer*

History is written by winners so it will remain largely unknown to most that the Kosovo rebellion was a civil war covertly designed, organized, (essentially started) and supported by the same governments militarily imposing the Rambouillet accords. The *Worker's World* describing a German documentary brought a part of the reality of the Yugoslav destabilization to light:

> "Finally, long after the war, some of the truth began to break into the media. On Feb. 8, the major German television network ARD broadcast a special on the war entitled "It Began with a Lie." This showed that the charges of mass murder, genocide and organized "ethnic cleansing" made against Belgrade were inventions of the U.S., German and other governments.[5]

The Serbs, however, refused to sign away their sovereignty and may have reacted to the bombing by expelling the Albanian Kosovo population.[a] The "free" press should be called to account for not alerting the public that it was NATO members acting and Yugoslavia doing the reacting. It was Yugoslavia, and no one else, under threat all the time. Yugoslavia was not threatening anyone outside its borders and was not threatening anyone within their borders until they were being destabilized as described above. During that destabilization homes were destroyed as the KLA were rooted out of the houses from which they were firing on Serb soldiers but no

---

[a] We say "may have" because there is the high probability that the KLA engineered the ethnic Albanian exodus from Kosovo under the coaching of Western Intelligence services who were carefully writing history to justify the destruction of Yugoslavia. Only an alert researcher on the ground in Kosovo can research the truth. Jared Israel, "Why Albanians Fled the NATO Bombing: The Truth About What Happened," Interview with Cedda Pralinchevich, http://emperors-clothes.com/interviews/keys.htm, will provide insights into what questions to ask. Cedda Pralinchevich is very persuasive that Albanians were fleeing upon orders of their leaders and in their culture not obeying was not an option. The website http://emperors-clothes.com has extensive well-researched and solidly-sourced information on the destabilization of Yugoslavia.

Serbian ethnic cleansing occurred before or after NATO started bombing Yugoslavia.[a]

The original propaganda figures of over 100 massacres with 100,000 to 500,000 Albanian men missing and thought to be slaughtered were reduced to a still sensationalized 10,000 expected to be found in mass graves when NATO first entered Kosovo. Instead of massacres, inspection of the alleged 30 mass gravesites by an American FBI team turned up 200 bodies and the Kosovar externally orchestrated civil war body count became 2,108 killed by all participants—the Serbs, the KLA, *local grudge settlements*, and NATO bombs. Emilio Perez Pujol, the head of the Spanish Forensic team conducting the investigation, said "not one mass grave was found."[6]

The lack of mass graves and this low body count testifies to a successful NATO propaganda blitz (that *Mighty Wurlitzer* again) that has never been addressed in depth by the media of record. How could they? It is they who blazed the propaganda from their headlines.

When to the above disinformation we add the Pentagon wordsmiths' claim of the destruction of one-third of the Serbian military (122 tanks, 454 artillery pieces, and 222 armored personnel carriers) and the postwar investigation by General Wesley Clark, the West's commander of that war, that only 14 tanks, 20 artillery pieces, and 18 armored personnel carriers" were destroyed, it is obvious that this was a planned propaganda campaign.[7]

The American/NATO assault on Serbia/Kosovo destroyed only about 50 of Serbia's major weapons of war and very few soldiers while killing more civilians than the accused nation, Serbia. However, that bombing blitz succeeded very well in creating massive destruction of the obvious real target, Serbia's civilian economic infrastructure.

Under the oxymoron of a "humanitarian war," which depicted the West as saviors while NATO bombed 15 defenseless cities around the clock for 78 days, the successfully destroyed real targets of precision bombing were: heating plants for entire cities, 344 schools, 33 clinics and hospitals, power plants, food processing plants, pharmaceutical plants, bus and train depots, electrical grids, bridges, factories, power stations, trains,

---

[a] A pattern has emerged. Military destabilization of these countries begins by training and financing dissidents to assassinate policemen and leaders and destroy economic infrastructure. Not knowing what is happening or exactly who is to blame, the targeted countries militarily suppress their own people. This provides a foundation for claims of human rights abuses internationally while weakening that nation internally. In the more important cases, like Yugoslavia, those suppressions are expanded by the "Mighty Wurlitzer" into an excuse for direct intervention.

The same methods are used to destabilize potential political groups internally. In the FBI's Operation COINTELPRO and other American internal destabilizations, "agent provocateurs" were inserted into civil rights, and other progressive, groups. Not only did the FBI receive intelligence on the groups, those inserted agents were to attempt to lead the group into violent acts for which they could be arrested. Run a Google Internet search.

airports, water supply systems, warehouses, oil refineries, fuel storage, chemical factories, museums, and TV and radio stations. Among the commercial buildings destroyed were twin tower skyscrapers eerily reminiscent of the World Trade Center twin towers destroyed in the 9/11/2001 terrorist attack on America.

After the destruction of Yugoslavia was carried out under the false flag of oppression and genocide in Kosovo by Serbia, 350,000 Serbs, Gypsies, Slavic Muslims, Croatians, Jews, Turks and anti-fascist Ethnic Albanians were driven out of Kosovo in a continuation of the Albanian ethnic cleansing that had been in progress since WWII (40% ethnic Albanian in 1945 increased to 80% by 1980 and is now over 90%). After defeating the defending Serbian army, the Kosovo occupation army claims not to have been able to prevent this ethnic cleansing by the very forces they financed, armed, and coached for eight years.

Policies-of-State to Control Resources and the *Wealth-Producing-Process*

We will quote from our previous book:

> Powerbrokers within NATO are concerned with Yugoslavia only as a small battle within one or more of four centuries-long struggles:
> 1. The splitting of the Roman Empire into Eastern Orthodox Christianity and Western Christianity starting in the fourth century. This created the Orthodox Christian East and Western Christians that are fighting over territory on the boundaries between those sister religions yet today. It is obvious that, without the support of Western Christian nations, Yugoslavia's Western Christians would not have had the political strength to shatter that once peaceful federation.
> 2. The 1,300-year struggle pitting Eastern and Western Christians against Muslims was a battle between the Muslim East and the Christian West. The current alliance of the Christian West with Balkan Muslims against Eastern Orthodox Christians is only a strategic decision of *managers-of-state*.
> 3. The 70-year battle between communism and capitalism, the Cold War. Most, but not all, communists are currently Eastern Orthodox and most, but not all, capitalists are currently Western Christian. This is the historic in-step march of religion and governments as empires expand and contract.
> 4. And then, the centuries of battles over who will control the *wealth-producing-process* and thus who will lay claim to wealth, the primary subject of this book. This battle over the world's wealth is between the fragmented periphery of empire and the same allied, coordinated, and powerful West.
>
> That last struggle, *managers-of-state* utilizing religious and political loyalties to control the *wealth-producing-process*, is the one that counts. At any one moment, what is motivating any one person or one's vision of these historic events

depends upon that person's position and loyalties within those four struggles. For those deeply committed to religion, or moderately religious and not interested in politics, which covers most of the masses, religious loyalties will determine their opinions. Those committed politically will be on one side or the other of the battle between capitalism and any form of cooperative society. If one is a corporate strategist, a Manager of State, or aware that one's livelihood is deeply affected—either positively or negatively—by the inequalities of trade, then some subdivision of the battle over world trade will be primary in their considerations.[8]

Clinton's Energy Secretary Bill Richardson spelled out America's Balkan policy a few months prior to the 1999 bombing of Yugoslavia:

> "This is about America's energy security... It's also about preventing strategic inroads by those who don't share our values. We're trying to move these newly independent countries toward the West... We would like to see them reliant on western commercial and political interests rather than going another way. We've made a substantial political investment in the Caspian, and it's very important to us that both the pipeline map and the politics come out right."[9]

Again we will quote from our previous work:

> The breakup of Yugoslavia is little more than Western Christianity's continuation of pushing of the line between Western Christianity and Eastern Orthodox Christianity (or capitalism and communism if politics is one's motivation) further East to build a coalition of friendly nations between Europe and the world's last great pool of oil in the Caspian Basin. The *policies-of-state* here are obvious, isolating Russia politically, reducing its control over the oil and gas deposits in the Caspian basin, and piping those hydrocarbons to Europe. Germany reached an agreement with Croatia (announced in the UN) for a pipeline through its territory and—even as the bombs were falling on Yugoslavia—officials of Georgia, Ukraine, Uzbekistan, Azerbaijan, and Moldova were in Washington, DC, signing a regional alliance (GUUAM) that included discussions of oil pipeline export routes to the West. There was also high interest in turning the rich minerals of Kosovo (the Trepca mining/manufacturing complex, which was too valuable to bomb and now arbitrarily turned over to Albanian Kosovars), the suspected oil and gas deposits within the Dinarides Thrust, and other mineral wealth of Yugoslavia (coal, bauxite) towards Europe. This—through the breakup of Yugoslavia—will deprive Eastern Orthodox Christians of that wealth, will weaken that tiny enclave of socialism, and all while simultaneously increasing the wealth of Western Europe. Thus we see that the foundation of all property rights is military power.[10]

While the Trepca mines rich in lead, zinc, cadmium, gold, silver, and coal were considered the most valuable piece of real estate in the Balkans, through Yugoslavia is the shortest route to Europe for oil from the Caspian Sea region.

Both Iraq and Yugoslavia were working hard to maintain their independence and control their destiny. But both nations reputations and economies were destroyed by propaganda and bombing, (Very similar to the massive propaganda deployed almost 200 years ago to destroy the reputation of Napoleon in the attempt to reclaim the excessive rights of aristocracy, a system which the Napoleonic Codes—established as the fundamental law in over 30 countries—eventually destroyed.)

The natural wealth, the industrial wealth, and the future wealth of Yugoslavia have been delivered to predatory Western finance capital. Though the human cost is greater today this is a replay of the Middle Ages when the raiding parties from the cities of Europe destroyed the industrial capital of the countryside to maintain its dependency upon a city.

That an empire manufactures excuses for war whenever it wishes to gain the support of the people to destroy a potential rival is documented history.[11] Obviously the death of 2,108 people (both Albanian and Serb Kosovars, killed by the Serb military, the Kosovo Liberation Army, and by NATO) in Kosovo's NATO designed and supported civil war was not the reason for NATO's bombing of Yugoslavia. (Note how the whole story is told in that one sentence.) Two-hundred thousand Iraqi soldiers were killed in the Gulf War and over 1-million, largely children and weaker old people, perished in Iraq due to the American-led sanctions. One-third of the East Timorese (200,000) died in that Indonesian suppression of rights (America supplied the weapons and gave the green light). The ethnic cleansing in Rwanda killed 500,000 over a period of five years. The 20-year conflict between Ethiopia and Eritrea (a province of Ethiopia, the independence of which was covertly supported by America during the Cold War to weaken Ethiopia) caused the deaths of 50,000. The 16-year struggle in Sudan extinguished the lives of 2-million. Eighty thousand were killed up to this point in time in Russia's Chechnya suppression. And, in the early stages of the Yugoslav destabilization, tens of thousands were killed when Croatia— with the backing of the United States and Germany—"ethnically-cleansed" her territory of over 500,000 Serbs.[12]

Eastern Europe could not be totally restructured along Western political and economic lines so long as Yugoslavia remained intact with her citizens well cared for and her industry underselling Western products throughout Eastern Europe. An opposing ideology with an intact military could not be permitted west of the planned new line of NATO defense, Romania, Bulgaria, and Greece. Thus the Western Christian nations of Romania, Bulgaria, Hungary, Slovenia and Croatia surrounding the Eastern Orthodox Serbia are being brought within NATO. Serbia is now expected to become one of the poorest nations in Europe. It cannot maintain a powerful military and it cannot arise as an example for other dependent countries. Such was the *Grand Strategy* behind the destabilization of Yugoslavia.

The gains to *Imperial-Centers-of-Capital* are Huge

NATO countries were after quicker and larger financial returns than described above. The Yugoslav economy was a socialist market economy with industries managed by labor.[13] The destruction of Serbia's industries, along with the embargo, opens the entire Eastern European market to western European products and services (construction) that the well-educated, well-organized, hard-working, and knowledgeable Yugoslavs could have produced.

As products and services produced under the management of labor and direct financing of industry by the central bank could be sold or contracted much cheaper than Western products (there was not the massive unearned monopoly profits as in a subtly-monopolized economy, see below), without the fragmentation and embargo of Yugoslavia it is the Yugoslavs which would have dominated many of those markets. It is they who would have become wealthy, and, the most dangerous of all, the rest of Eastern Europe had a similar industry/labor history and they and the entire world would have observed the Yugoslav success under a social structure that had totally broke with *exclusive feudal title* to nature's wealth.

Thus, in final analysis, the *managers-of-state* in the West understood well that protection of the markets of Eastern Europe for Western industry and emerging Eastern European industry structured in their image—and possibly the very survival of Western neo-liberal economic philosophy—required the destabilization of Yugoslavia, severe crippling of their industrial infrastructure, and that of any other nations that dared maintain their independence.

So long as those targeted for destabilization cannot or dare not respond, wars are still profitable. A full accounting of the profits from those Eastern markets as well as the multiplier factor (as the money from locally employed labor circulates within the economies of Western nations) will show that, to the winners, the breakup of Yugoslavia was one of the most profitable combinations of economic, financial, covert, and overt warfare in history. Only by the full destruction of the cooperative societies to the East could Eastern Europe be rebuilt in Western Europe's image. When the losers of these battles for resources and markets collapse those societies become impoverished.

Control of those Eastern and Central European resources have been Germany's goal for 100 years and was the specific goal of Hitler's thousand-year Reich. Western imperial nations have given up on the battle between themselves over the world's resources and markets and have allied together for the huge gains possible from controlling the resources and the *wealth-producing-process* of their neighbors to the East.

Turning the Screws Tighter

In September, 2000—the very month the first edition of this author's *Economic Democracy* came out with the above revelations—it became common knowledge that American money was covertly financing elections in both Serbia and Montenegro. The U.S. Congress openly authorized over $10-million to Serbs and Montenegrins economically and politically breaking ranks with their government. Those funded became prime prospects as puppets to run that part of the world.

This standard covert policy of the Cold War was unknown to most citizens of Western nations. Where previous funding of elections was covert, ever since the collapse of the Soviet Union (with the exception of China and a few other countries) the U.S. has been covertly and overtly financing elections of emerging nations. That, of course, is illegal under both American law and the laws of the countries being compromised.

All who follow how overthrows of governments were accomplished all over the world by the imperial nations during the Cold War knew that the leaders of the mob which burned the Yugoslav parliament and other centers of power of the Milosevic government were coached, financed, and even armed by German and American intelligence. The final destabilization of Yugoslavia provides a textbook example of the *Mighty Wurlitzer* destabilizing functional democratic governments throughout the Cold War of governments that were not accepting control from the imperial center:

- A ring of radio stations were established around Serbia beaming in propaganda.
- Suitcases full of American and German cash were given to opposing newspapers, news agencies, broadcasters, political parties, think-tanks, student groups, "human rights" organizations, and trade unions.
- The media loyal to the Serbian government were denied access to satellite communications while the opposition media were given access.[a]

---

[a] *Los Angeles Times*, September 26, 2000; New York Times, September 20, 2000; Senator Joseph Biden's Senate Hearings on Serbia, July 29, 1999; Serbian Democratization Act, HR1064, September 5, 2000; cited on various webpages at http://emperors-clothes.com. We have barely opened the door on the all-out financial, economic, covert, and overt warfare destabilization of Yugoslavia. The definitive books have not yet been written on this deeper history. We suggest early readers to study the website http://emperors-clothes.com and later readers watch for books and articles by Michel Chossudovsky, Jared Israel, Peter Gowan, Greg Palast, Michael Parenti, Noam Chomsky, and authors in Eastern Europe, Yugoslavia and Russia. In "Regime Change: A Look at Washington's Methods and Degrees of Success in Dislodging Foreign Leaders," *The Christian Science Monitor*, January 27, 2003, Peter Ford outlines the 50 years of America destabilizing other governments we are addressing, including the

- In the final push mobs were armed, coached, and financed to take over all the media. The Serbs no longer controlled a media within their own country.

In any of the nations allied against Yugoslavia, any opposition political group would be arrested if they were funded by outside powers trying to overthrow the government. Yet, even as they were being labeled as dictators by the West's *Mighty Wurlitzer* the Yugoslav government was not even arresting those openly funded by the very outside powers overthrowing them. How this money was pouring in and funding the opposition was, until the takeover of that media, openly discussed on Serbian news.

Even as Western media parroted Western intelligence service wordsmiths as Yugoslavia being a "dictatorship," Canadian observers reported the election as open as any election in Canada, with no police visible, and opposition literature widely distributed. But those observations were not what the world heard. The only "news" that reached the masses, and what was recorded in the media of record for historians, was that of dictators and genocidal murderers.

When a nation is targeted for destabilization, or there is need to suppress a tendency for independence in countries already under control, the National Endowment for Democracy (NED) funds opposition groups (such as: The Center for International Private Enterprise, Humanitarian Law Center, Center for Democracy Foundation, Belgrade Center for Human Rights, European Movement of Serbia, G-17 economists, Center for Anti-War Action and Media, think-tanks, student groups, and many others), all claiming to be private groups but actually funded by the American congress through the NED and other means (such as George Soros' *destabilization foundations* of which his Open Society Institute is only one), provides the crucial service of funding puppet media and politicians.[a] This covert funding of opposition forces through NED is standard practice worldwide. In short, Western powers were practicing total dictatorial control of governments and media and military suppression of dissent, the very things of which they accuse every country not safely under their empirical umbrella.

---

demonization of progressive leaders like Milosevic and how George Soros' *destabilization foundations* work.

[a] When knowledge of American covert funding of other nations' elections surfaced, the U.S. Congress established the National Endowment for Democracy (NED) in 1983 to fund openly a part of what the CIA had been funding covertly (*Washington Post*, September 21 and 22, 1991 and William Blum, *Rogue State: A Guide to the World's Only Super Power* [Monroe, ME: Common Courage Press, 2000], Chapter 19). Run a Google Internet search using many combinations of keywords and countries.

Before they had even taken office, Serbian opposition leaders met in Bulgaria with the IMF, the World Bank, and the leaders of NATO countries to finalize the fine points on the takeover of Yugoslavia[14] which included all the structural adjustment and abandonment of protection of citizens imposed upon most nations on the periphery of empire which would eventually mean the takeover of their economy by the German mark and eventually the European euro.

Once the various former Yugoslav provinces use the German mark or the euro as their currency (as all but Serbia now do including Kosovo and Montenegro), Serbians can no longer create their own money and their funding of essential industries and services will be severely curbed. The Balkans will have become the "countryside" for the West European economy; an expanded version of the vision of Germany for the past 100 years.

With the Western-imposed new leaders of Croatia, Slovenia, and other regions being direct descendents of Hitler's Ustase death squads with every intention of making second-class citizens of their Eastern Orthodox neighbors, the new leaders of Serbia have no illusions as to the hard future the West will be imposing upon them. After all, poverty is many times higher in the collapsed Eastern Europe and the former Soviet Union than it was under Communism. Even the Ukraine, the breadbasket and industrial heartland of the East—which dutifully followed all the prescriptions of the IMF, the World Bank, and NATO—is prostrate and essentially begging the West for food. Of course, these leaders are aware that Western promoted structural adjustment prescriptions created that poverty but they are equally aware that they have been left with no other choices.

President Milosevic is being tried in The Hague, as a war criminal. The winners write history and the current International Criminal Tribunal was designed specifically to write history with the former leaders of Yugoslavia as the war criminals even though it was international capital, through their control of the policies of America and the nations of Western Europe, which directly orchestrated the destabilization of the once peaceful and prosperous Yugoslavia. (In his defense, Milosevic's defense outlined the entire process of the West's destabilization of Yugoslavia more thorough than we have outlined it here. A lady spectator who came for the purpose of seeing Milosevic convicted said, "We have been deceived." As that deception will not leak out through the media or into the history books for the reasons outlined in Chapter 3, sincere researchers will have to study Milosevic's defense to write honest history.) Many were killed and brutalized in that war so the West will have no problem finding something somewhere to convict Milosevic. But surely the original destabilizers are the one's responsible for all the death and destruction.[15]

The war against the Taliban in Afghanistan is instructive. It seems the policy was primarily to take no prisoners and relatively few were taken.

Those essentially executed rather than taken as prisoners are enemies of the countries financing the current War Crimes Tribunal.[a] Although this is against the rules of both decency and war, one can be sure there will be no War Crimes Tribunal against those responsible.

The new Serb government had no choice. The shattered Serbian economy was to receive no financial support or access to markets until the Serbs turned Milosevic over to the War Crimes Tribunal. Such is the unacknowledged power of monopoly capital which exercises enormous financial and economic control in virtually every nation in the world except China and even that powerful country must be very careful.

The *managers-of-state* of the now *allied imperial-centers-of-capital* know well their power, use it ruthlessly, and leave weak countries no alternative. Key countries targeted for destabilization and takeover by the West who try to maintain independence and who have no powerful nation to protect them risk the same devastation by Western military power as was visited on the once independent and relatively prosperous Yugoslavia. Once the powerful Soviet Union was destabilized, virtually every country in the world was at the mercy of the allied, well-organized, *imperial-centers-of-capital*.

A NATO Alliance all the way to Russia's Border

Under the *Grand Strategy* of the organized and allied NATO countries, all Eastern European countries up to the border of the old Soviet Union, with the possible exception of Serbia, are to become allies. But they will not be allotted equal rights. The guarantees of all Yugoslav workers for jobs, free health care and education, pensions, paid maternity leave and vacations, low-cost recreation, and cheap food and rent has been replaced in all the breakaway provinces, now allied with the west, with 20% unemployment, high prices, and a far lower average standard of living.

What will happen to these Eastern Orthodox cultures, whose citizens have historically been second class citizens within territories controlled by Western Christians? A clue is provided by remembering that the opposing Eastern and Western cultures enslaved each other's citizens for centuries. The very word "slave" is derived from what are now the Eastern Orthodox Slavic people of Eastern Europe.

Another clue can be ascertained by viewing what is happening to the laboring classes in former Eastern and Central European counties who are religiously and culturally tied to the West. Those Western Christian cultures will surely be treated better than Eastern Orthodox Christians.

Analyzing the still low living standards of the dozen or so Eastern European countries religiously and culturally tied to the West and slated to

---

[a] For a view of the threat to the West of an unbiased International Criminal Court read: Tuva Raanes, "A Divine Country All on Its Own," *World Press Review*, October 2002, p. 17.

be allies, provides a clue to the bleak future of countries not religiously and culturally tied to the West (Eastern Orthodox Christian Serbs) and not viewed as natural allies.

When Eastern Europe collapsed under the pressure and coaching of the West as outlined above, the economically efficient Czechoslovakia disintegrated into two inefficient countries, the Czech Republic and Slovakia. The fate of the highly efficient VSZ steel complex in Slovakia (a Western Christian nation) provides a glimpse of their future. With the breakup of Czechoslovakia, the collapse of all Eastern European countries, and the imposition of IMF/World Bank structural adjustments, the local markets for VSZ steel disappeared. Markets in the West were protected from VSZ's low priced—high quality—steel, the once-booming steel complex ran out of money, and under IMF/World Bank rules they could not be financed by the Slovakian central bank.

This prostrate industrial jewel was picked up by America's U.S. Steel for the bargain basement price of $450-million and it now provides 25% of their steel making capacity. Slovak steelworkers are paid roughly $2 an hour against U.S. Steel workers pay in America of $35 to $45 an hour.[16] High quality Slovakian steel will be sold on world steel market, those mills will operate at full capacity, any over-capacity will be alleviated through lowered production in America, Western Europe, or Japan and the huge profits generated in the Slovakian mills will disappear into the accounting books and profit distributions of U.S. Steel. In short, the labor of America and Europe will take a loss, the labor of Slovakia will hold though at a low pay level, and all gains will go to the owners of U.S. Steel. This same scenario will play out in other industries.

Like the underpaid developing world, Eastern Europe will gain only a little because their pay is too low to provide adequate buying power. Labor in the developed world will eventually lose buying power as their jobs are taken by underpaid Eastern European workers. Germans, Japanese and other steel producers will have to lower steel and labor prices or lose market share. This will be the well-understood cyclical crisis of over production of capitalism compounded by the abandonment of economies once seen as crucial to protect against fast expanding socialism (Japan and the Asian tigers) and further compounded by the melding of high-paid capitalist economies of Western Europe with equally-productive low-paid former socialist economies of Eastern and Central Europe.

Economic statistics showing a steadily advancing world economy are ignoring the shrinking of 40% of the world economy. The collapse of the currencies, buying power, and industries of Mexico, Southeast Asia, Latin America, and the former Soviet Union meant their citizens were impoverished as their resources and the production of their labor were purchased by the imperial centers far below the previous norm.

In the same way that low-priced oil maintains healthy economies for the imperial centers (the primary reason for the current takeover of Iraq), a rapid lowering of the price of any resources or production of labor from the periphery of empire will, so long as the markets of the imperial center can be protected, be a boon to those economies of the center of empire even though the periphery may be devastated.

Protecting the markets of the imperial centers may be relatively easy in the short run as the periphery collapses but will be tough in the long run. Underpaid labor on the periphery will not be able to buy their own production while the products produced with that low-paid labor and lower-valued capital can undersell producers in the wealthy world.

This will be tempered by capital of the imperial center purchasing much of the industrial capital of the periphery at bargain prices but, as outlined with the Slovakian VSZ steel mill above, this melding of cheap-cost industries with high-cost industries only means it takes a little longer for the cycle of lost buying power and collapsing values to work its way through the economy. And even that extended time span will collapse if stock market and land values in the imperial centers collapse and destroy buying power and consumer confidence.

Collapse of the *Invisible Borders* between the High-Paid Imperial Center and the Low-Paid Periphery

Lets us look at the world economy today:
- Instead of a world economy expanding from investment in basic production, we now have a collapsing periphery while the imperial centers expand from wealth pouring into America and Europe through massive inequality of pay for equally-productive labor (as per the wealth appropriation formula in Chapter 2).
- Forty years ago 30% of the American economy was services and 70% was industry; today it is 70% services and 30% industry.
- The price of wages and commodities on the periphery of empire keeps dropping lower and lower. Thus the price of commodities imported dropped 60% in the 30 years preceding 1996. With the currency collapses in 1997, commodity prices have possibly dropped another 50%.

Those losses on the periphery were the gains that the imperial centers admired as they measured their increase in wealth. The world cannot, and will not, tolerate a wealth appropriation rate that high. The extreme difference in wealth between the imperial centers and the periphery must collapse of its own weight. After all, those lower commodity prices represent loss in buying power on the periphery.

One-third of the world's productive capacity is now idle (Professor Lester Thurow). The substantial industry built on the periphery of empire is a change from past economic crises. Just trying to survive, those periphery industries have to pour products into the imperial center. Buying those products cheap, selling those products cheaper than past norms but still with a high margin, and banking the profits was America's great gain in wealth between 1992 and 2000. The steadily rising stock market based on those profits was creating wealthy people, thus creating buying power and the masses also received value (wealth) via those lower prices.

Market value has a relationship to use-value. Cheap resource imports are manufactured into valuable consumer products and cheaply manufactured, high use-value consumer products have value. If imported product costs drop by half (those low wages on the periphery for equally-productive work), the trader can bank more value even as the consumer gains more value. If better materials and technology double the useable life or productive use of a product, the value to the consumer doubles. (Note: The productivity of computers doubles every few years and cars which ran only 70,000 miles 40 years ago now run 200,000 to 300,000 miles.)

As I write this, a friend shows me a sale ad for a power tool for $250. He said, "I just bought an identical tool at Harbor Freight for $75, saving $175." Obviously the Harbor Freight tool was manufactured in low-wage China and then offered at only a modest price markup permitting my friend, the final buyer, to gain wealth. Assuming the same $250 tool was imported for the same low price but the trader raised the price to the $250 price of the competition, it is the trader who would have gained the $175, not the final consumer. But in both instances $175 in wealth would be gained by America. Another friend paid $130 for a rotary drill press from Harbor Freight that he knew should cost $800. Other similarly discounted bargains can be spotted. If all products could be bought overseas at that 80% discount the imperial centers would gain enormous wealth. [a]

---

[a] In the December issue of Economic Reform William Krehm points out that due to low wage costs in China Television prices have dropped 9% a year for the past 3 years, tool prices dropped 1% per year, and sports equipment dropped 3% a year. We mentioned how Harbor Freight, through dropping tool prices roughly 60%, appears to be an honest trader and permitting the final consumer to accumulate that wealth. Either Harbor Freight's low tool pricing was before 1998 or the drop in those prices are far understated.

Through rapid expansion of graduate engineers, China is rapidly expanding production and sales of high technology items (over 50% a year at this time but that is on a low base). It is not unreasonable to assume that competition between China and the Asian Tigers could lower product prices in the imperial centers 5% a year. Assuming protective measures are not put in place, and to do so will be both ideologically and actually difficult, eventually the excess profits of traders will disappear. The loss of those profits would normally mean a collapse of stock prices.

But if the military/legal lock on the rest of the world can be maintained, the economies of the imperial centers may not collapse. It will take the sale of only a few

Those examples indicate the power of traders to maintain wide margins is weakening. Expand that concept to all consumer products and you see how the consumers of the imperial centers can rapidly accumulate wealth even as the periphery becomes poorer. Only a few high priced products and services exported would pay for those cheap, yet valuable, imports. This accounts for the great wealth accumulated by the imperial centers during the 1990s as the periphery collapsed. To my knowledge this simple mechanism for transferring wealth from the low-paid to the high-paid is not addressed in economic or foreign policy literature.

When stock market values on the periphery start dropping and import values to the imperial centers (the periphery's export values) keep dropping, the periphery of empire loses both value and buying power. But, so long as other values in the imperial centers (primarily real-estate) hold or increase, the values to borrow against, and thus the buying power, will hold. But if the stock markets in the imperial centers fall, other values will plateau or start to fall and, at some point, the values to borrow against will not be there. The buying power in those once-wealthy nations will then start falling. As buying power has already shrunken rapidly on the periphery, the buying power to keep the world economy afloat will have shrunk drastically, prices will drop, and more of the world's productive capacity will have to close down. (It may not happen. Monthly income in the imperial centers once budgeted for discretionary spending is now free to invest in property, especially homes, and increased home values mean more buying power.)

The imperial centers can print money to provide buying power to their citizens and increase values. (Periphery nations are effectively denied that right.) If commodity import prices to the imperial centers continue to shrink, values will continue to be imported or produced in those imperial centers even as values continue to drop on the periphery. The balance between wealth in the imperial centers and wealth on the periphery can, within reason and depending upon the military power of the imperial centers, be held at either a high or low differential. Today it is being held at a high, and growing, differential. Wealth on the periphery is shrinking while wealth in the imperial centers is, or at least was, still growing.

---

products and services at a high price to pay for those massive products imported at a low price. If that were to happen, we would be observing what has previously only been analyzed in economic theory, the import of products at almost no cost (the same as the theory the production of all products at almost no cost) and all that is necessary for a healthy economy is for citizens to provide each other with services. The imperial centers are approaching that utopian stage. Forty years ago, American labor was 70% industrial and 30% services. Today it is 30% industrial and 70% services. Surely before that utopian state is reached the periphery will become aware their resources and labors will be providing most of the consumer products of the imperial centers.

Siphoning from the periphery of empire to the imperial center at the rate of 25-to-1 through a 20% differential in pay for equally-productive labor, as discussed in Chapter 2, will increase exponentially if currency values widen. If that wealth differential continues to grow as the wealth of the periphery pours into the imperial center, or if the citizens on the periphery of empire figure out why it is that they are so poor while it is their resources and labor producing the wealth for the imperial centers, a flashpoint will have been reached.

As the imperial centers hold, and though this reality is not acknowledged, the periphery has collapsed to the extent that the average standard of living worldwide has dropped substantially. With the exception of East Germany, the standard of living in virtually every East European country is lower than in 1985, most far lower. Russia and the former provinces of the Soviet Union have seen their standard of living drop in the range of 50%. Argentina's per-capita annual income dropped by 60%. The economies of Brazil, Uruguay, Bolivia, and others threaten to mimic Argentina. Most of Africa has seen their living standards steadily erode. Japan's economy is shrinking (their wealth is down $18-trillion). And, although their balance of payments have stabilized, the former Asian Tigers have not regained their pre-1997 per-capita living standard. Such immense economic crisis in previous history has created wars. It will take an enormous military to maintain the current immense rate of transfer of wealth from the periphery to the imperial centers.[a] The current power-structure understands this well. America's roughly $280-billion military budget climbed to $320-billion and appears headed to over $450-billion. That is more money spent on the military than the rest of the world combined and most those are allied with, or at least friends of, America.[17]

If the U.S. is so militarily secure, why does America have such a violent foreign policy? It is because students of foreign policy are not taught peace. Instead they are taught that no other nation can be trusted so give no quarter and to take all they can get.[b]

Every sober citizen wants an end to wars. Only when faced with power have imperial nations ever abandoned their claims upon the wealth of the

---

[a] The same transfer of wealth from the weak to the powerful is on-going within the American economy. If the share of the nation's wealth between the wealthy and the poor had remained stable the past 30 years, the annual income of the lowest 10% would be double what it is today. But a standard analysis is deceiving. If the wage of American citizens can buy two to three times the consumer products as per the Harbor Freight example above, they are far wealthier. Only a powerful military and successful financial and economic warfare can maintain such levels of appropriation of others' wealth.

[b] Which is just what they do. All foreign policy planners are doing exactly the opposite of what they are telling the masses. For that policy laid bare read Michel Chossudovsky's work (*War and Globalization*). As we chose to show the fictions of economics as taught today and to lay out an honest world development philosophy, he addresses foreign policy in much more depth than we do.

periphery. Those imperial centers cannot control billions of people if they ally together. The periphery must organize to peacefully reclaim their share of the world's wealth produced by the world's resources and the *wealth-producing-process*. After all, most those natural resources are within their borders.

The enormous wealth flowing into the imperial centers from the periphery is consumed in part by the huge expenditure on arms necessary to control the resources on the periphery and thus control the *wealth-producing-process*. The economic multiplier from these wasteful expenditures creates the good life for citizens in those imperial centers. This system of theft is then hidden from the social mind by massive *propaganda* portraying the suppressed as dangerous enemies and the suppressors as a benevolent people attempting to bring *peace, freedom, justice, rights*, and *majority rule* to the world.

We now address how the legal framework for siphoning the wealth of the world to *imperial-centers-of-capital* is established through the economic and financial philosophies of the imperial centers.

Notes

[1] See above footnote.

[2] Ibid and Parenti, *To Kill a Nation*, Chapter 10, p. 105. check *Jane's Defense Weekly*, especially the May 10, 1999 issue. In *Dollars for Terror*, Chapter 10, Richard Labeviere explains that Special Operations Command (SOCOM) overseas MPRI and other private military groups and interfaces between those groups and the Pentagon; Linda Robinson, "America's Secret Armies," *U.S. News & World Report* (November 4, 2002), pp. 38-43. Run a Google Internet search.

[3] Ibid; Be sure and check later articles and books by those same authors; Parenti, *To Kill a Nation*, Chapter 11.

[4] Parenti, *To Kill a Nation*, Chapter 15, p. 12, 28-29; Fidel Castro, *Capitalism in Crisis: Globalization and World Politics Today* (New York: Ocean Press, 2000), p. 209.

[5] "Big Lie Exposed," *Workers World*, April 12, 2001.

[6] Parenti, To Kill a Nation, Chapter 14.

[7] See endnote 1. For reduced Serbian losses: Parenti, *To Kill a Nation*, Chapter 16; Richard J. Newman, "A Kosovo Numbers Game," *U.S. News & World Report*, July 12, 1999, p. 36.

[8] J.W. Smith, *Economic Democracy: The Political Struggle of the Twenty-First Century*, updated and expanded 3rd edition (www.ied.info/cc.html: The Institute for Economic Democracy, Chapter 7.

[9] George Monbiot, A Discreet Deal in the Pipeline, *The Guardian*, 15 February 2001.

[10] Smith, *Economic Democracy*, updated and expanded 3rd edition, Chapter 7.

[11] Fidel Castro, *Capitalism in Crisis: Globalization and World Politics Today* (New York: Ocean Press, 2000), pp. 215-17. James Bamford, *Body of Secrets: Anatomy of the Ultra Secret National Security Agency* (New York: Doubleday, 2001), pp. 70-75. Run a Google Internet search.

[12] Parenti, *To Kill a Nation*, pp. 12, 28-29, Chapter 15.

[13] Jaroslav Vanek, *The Labor Managed Economy* (London: Cornell University Press, 1977).

[14] *United Press International*, September 27, 2000.

[15] Parenti, *To Kill a Nation*, Chapter 12.

[16] Deirdre Griswold, "Marxism, Reformism and Anarchism: Lessons from a Steel Mill in Slovakia" *Workers World* (December 14, 2000).

[17] James Petras, "Argentina: Between Disintegration & Revolution," *CovertAction Quarterly* (Fall 2002.), pp. 27-33; Michel Chossudovsky, "United States War Machine: Revving the Engines of World War III, *CovertAction Quarterly* (Fall 2002), pp. 41-46. For the latest information not on your evening news run a Google Internet search.

7. Inequality Structured in Law

The entire world wants TVs, stereos, cars, nice homes, and all else they see in movies and on TV screens. So globalization is going to happen. The problem is not globalization per se; it is corporations structuring world property rights to their advantage, a continual expansion of *residual-feudal exclusive* property rights.

Structuring inequality into law (restricting rights to the commons for some and expanding the rights of others) has been an integral part of the formation of civilizations. The first person powerful enough to claim title to a piece of valuable and productive land could claim the wealth produced while sitting in idleness and splendor.

Anyone claiming such rights in primitive societies would be immediately challenged. Communal rights were established so each could claim their share of the fruits of the earth. But those claims of private ownership were eventually made by powerful people who continually structured the laws to claim more and more of the rights to the commons of weaker peoples. Powerful people (those first powerful, idle people, eventually called aristocrats) over the centuries, piece by piece, claimed title to the land and at the peak of aristocratic power there was no common-use land left. Excessive rights for the powerful to the wealth produced by money and technology were also structured in law.

The origin of the West's exclusive property titles to nature's wealth was feudalism. The revolts of the common people (the America Revolution, especially the French Revolution, and many internal political battles) slowly eroded *feudal exclusive* rights to nature's wealth.[1] Due to those revolts, some of the rights of the commons were returned to the people through the common people being permitted *residual-feudal exclusive* title to land.[a]

---

[a] Due to revolutions and threats of revolutions, aristocracy had to share rights or lose all excessive rights. This set the pattern of today's rights. Each time a power-structure is under threat, to gain loyalty more rights are given to the people. This is seen most clearly in access to technology, finance capital, and markets being given to a prostrate Western Europe, Japan, and the Asian tigers after WWII so as to stop fast expanding socialism. The unwritten contract to pay labor well while that battle was being fought (the Cold War) was also an increase in rights protecting the powerful's superior rights.

Before the crisis of fast expanding socialism, which was little more than reclaiming the commons, the operative economic philosophy was to give nothing to anybody, charge all the market would bear, and pay the lowest possible price. That this was little more than a philosophy to protect wealth and power (a monopoly) can be easily

Rights for the people expanded further through rights granted to organized labor and some of those rights expanding to unorganized labor. With better pay labor even bought stock and gained some of the *residual-feudal exclusive* rights of capital.

With the possible exception of when the masses were granted rights to land and technology as Europeans settled America and the rights granted during the Great Depression under the threat of a ballot box revolution, the greatest gain of rights for the common people was after WWII. The powerful were frightened that communism (those communal property rights where the struggle started) was going to replace capitalism throughout the world. Under that threat, countries on the borders of fast expanding socialism (all Western Europe, Japan, Taiwan, and South Korea) were given access to technology, finance capital, and American markets. More important was the unwritten contract with labor that they would be well paid in this massive struggle between capitalism and communism (private property and communal property). It is that unwritten contract, and the massive funds spent in that struggle, that provided the high standard of living that has become common in America, Europe, Japan, Taiwan, and the Asian tigers.

But, as will be shown in these final chapters, the massive wealth distributed is only a small part of what could have been produced and distributed under *democratic-cooperative-capitalism* (a legal structure for where all receive their share of the wealth of a modern commons; even as they retain and even increase their competitive private property rights). The excessive rights of subtle monopolies claim too great a share of the wealth produced and too much is wasted in capital destroying capital and much more is wasted in wars. But if all had rights to a modern commons through elimination of subtle monopolization, as described in the next chapters, unearned wealth would no longer be claimed by the excessive rights of non-productive monopolists.

Such monopolies are non-productive because they lower distribution efficiency and thus lower production far below society's potential. Under *democratic-cooperative-capitalism*, there would be instant distribution of wealth to all relative to their provision of services and contribution to the production of wealth. As the massive increase in wealth produced and distributed under *democratic-cooperative-capitalism* proves, monopolists do not produce. Their interception (not production) of wealth is through *residual-feudal exclusive* rights (monopolies) structured into law for centuries by their predecessors.

There is a continual struggle over who will receive the wealth produced from the gains in efficiency of the *wealth-producing-process*. The shrinkage in

---

ascertained by noticing how fast the wealth spread when allies were needed and Adam Smith philosophy was replaced by Friedrich List philosophy, give them access to technology, finance, and markets and protect tender new industries and markets.

the buying power of hourly labor throughout the imperial centers as the buying power of the owners of capital expands proves that greater inequality is yet being structured in law. Capital is not only receiving all the efficiency gains from improved technology, they are claiming a part of what once went to labor.

Structuring inequality in law is ongoing as the *imperial-centers-of-capital* establishes the rules of unequal world trade. "The heart of the GATT—Bretton Woods system is what is known as MFN—most favored nation."[2] GATT, NAFTA, WTO, MAI, GATS, and FTAA, though supposedly defining equality, bend the will of weak nations to that of powerful nations. That process determines which nations will industrialize and which will remain as providers of resources for the *imperial-centers-of-capital*. Those permitted to industrialize will accumulate capital and those consigned to provide the natural resources to feed those imperial centers will remain poor and in debt:

> Many people learned for the first time at Seattle (2001) of the existence of the QUAD, the Quadrilateral Group of Trade Ministers, which was formed in 1981 and acts as an informal committee guiding the global trade regime. Before public meetings of the WTO, members of the Quad—the United States, The European Union, Japan, and Canada [all CEOs of, or closely connected with, global corporations]—meet privately, making key decisions without the participation of other representatives of the world community. Once the QUAD reaches agreement, a larger, select group of twenty to thirty countries are invited to come together in informal meetings. Only after that do the 143 members of the WTO discuss and vote on proposals that are typically, by this point, faits accomplis. The poor countries of the world are forced to fall in line by the pressure of the economic and political muscle arrayed against them.[3]

Howard Wachtel understood this process well:

> When the WTO replaced GATT on January 1, 1995, all of the GATT rules and its 47 years of precedents were folded into the WTO.... The WTO is an organization of some 500 highly paid professionals, mostly lawyers ... [which] make significant decisions about international trade out of the public's view. It has no written bylaws, makes decisions by consensus, and has never taken a vote on any issue. It holds no public hearings, and in fact has never opened its processes to the public.... Its court-like rulings are not made by U.S.-style due process. Yet WTO today [because it has a dispute settlement mechanism with enforcement powers] rivals the World Bank and International Monetary Fund in global importance.... Three minimalist GATT principles continue to operate through the WTO. The first is the famous most-favored-nation status (MFN): Products traded among GATT members must receive the best terms that exist in any bilateral trading agreement.... [The second:] Goods produced domestically and abroad must receive the same "national treatment"—equal access to markets.... [The third] is "transparency," which requires that any trade protection be obvious and quantifiable—like a tariff.... The WTO has the authority to resolve disputes and to issue penalties and sanctions.[4]

The plan was to

> give GATT a "legal personality," known as the Multilateral Trading Organization (MTO) [later organized as the World Trade Organization or WTO], that could strictly enforce global trading laws.... MTO [now WTO] will have the power to pry open markets throughout the world.... The proposed agreement would also extend GATT oversight from "goods" (machinery for instance) to "services" (insurance, banking). In order to protect trade in services, GATT would guarantee intellectual property rights—granting protection for patents and copyrights.... MTO would have the authority to restrict a developing nation's trade in natural resources (goods) if it didn't allow a first world country's financial service company sufficient access to its markets.... GATT panels may some day rule on the trade consequences of municipal recycling laws or state and local minority set-aside programs. In any trade dispute, the nation whose law is challenged must prove its law is not a trade barrier in secret hearings. The new GATT says plainly, "Panel deliberations shall be secret." Under this system, newly elected federal executives could allow the trade or environmental laws of their predecessors to be overturned by mounting a lackluster defense of the laws. And since the defense would occur in secret, without transcripts, interest groups and the public would never know the quality and vigor of the defense. Environmental or health and safety laws (and possibly labor rights and human rights laws) affecting another nation's commerce, no matter how well intended, will be more easily challenged. Again, the executive branch from the challenged nation would defend the law in star-chamber proceedings in Geneva—out of view of media and interest groups back home.[5]

David C. Korten points out,

> the burden of proof is on the defendant to prove the law in question is not a restriction of trade as defined by the GATT.... Countries that fail to make the recommended change within a prescribed period face financial penalties, trade sanctions, or both.... The WTO is, in effect, a global parliament composed of unelected bureaucrats with the power to amend its own charter without referral to legislative bodies.... [It] will become the highest court and most powerful legislative body, to which the judgments and authority of all other courts and legislatures will be subordinated.[6]

After WWII, the U.S. State Department "devoted a great deal of time and energy formulating the legal structure" to limit others' rights to place conditions on trade within their country:[7]

> [A]ny member can challenge, through the WTO, any law of another member country that it believes deprives it of benefits it is expected to receive from the new trade rules. This includes virtually any law that requires import goods to meet local or national health, safety, labor, or environmental standards that exceed WTO accepted international standards.... [Both national and local governments] must bring its laws into line with the lower international standard or be subject to perpetual fines or trade sanctions.... Conservation practices that restrict the export of a country's own resources—such as forestry products, minerals, and fish products—could be ruled unfair trade

practices, as could requirements that locally harvested timber and other resources be processed locally to provide local employment.[8]

The equality and transparency in world trade supposedly guaranteed by GATT, NAFTA, The WTO, MAI, GATS, or FTAA are fraudulent. While weak nations are forced to open their markets, legal structures, and financial institutions, tariffs between the organized and *allied imperial-centers-of-capital* remain one-quarter that between the developing world and those imperial centers. And the buying power of developing world export commodities and labor continue to fall as the imperial nations continue to tighten the screws of financial, economic, diplomatic, covert, and overt warfare.

Cuba was able to develop an education and health system equal to America precisely because she escaped the clutches of the IMF/World Bank and the structural adjustments they would have imposed.[9] When former World Bank Chief Economist Joseph Stiglitz was forced out of the Word Bank for suggesting relaxing structural adjustment rules he was asked by interviewer Greg Palast of the *London Observer* if any nation avoided the fate of structural adjustments. Stiglitz replied, "Yes! Botswana. Their trick? They told the IMF to go packing."

Good people within the IMF/World Bank keep sending Palast internal papers which prove there is no intention that the periphery will successfully develop. A reading of Palast's *The Best Democracy that Money can Buy: The Truth about Corporate Cons, Globalization, and High-Finance Fraudsters* (2003) will convince one that the purpose of this unspoken and disguised economic warfare through imposed structural adjustments is specifically to hold down the price of developing world resources and labor and to transfer that wealth, natural and processed, to the imperial centers. In 2001 Joseph Stiglitz was awarded a Nobel Prize in economics for his courageous stand.[10]

The Kuznet's Curve is used to prove that Adam Smith free trade will develop the impoverished world. In WTO meetings charts were pulled out which admitted these structural adjustments initially make life worse for poor countries. The Kuznet's Curve supposedly proved that over time their average standard of living would improve. As the *imperial-centers-of-capital* would never dream of inflicting such pain upon themselves, one can safely conclude that the Kuznet's Curve is just one more tool to keep the masses satisfied and passive. Think of it like this: if we were working together building for the future, would you allow me a higher share of the wealth produced upon my claim that your sacrifice would make you better off in the future? Under capitalism, those who can accumulate capital are the winners; Kuznet's curve shows the already wealthy initially gain the most under those structural adjustment rules. It is they who then have even more to invest. The wealth accumulated continues to widen and that alone disproves Kuznet's thesis.

Structural adjustment rules get ever tighter. MAI was described by *Business Week* as, "The Explosive Trade Deal You've Never Heard Of."

Then Director General of WTO called the secretive MAI rules as, a "Constitution for a single global economy."[11] Under IMF/World Bank/GATT/NAFTA/WTO/MAI/GATS/FTAA structural adjustment rules, governments of the developing world could not provide supports to their industry and severely restricted supports to education and health care.

This is the secret of resource-rich impoverished countries and resource-poor wealthy nations. Weak nations are forced to participate in the world economy under exactly the opposite rules under which every powerful nation developed. All wealthy nations provide enormous subsidies to their industries and agriculture. They all placed, and some still place, high tariffs on manufactured imports and low or no tariffs on raw material imports. Subsidies and tariffs in the imperial centers are increasing even as those on the periphery are denied that right. There are also land donations, tax breaks, and below cost services in bidding wars in those wealthy nations so as to gain or retain industry as well as wage subsidies, and outright cash incentives. Frances Moore Lappé points out that "More than a third of annual U.S. government spending, an estimated $448-billion, consists of direct and indirect subsidies for corporations and wealthy individuals, in direct violation of free-market principles."[12]

Even as structural adjustment rules deny the periphery of empire the right to control their imports and exports or subsidize their industries, as we just described is done by the developed world, the *imperial-centers-of-capital* maintain some level of embargo against over 70 countries.[13]

These embargoes are pressures forcing those countries to bend to the dictates of the *imperial-centers-of-capital*. Not only are direct and indirect subsidies provided within the imperial centers, the highly developed infrastructure (roads, ports, and airports) in the developed world, as well as basic research, which greatly cheapens production costs, are largely paid for and maintained by public funds.

Free Food is horribly expensive

. At first look it would appear that giving millions of tons of cheap Western grain to the impoverished world is very generous. However, both cheap and even free imported food can be one of the greatest disasters to befall a country:

> Where would Western business and labor be if a powerful nation exported food to it below the price of local production? Their farmers would go bankrupt, the tractor and machinery companies would go bankrupt, the millions of people depending on these jobs would be without work production of remaining industries would have to be sold to other societies to pay the import food bill, and the West would quickly become impoverished.[14]

This is just what happened to the Ukraine. Cheap grain poured into that country after the Soviet collapse, the farmers could not sell their grain for enough money to pay costs, so they quit planting. That breadbasket of the former Soviet Union became hungry and depended on the world for food handouts. As buying power has been destroyed, this can only have been equally as devastating on all other industries in the Ukraine:

> Exporting food may be profitable for the exporting country, but when their land is capable of producing adequate food, it is a disaster to the importing countries. [Note that many of the poor nations today are rich in natural resources and arable land.] American farmers would certainly riot if 60% of their markets were taken over by another country. Not only would the farmers suffer, but the entire economy would be severely affected.
>
> Imported food is not as cheap as it appears. If the money expended on imports had been spent within the local economy, it would have multiplied several times as it moved through the economy contracting local labor (the economic multiplier).... This moving of money through an economy is why there is so much wealth in a high-wage manufacturing and exporting country and so little within a low-wage country that is "dependent" on imports. With centuries of mercantilist experience, developed societies understand this well.... [S]ubsidies, tariffs and other trade policies eliminate the comparative advantage of other regions to maintain healthy economies in the developed world.... The result of these First World subsidies [for export] are shattered developing world economies.[15]

The economic multiplier is the health of an economy. A nation's farmers selling their crops provide them with the money to purchase products and services produced by others within the country. Those selling their products and services to the farmers use their income to purchase what is produced by the labor of other producers in the country or region. The economic multiplier, through balanced production within a country or region, creates a healthy, wealthy economy. When a country imports food or any other product, and there are insufficient compensating exports of equally high value (meaning both high value-added products and the labor that produced them were equally paid), that country becomes poorer, not richer.

Zambia had 40 small industries producing clothes for Zambians. A flood of used clothes from America undersold those producers forcing them to shut down, the multiplier factor went into reverse, and the number of impoverished Zambians rose rapidly. A small donation from the exporting country became a big loss for the importing country.

Financial Warfare

In response to the West's economic warfare that maintained low oil prices, oil countries formed OPEC and raised the price of crude oil. Enormous sums of money immediately started moving from the West to the East. This was a crisis of the first order. As the West controlled the money creation process, they turned to financial warfare to rectify the problem:

In the early 1970s, the United States and, to varying extents, the other OECD countries, responded to OPEC's increases in oil prices by heavily expanding the money supply. The resulting inflation, together with the administered pricing policies in many basic U.S. industries, sharply increased the prices of U.S. exports and thus the cost of many imports to the developing world. Such an inflationary policy enabled the OECD countries, as a group, to keep their current accounts in balance, despite the large oil prices.... In effect, the United States largely insulated itself from the oil price hikes by passing the burden on to the developing world, whose current accounts deficit mounted. The developing world, in turn tried to ease this burden by borrowing heavily rather than by deflating.[16]

We will quote from our previous work:

> In short, those petrodollars were transferred to the developing world, then returned to the developed world through export purchases and capital flight, and then dollars were printed to lower the value of Arab petrodollar deposits. If the petrodollars lent to the developing world had been used to build industrial capital and agricultural self-sufficiency, inflating the dollar would have effectively reduced their debts along with the intended reduction of developed-world debts to the oil cartel.
>
> But, as this money was spent on consumer goods (that properly should have been, on the average, produced by themselves) and funneled into personal bank accounts in the developed world, the developing world gained only the debt. The gains of the Arab cartel were largely erased as the value of their money was essentially halved and the developed nations retained their subtle monopolization of world capital in the form of a $1.7-trillion debt trap for the developing world (1998 [now $2-trillion, 2002]) which could only be paid off through sales of valuable resources.[17]

Petrodollars not consumed by wars were deposited in American and European banks and then lent to the developing world for non-productive purposes:

> Banks everywhere, flush with petrodollars, had to struggle to find big customers to whom they could make big loans. Brazil, Mexico, Argentina, Nigeria, and others were wonderful customers, borrowing hundreds of billions worth of these "recycled petrodollars," as they were called.... Just moving that money out the door was an achievement because the sums were so vast. Bankers had to struggle to find clients. Never mind that at least $500-billion of those loans turned sour. Never mind that for a decade the biggest borrowers did not make a single payment. Nor, in all likelihood, will they ever.[18]

If labor in the developing world had been better paid, surplus finance capital would have built industry to service that market. But the combination of low wages on the periphery of empire, low commodity prices, and debt, is an excellent method of guaranteeing the world's natural resources are reserved for populations within the *imperial-centers-of-capital*.

> Debt is an efficient tool. It ensures access to other peoples' raw materials and infrastructure on the cheapest possible terms. Dozens of countries must compete for shrinking export markets and can export only a limited range of products because of Northern protectionism and their lack of cash to invest in diversification. Market saturation ensues, reducing exporters' income to a bare minimum while the North enjoys huge savings.... The IMF cannot seem to understand that investing in ... [a] healthy, well-fed, literate population ... is the most intelligent economic choice a country can make.[19]

By 1996, developing world commodity export prices had fallen 60% and the worldwide currency collapses on the periphery of empire since may have dropped those prices, plus developing world labor values, another 50%.[20] The steadily lowering of commodity export prices and the resultant steadily increasing poverty in the developing world, is a record of the success of the IMF/World Bank/GATT/NAFTA/WTO/MAI/GATS/FTAA/military colossus in maintaining access to, and low prices for, the world's labor and natural resources:

> Structural Adjustment [demanded by the IMF] is best summed up in four words: earn more, spend less. While such advice might be valid if it were given to only a few countries at once, dozens of debtors are now attempting to earn more by exporting whatever they have at hand; particularly natural resources including minerals, tropical crops, timber, meat and fish. With so many jostling for a share of limited world markets, prices plummet, forcing governments to seek ever-higher levels of exports in a desperate attempt to keep their hard currency revenues stable. The "export-led growth" model on which the fund and the World Bank insist is a purely extractive one involving more the "mining" than the management—much less conservation—of resources.[21]

Countries without the industries to produce for themselves are far underpaid for their resources and labor. A share of what is earned is intercepted and diverted by corrupt managers, the developing world must borrow to survive, and their debts grow ever bigger. William Greider describes the inevitable steady spiral into debt when too great a share of a country's resources and labors are "confiscated" by predatory capital and the locally corrupt:

> A debtor who repeatedly borrows more than the surplus his labor or business enterprise produces will fall further and further behind in his obligations until, sooner or later, the inexorable pressures of compound interest defeat him.... Interest [is] usurious when the borrower's rightful share of profit [is] confiscated by the lender.... The creative power of capital [is] reversed and the compounding interest [becomes] destructive.[22]

Professor Lester Thurow explains:

> The fundamental mathematics is clear. To run a trade deficit, a country must borrow from the rest of the world and accumulate international debt. Each year interest must be paid on this accumulated debt. Unless a country is

running a trade surplus, it must borrow the funds necessary to make interest payments. Thus the annual amount that must be borrowed gets larger and larger, even if the trade deficit itself does not expand. As debts grow, interest payments grow. As interest payments grow, debt grows. As time passes the rate of debt accumulation speeds up, even if the basic trade deficit remains constant.[23]

Loans to the developing world were made irresponsibly:

> [E]xternal loans were not used to finance large-scale industrial or other projects designed to improve the productivity of the national economy. The military dictatorships used them instead to open up domestic markets to imports in order to allow the middle classes a brief, and therefore all the more passionate, frenzy of consumption.... [Those debts] are still being paid for today with even greater poverty, unemployment and destitution for the majority of the population. Much of the contemporary wealth of such nations, including Argentina, can be found in numbered Swiss bank accounts rather than between Terra del Fuego and La Plata.[24]

As American citizens have won lawsuits against banks for their defaulting on loans that were loaned less blatantly irresponsible—and as "every debt crisis in history since Solon of Athens has ended in inflation, bankruptcy or war"[25]—the wealthy world should cancel those unpayable, unjust debts. With a market value as low as 14.75-cents on the $1 and an average of 28-cents on the $1,[26] the supposed value of those $2.5-trillion in loans are already largely gone anyway and the remaining value will melt if, or should we say as, the crisis deepens. As America defaulted on much of its development debt in the 1800s, precedent for forgiving that debt is well established. And any honest accounting of underpaid labor and resources would show the wealthy world owing the impoverished world.

As money will flee back to the safety of the *imperial-centers-of-capital* when a financial crisis on the periphery occurs, the center gets stronger (initially) as the periphery gets weaker. (Equality of pay for equally-productive labor would eliminate the current *invisible borders* of monopoly capital and thus eliminate those collapses caused by the flight of capital. There would then be no need to flee as there are now no borders.) Since the collapse of the Soviet Union and the acceptance of the Western model by China, there is no fear of losing the periphery to democratic forces in those countries and thus there is no reason for the already allied imperial centers to provide protection to any needy country.

But will the world return to a balance of a wealthy center with an impoverished but functioning periphery (successful financial warfare)? Will the world economy stabilize with a secure allied center and even lower prices for a collapsing periphery (super successful financial warfare protected by a powerful military)? Or has control of technology and control of trade been lost, resulting in ultra-cheap manufactured products pouring into, and collapsing, the allied center (another great depression and failure of financial warfare)?[27]

The American stock market gained $11-trillion between 1989 and 2000, created in part by money fleeing the periphery, but lost $5-trillion of that in the next 26 months. But the gain in real estate and bond markets has, so long as land prices hold, cancelled out those losses. So, at least until the World Trade Center/Pentagon bombing of 9/11/2001, the economies of the imperial centers were still strong even as the periphery economies worldwide were collapsing.

To gain allies to fight the Cold War, a few key countries on the periphery (Japan and the Asian Tigers) were allowed rights within the subtle monopoly banking and trading system. Their collapse was a substantial loss of rights to participate as equals in the world economy. But once a population has enjoyed those rights it is very politically difficult to take them away. If denied relatively equal trading rights those once successfully developing nations will understand those economic warfare maneuvers and may ally together and successfully withdraw from the system (www.narconews.com, Heinz Dieterich Steffan, Rebelisn [sic]).

So an attempt will be made to soften the current collapse on the periphery. It remains to be seen if finance capital will flow back to the periphery after the 9/11/2001 terrorist attack. But if that money does flow back, many developing world industries will have new owners. Finance capital monopolists of the imperial centers will have, during that financial crisis, bought title to those industries and resources for a fraction of its true value (again Kuznet's Curve is disproved). With local capitalists on the periphery now owning much less of their nation's wealth, economic activity within those nations cannot return immediately to its previous vigor:

> However, if the increased wealth flowing to the center of empire trickles down to the masses through both lower prices and buying power generated from stock market profits, it is possible for the center to be more vigorous than ever. But a collapse of Western stock markets would eliminate the trickling down of wealth and reduce purchases. That reduction could multiply through the economy, and the recessions and depressions on the periphery will have come home to the imperial-centers-of-capital. A substantial softening of European and American economies would blow back upon the already collapsed economies of Southeast Asia and put heavy pressure on the Chinese economy. If economies fall to that level, only relaxing the monopolization of finance capital and restructuring world trade (meaning equal rights, equal access to technology and capital, equal trade, etc., along the guidelines of *democratic-cooperative-capitalism*) can establish a *vigorous* world economy. [28]

Equal Trade as opposed to Unequal Trade

Financial power, economic power, and military power (financial warfare, economic warfare, covert warfare, and overt war) maintain the unequal pay between the *powerful imperial-centers-of-capital* and the weak on the periphery. As per the wealth-accumulation-process outlined in Chapter 2, this unequal pay forms unseen borders that define the well-cared-for protected within those *invisible borders* and the impoverished outside those borders.

These *unseen borders* created by legal structures established over the centuries to protect power and wealth can be proven by a simple mental exercise: All wealth is processed from natural resources and most of the world's resources are in the impoverished world. Pay labor on the periphery of empire equally for equally-productive work, permit them industrial capital (technology) to produce for themselves, allow them equal access to world markets, and soon all people will be relatively equal. They will be building and producing for themselves and the world, not just producing for the wealthy world. There are no longer any borders guiding the world's wealth to those imperial centers. The periphery of empire, previously a huge plantation system providing resources and labor to the *wealthy imperial-centers-of-capital*, will have gained control of their destiny.

Capital destroys Capital

> The excessive accumulation of capital by stateless corporate imperialists, and the denial of capital to the world's powerless and their lack of prosperous internal market economies, are two sides of the same coin. There is too little buying power among the dispossessed to purchase all the production of industrial capital. When there is already a surplus, capital building more industry without developing more consumer buying power will destroy other capital.[29]

Michael Moffit points out:

> "Until we get real wage levels down much closer to those of Brazil's and Korea's, we cannot pass along productivity gains to wages and still be competitive." With factory wages in Mexico and Korea averaging about $3 an hour, compared with U.S. wages of $14 or so, it looks as if we have a long way to go before U.S. wages will even be in the ball park with the competition. That the decline of U.S. industry is the natural and logical outcome of the evolution of the multinational corporate economy over the past twenty-five years has been a bitter pill to swallow and it will become increasingly distasteful as time goes on. *One consequence will be a nasty decline in the standard of living in the United States....* [W]e have the outlines of a true vicious circle: the world economy is dependent on growth in the U.S. economy but the U.S. domestic economy is [now] skewed more towards consumption than production and investment, and this consumption is in turn sustained by borrowing—at home and abroad.... The deal with surplus countries essentially has been as follows: you can run a big trade surplus with us provided that you put the money back into our capital markets.[30]

Instead of sensibly and ethically increasing the wages of poorly-paid but equally-productive labor to the level of the well-paid, capital plans to lower the wages of the well-paid to the level of the underpaid. Though capital may see short-term gains, in the long run it is a race to the bottom:

> So long as global productive capacity exceeds global demand by such extravagant margins, somebody somewhere in the world has to keep closing factories, old and new.... South Korea will be losing jobs to cheap labor in Thailand and even China may someday lose factories to Bangladesh.[31]

Japan's industry has operated at 65.5% capacity for 12 years. By 2003 the entire industrialized world was producing at the same two-thirds capacity.[32] The low wages in the industries of the latest countries to attempt to develop and the lowering of wages within previously fast developing countries whose economies and/or currencies have collapsed does not permit those workers to buy the products they produce. Thus most of that production must, under fierce competition, be marketed to the wealthy world. So long as free trade is practiced, the low prices those products can command will eventually hollow out the economies of America and Europe:[a]

> The world's existing structure of manufacturing facilities, constantly being expanded on cheap labor and new technologies, can now turn out far more goods than the world's consumers can afford to buy.... The auto industry is an uncomplicated example: Auto factories worldwide have the capacity to produce 45-million cars annually for a market that, in the best years, will buy no more than 35-million cars.... Somebody has to close his auto factory and stop producing.[33]

This is economic insanity. Perfectly good industries are shut down in the imperial centers and rebuilt on the periphery. When industries in the imperial centers shut down, local businesses close for lack of customers and the values of both homes and commercial property collapse. But, due to their underpaid labor, equal values are not established on the periphery. *"There is currently no mechanism within the market system to build consumer buying power and implant this new technology where it is badly needed while keeping the already producing factories servicing the already established market."*[34]

Under the current monopoly system designed to reserve the wonders of the *wealth-producing-process* for the powerful, those industries can be built quickly. But the markets of an efficiently functioning economic infrastructure (roads, schools, universities, businesses, homes, postal system, trucking companies, and airlines) can only be built slowly.

The struggle over the *wealth-producing-process* thus wastes more than wars. As shown below by developing an efficient economic infrastructure under *democratic-cooperative-capitalism*, all that waste and the waste of those wars can be eliminated and an efficient economic infrastructure quickly built by

---

[a] We must remember that true free trade has never been permitted, and is unlikely to be permitted now. So, to understand this scenario as it evolves, developing world economists must study on the many methods of protecting markets within those imperial centers.

simply building industries on the periphery and paying equally-productive labor equally. That new production would be affordable for the periphery where equally-paid labor now has purchasing power.

Money is used to combine three factors of production—land (natural resources), labor, and industrial capital—to produce an economic infrastructure and consumer products (true wealth). When money is created to establish an economic infrastructure (industry, businesses, universities, homes, et al.) the value of the wealth created backs that created money.

Currently, "the immediate discounting of a nation's currency on the periphery of empire if it attempts to print money [to produce industry or infrastructure] exposes how control of trading currency monopolizes buying power for *imperial-centers-of-capital*."[35] Reversing those financial warfare rules makes it clearer yet. Equal pay on the periphery of the abandoned empire, along with the right of the periphery to create currency in step with the increased value of the economic infrastructure being created, will expand buying power in step with increased industrial capacity. As that industrial capacity expands money circulation, more buying power is created and poverty decreases. Elimination of subtle monopolization allows the magic of the economic multiplier to function freely and produce a healthier and wealthier society.

Sincerely Sharing the *Wealth-Producing-Process*

Powerful countries have lots of experience in calculating needed resources and how to obtain them for their own needs. If they were sincere in wanting to develop the developing world they can easily calculate the waste of the current economy, the waste of wars, take inventory of the world's resources, and draw up a working plan for sustainable development of poorer nations. Western Europe integrating its production of coal and steel (specifically to eliminate war) and later the European Union integrating Western European economies provide models.[36]

It is necessary to expand those principles to all regions of the world and for all people within a region to share equally. Since this would mean big adjustments in the structure of their economies, it is highly unlikely we will hear those options suggested by the imperial centers. Power only responds to equal power. Only by allying amongst themselves and thus gaining power can weak nations force the imperial centers to open up sincere development options.

Under the current world trade structure, the developing world cannot compete with the developed world. But they can compete with each other. All true wealth is processed from natural resources and most the world's resources are in the impoverished world. By forming trading alliances, bartering their resources to the wealthy world in trade for technology and access to markets, creating their own trading currencies manufacturing their own consumer products, and by trading within that alliance and wherever else the trades would be equal, those nations can quickly develop.

These are all rights under which every industrialized nation developed and those same rights are now denied the periphery through imposed structural adjustments. Any nation that seriously considers taking control of its own destiny faces immediate embargo and covert destabilization. If they cannot be covertly destabilized they face overt war. Only by allying together can the periphery gain the power to negotiate equally with *powerful imperial-centers-of-capital*.

As the multiplier factor from production and distribution within a country is the health of an economy, a region (not a small or even a medium sized country) should be designed to be largely self-sufficient in food and industry. With adequate resources within their borders, this region could barter access to resources for the developed world for their access to technology and capital. More capital can be obtained from an equalizing surcharge on those resources (export tariffs equalizing unequally paid labor, the negotiations spoken of above) and radically simplified and more equitable methods of capital accumulation that we will be discussing in the next chapter.

It is possible to turn "win-lose" or "lose-lose" trade wars into "win-win" equalizing managed trade. A wealthy importing country should pay an equalizing surcharge based upon equitable landrent and labor values on imports from the region which has lost title to its resources and whose labor is underpaid. Surcharges on trades between regions would be relative to inequality of wage rates and to equalize costs between rich and poor deposits of natural resources.

Through those surcharges, natural resources should be priced relative to the cost of mining the world's poorer mineral deposits in the resource-poor developed world. Those monies should not go directly to the typically corrupt developing world nation. They should go into a compensation/development/ecosystem protection fund to pay directly for developing a region's infrastructure, constructing developing world industries (industrial capital), developing renewable energy resources, developing environmentally sound products, designing and implementing ecologically sustainable lifestyles, rebuilding soils, and cleaning up and revitalizing the world's ecosystems. Those surcharges should be lowered in step with the industrialization and increase in wages of the developing nation.

Once roughly equal in technology and labor equally paid, surcharges would be eliminated and honest free trade would flow between those regions. Trade between unequal regions should be managed trade while trade within regions and between roughly equal regions would be free. As technology, labor skills, and capital accumulation equalize, protections would be lowered.

Undeveloped world industry would be protected from the deep pockets and experienced industry of the developed world and labor and industry in the wealthy world will be protected against low-paid labor of the developing world. The now allied undeveloped regions should develop competitive and balanced economies. A resource-depletion tax, a renaming of the equalizing surcharge, would be retained for rebuilding soils and funding sustainable lifestyles:

> If wages paid in basic industry are equal to wages paid by the consumer of those products (Adam Smith's concept of labor retaining the value of what it produces[37]), this will create initial buying power and the expenditure of those wages on consumer needs will produce more buying power (the economic multiplier and development of a market economy). Once the internal market economies of impoverished nations are developed and a skilled labor force trained, those countries should be integrated with, and enjoy free trade between, other developed regions using the maximum efficiencies (comparative advantage) of each region. "What is needed is a global regulatory framework for multinational corporations—a set of common standards for labor rights, tax and wage rates, and environmental protection—as well as the means, both national and international, to enforce them." Instead of policies that bring well-paid labor down to the wages of the lowest paid, equalizing managed trade would be raising the wages of the poorly paid to those of the better paid.[38]

William Greider says it well:

> [The developed world] ought to reject any new trade agreements that do not include a meaningful social contract—rules that establish baseline standards for health, labor laws, working conditions, the environment, wages. The world economy needs a global minimum wage law—one that establishes a rising floor under the most impoverished workers in industrial employment.[39]

Wealth is only the representative value resulting from combining natural resources (land), labor, and industrial capital. By peripheral nations using the currency of an imperial center as its trading currency, the imperial center can actually print money to own industry within those periphery countries. A country is not free when another country has such leverage over its entire economy. By forming regional trading blocs and printing its own trading currency to establish industries, the developing world has all three requirements for the production of wealth, natural resources, labor, and industrial capital. Money should not be created for consumption as no values are created. Properly money can only be created to build wealth. The industries built and the wealth produced provides the value to back the newly printed money:

> It must be emphasized that when this capitalization is complete each country will have equal rights (within its region) to resources, industrial capital, and markets. Those rights automatically translate into the ability of that nation's citizens to feed themselves and job rights that, in turn, translate into buying

power and that society's share of social wealth. Nations that are poorer in resources need to be assigned a higher level of industrial capital. But the regional average should still be that all-important ratio of approximately one unit of industrial capital to thirty units of social capital (see below); and all capital should, on the average, be regionally and locally owned.[40]

Most of the recommendations above were applied when Greece, Portugal, and Spain joined the Common Market: The European Union planners "implemented a fifteen-year plan which included massive transfers of direct aid, designed to accelerate development, raise wages, regularize safety and environmental standards, and improve living conditions in the poorer nations."[41] These suggestions equalize the rights of capital and labor and return the world's natural resources to their rightful owners:

> Currently the cost of minerals in the United States is only 1.7% of GNP and the cost of fuel only 2.0%. This demonstrates that there is plenty of room to increase the price of minerals and carbon fuels to a level that the lower grade deposits in the developed world can be mined and renewable energy utilized. The recycling of minerals would then be profitable and renewable energy would be competitive.
>
> With labor equally paid, initially through tariffs and resource depletion (landrent) surcharges balancing production costs, the world can then mine all deposits (rich and poor), maximize product life (because consumer products now appear expensive), and can recycle (because they are actually now cheaper) the consumed minerals, paper, plastic, and other materials. Though developing-world resources may appear higher priced under these rules, they are really cheaper. Far more people will be provided with the amenities of life even as the world's resources and ecosystems are protected, which is the proper measure of cost.
>
> Once resources are no longer wasted producing arms—and social efficiencies such as those outlined in the classics of Thorstein Veblen, Stuart Chase, Ralph Borsodi, this author's previous work, and many others documenting the enormous wasted labor and resources—are instituted, the developed nations can afford to use their poorer deposits, develop new technology, or trade (equally now) with those who have rich deposits.[42]

Military power is the final arbiter on control of resources and markets. If the undeveloped world is organized broad enough, the military power of the imperial centers can be offset. A large military would now be an expensive handicap. Starting with the periphery, the world should disarm and a restructured, fully democratic, United Nations force should provide security for all. Industry, labor and finance capital formerly producing and maintaining arms can now produce for the world's true needs. The world's intelligence services should be maintained with their primary duty being detection of unrest and terrorism.

With $21-trillion worth of social capital and $1-trillion worth of industrial capital (1990), less industry wasted by the military, America has roughly one unit of civilian industrial capital to thirty units of social capital.[a] The developed world need only supply those all-important industrial tools (3.3% of the wealth in a balanced economy); with those tools the developing world can produce their own social capital (96.7% of the wealth).[b] By avoiding the American throw-away economy model, a secure, quality life is possible with only 20% the resource consumption of Americans.[43] As industry will no longer be producing for the military and there will be at the same time technological efficiency gains, we can safely reduce industrial needs to 14% of America's level in 1990:

> We have calculated that a society can be well cared for at 20% of the American consumption rate, or with as little as 14% of U.S. per-capita industrial capacity at the peak of the Cold War. As of that date (1990), the value of industrial tools stood at about $5,600 per person in the United States. (Homes, cars, roads, bridges, electric power, water systems, sewers, etc., are social capital. Steel mills, factories, and so forth are industrial tools.) By the above calculation, one would consider 14% of that—or under $900 industrial capacity per person—as adequate for an efficient, peaceful society.[c] Allowing 3.5-billion people without modern tools, $3.15-trillion of industrial capital is needed to develop the world to a sustainable level. That is 18.5% the amount spent on arms by the world since WWII.
>
> Assuming it would require 45 years for the developing world to be educated and to build social capital as it was being given industrial capital, and assuming a doubling of the developing world's population in that time span, it would require $6.3-trillion. That larger figure would be only $140-billion annually, or 14% of the $1-trillion spent on arms each year worldwide at the time of the Soviet collapse. Until that collapse, NATO and Warsaw Pact countries accounted for 86% of that expenditure, or about $860-billion (1990), and the Western alliance spent well over half of that. *Thus it would*

---

[a] *Statistical Abstract of the U.S., 1990,* pp. 463, 734, charts 752, 1295 (check gross stock, total; value added by manufacture; gross book value of depreciable assets). These statistics demonstrate that each factory reproduces its value every ten months and that there is approximately $21-trillion worth of reproducible social capital and $1-trillion worth of industrial capital. Professor Seymour Melman, probably the leading authority on military waste; Mr. Greg Bishak, of the National Commission for Economic Conversion and Disarmament; and William Greider, *Who Will Tell the People?* (New York: Simon and Schuster, 1992), p. 370, judge U.S. industry wasted on arms at roughly 20%.

[b] We are only calculating sustainable development at the level of technological efficiency of the year 2000. Paul Hawkens, Amory Lovings, and L. Hunter Lovins, in their pathbreaking work *Natural Capitalism: Creating the Next Industrial Revolution,* point out that increased efficiencies of technology will eventually be able to produce "four, ten, or even a hundred times as much benefit from each unit of energy, water, materials, or anything else borrowed from the planet and consumed." Paul Hawken, *Natural Capitalism: Creating the Next Industrial Revolution* (New York: Little Brown and Company, 1999), p. 8. See also Brian Milani, *Designing the Green Economy: The Postindustrial Alternative to Corporate Globalization* (New York: Rowman & Littlefield, 2000).

[c] That is about $3,600 worth of industrial capital per family and $100,000 worth of social capital.

require only 14% of the money habitually spent on arms by the world during the Cold War to industrialize the world. As the Eastern bloc has collapsed, this leaves only the West, but the $140-billion a year needed to industrialize the world is only 28% of that spent by the West to win the Cold War (48% of that spent annually by the United States alone).[a]

Once a region is developed, industrial needs drop sharply.[b] A 1998 report by the United Nations Development Program calculated the annual cost for universal access to a number of basic social services for all people in all needy countries at: $9-billion for clean water and sanitation, $12-billion for women's reproductive health, $13-billion to provide every person with basic health and nutrition, and $6-billion to provide basic education for all. The total, $40-billion, 5% the money spent on arms each year, would lift most the world's citizens out of deep poverty.

The US will spend twice that rebuilding the World Trade Center, much more each year protecting against terrorism, and those losses are only a tiny fraction of the losses worldwide from government-sponsored wholesale terrorism suppressing the world's breaks for freedom under the flag of a War on Terrorism. So restructuring to *democratic-cooperative-capitalism* and equal sharing of the world's wealth, thus eliminating terrorism, would be a good return on that investment. Obviously, if the developed world was sincere about eliminating poverty it could be done very quickly.

Much of Southeast Asia is highly industrialized and, in 2002, China alone graduated over 400,000 Ph.D.s in the hard sciences. We must remember it was Germany graduating 8-to-10 times more engineers than Britain (3,000 against 350) that made the German economy much more efficient than the British economy and it was Germany's efficient economy taking over British markets that led to World Wars I and II. A philosophy of sharing resources, sharing productive capacity, and sharing in the wealth produced can, however, avoid such Fascist attempts at military control of world resources which could easily turn into World War III as the educated developing world struggles to gain their space within the world economy.

---

[a] Smith, *Economic Democracy*, updated and expanded 3rd edition, Chapter 23. When one includes the National Security Agency, the CIA, and weapons programs carried out under the umbrella of the Atomic Energy Commission and Energy Department, the military budget was at least $350-billion, as opposed to the $292-billion official military budget we are using (those year-2000 figures will rise by 50% by 2007). Between $4-trillion and $5-trillion was spent on nuclear arms alone, mostly under cover of the Energy Department, since 1945 (Jonathan S. Landay, "Study Reveals U.S. Has Spent $4-Trillion on Nukes Since '45," *The Christian Science Monitor,* July 12, 1995, p. 3).

[b] Assume a region with no tractors was to build a tractor factory to produce the latest technology tractors. Allow 20 years to capitalize that region with tractors. Once capitalized, replacement needs will drop to under 20% the productive capacity of those factories. That holds true for all other machinery and products. This is why subtle-monopoly capitalism must look to export markets. It is either export or shrink in size.

America's and NATO's rapid reaction forces snuffing out resistance all over the world is only control of resources and control of the *wealth-producing-process* hiding under other excuses. If those economies on the periphery continue collapsing, and especially if the imperial centers implode, the people of the world will soon figure that out.

Instead of sustainable world development why is capital insisting on privatizing the world's water systems, electric systems, natural gas systems, et al, and doubling, tripling, and even quadrupling the charges? In spite of the enormous waste of capital destroying capital, despite the waste of wars, and despite the waste of monopolies within internal economies (see the first five chapters of this author's *Cooperative Capitalism*) capital accumulations are so enormous there are no other safe and profitable areas to invest it. An analysis of the capital and resources wasted within those three areas of the economy will conclude that the alleviation of poverty in 10 years and sustainable development of the world within 50 years under *democratic-cooperative-capitalism* can be accomplished.

We will now address the simplicity of restructuring an internal economy to provide full rights for all.

Notes

[1] J.W. Smith, *Economic Democracy: The Political Struggle of the Twenty-First Century*, updated and expanded 3rd edition (www.ied.info/cc.html: The Institute for Economic Democracy, 2003).

[2] Lester Thurow, *The Future of Capitalism: How Today's Economic Forces Shape Tomorrow's World* (England: Penguin Books, 1996), p. 131, 137.

[3] William K. Tabb, *The Amoral Elephant: Globalization and the Struggle for Social Justice in the Twenty-First Century* (New York: Monthly Review Press, 2001), pp. 9-10.

[4] Howard Wachtel, "Labor's Stake in WTO," *The American Prospect* (March/April 1998), pp. 34-38.

[5] Don Wiener, "Will GATT Negotiators Trade Away the Future?" *In These Times*, February 12-18, 1992, p. 7. See also Chakravarthi Raghavan, *Recolonization: GATT, the Uruguay Round & the Developing World*. London: Zed Books, 1990.

[6] David C. Korten, *When Corporations Rule the World* (West Hartford, CT, Kumarian Press and San Francisco, Berrett-Koehler, 1995), pp. 174-77.

[7] John Ranelagh, The Agency: *The Rise and Decline of the CIA* (New York: Simon and Schuster, 1986), p. 120.

[8] Korten, *When Corporations Rule the World*, pp. 174-75; Susan Strange, *The Retreat of the State: The Diffusion of Power in the Global Economy* (Cambridge, UK: Cambridge Studies in International Relations, number 49, 1998); Raghavan, Recolonization.

[9] Speech by Cuban President Fidel Castro at the Group of 77 South Summit Conference, April, 2, 2000. Run a Google Internet search.

[10] Joseph E. Stiglitz, *Globalization and its Discontents* (New York: WW Norton, 2002).

[11] Tabb, *The Amoral Elephant*, p. 196.

[12] Frances Moore Lappé, *World Hunger: Twelve Myths* (New York: Grove Press: 1998), p. 98; Ousseynu Gueye, "Let African Farmers Compete," *World Press Review* (October 2002), p. 12.

[13] Laura Karmatz, Alisha Labi, Joan Levinstein, Special Report, "States at War," *Time*, November 9, 1998, pp. 40-54; Donald L, Bartlett, James B. Steele, "Fantasy Island and Other Perfectly Legal Ways that Big companies Manage to avoid Billions in Federal Taxes," *Time*, November 16, 1998, pp. 79-93; Donald L Bartlett, James B. Steele, "Paying a Price for Polluters," *Time*, November 23, 1998, pp. 72-82; The Banneker Center's Corporate Welfare Shame Links, http://www.progress.org/banneker/cw.html; Thomas Omestat, "Addicted to Sanctions," *U.S. News & World Report*, June 15, 1998, pp. 30-31. Run a Google Internet search.

[14] Smith, *Economic Democracy*, updated and expanded 3rd edition, Chapter 13. See also Bhagirath Lal Das, *WTO: The Doha Agenda: The New Negotiations on World Trade* (London: Zed Books, 2003) and his many other books.

[15] J.W. Smith, *The World's Wasted Wealth 2*, (www.ied.info/cc.html: The Institute for Economic Democracy, 1994), pp. 66-67

[16] Arjun Makhijani, *From Global Capitalism to Economic Justice* (New York: Apex Press, 1992), p. 159.

[17] J.W. Smith, *Economic Democracy*, Chapter 14.

[18] Joel Kurtzman, *The Death of Money* (New York: Simon and Schuster, 1993), p. 72.

[19] Susan George, *A Fate Worse Than Debt*, (New York: Grove Weidenfeld, 1990), pp. 143, 187, 235.

[20] Lester Thurow, *The Future of Capitalism*, p. 67. See also, Peter Gowan, *The Global Gamble: Washington's Faustian Bid for World Dominance* (New York: verso, 1999), pp. 95-138, especially pp. 114-15; John Gray, *False Dawn* (New York: The Free Press, 1998) and Richard C. Longworth, *Global Squeeze: The Coming Crisis of First-World Nations* (Chicago: Contemporary Books, 1999.

[21] Susan George, *The Debt Boomerang* (San Francisco: Westview Press, 1992), pp. 2-3.

[22] Greider, *Secrets of the Temple*, pp. 707, 581-82. See also Susan George, Fabrizio Sabelli, *Faith and Credit* (San Francisco: Westview Press, 1994), pp. 80-84, 215.

[23] Lester Thurow, *Head to Head: The Coming Economic Battle Among Japan, Europe, and America* (New York: William Morrow, 1992), p. 232.

[24] Elmar Altvater, Kurt Hubner, Jochen Lorentzen, Raul Rojas, *The Poverty of Nations* (New Jersey: Zed Books, 1991) pp. 8-9.

[25] George, *Fate Worse Than Debt*, p. 196.

[26] CNN News (June 28, 1990); David Felix, "Latin America's Debt Crisis," *World Policy Journal* (Fall 1990): p. 734.

[27] Smith, *Economic Democracy*, updated and expanded 3rd edition.

[28] Ibid, p. 220.

[29] Ibid, p. 261.

[30] Michael Moffitt, "Shocks, Deadlocks, and Scorched Earth," *World Policy Journal* (Fall, 1987), pp. 560-61, 572-73.

[31] William Greider, *Who Will Tell the People?* (New York: Simon and Schuster, 1992), pp. 378-79, 399-400.

[32] Lester Thurow, *Building Wealth: The New Rules for Individuals, Companies, and Nations in a Knowledge-Based Economy* (New York: HarperCollins, 2000). See also, Jeff Faux, "The Austerity Trap and the Growth Alternative," *World Policy Journal*, (Summer, 1988), p. 375.

[33] Greider, Who Will Tell the People, p. 399.

[34] Smith, *Economic Democracy*, updated and expanded 3rd edition, Chapter 18.

[35] Ibid, p. 197.

[36] Dean Acheson, *Present at the Creation* (New York: W.W. Norton, 1987), pp. 382-84.

[37] Adam Smith, *Wealth of Nations*, Modern Library edition (New York: Random House, 1965), p. 64.

[38] Smith, *Economic Democracy*, updated and expanded 3rd edition, Chapter 22, quoting Gerald Epstein, "Mortgaging America," *World Policy Journal* (Winter 1990-91), especially pp. 37, 53.

[39] William Greider, *Who Will Tell the People?* (New York: Simon and Schuster, 1992), pp. 402-03.

[40] Smith, *Economic Democracy*, updated and expanded 3rd edition, Chapter 22.

[41] *AFL-CIO Task Force Bulletin on Trade*, 1992.

[42] Smith, *Economic Democracy*, updated and expanded 3rd edition, Chapter 22, first edition, citing Herman E. Daly, *Steady-State Economics* (San Francisco: W.H. Freeman, 1977), p. 109. See also Brian Milani, *Designing the Green Economy: The Postindustrial Alternative to Corporate Globalization* (NY: Rowman & Littlefield, 2000).

[43] David C. Korten, *When Corporations Rule the World* (West Hartford, CT, Kumarian Press, 1995), p. 35; Jeremy Rifkin, *Entropy: Into the Greenhouse World* (New York: Bantam Books, 1989), p. 233; Richard J. Barnet, John Cavanagh, *Global Dreams: Imperial Corporations and the New World Order* (New York: Simon & Schuster, 1994), pp. 177-178.

8. Equal Rights in Domestic Economies

Periodically a researcher of economic history will run into "The Tragedy of the Commons." This fable purports to prove the tragedy of the commons with an example of pastures used in common. Each farmer has rights to pasture his cattle. Self interest dictates that some will turn more cattle into that pasture so as they will make more money. With this perceived superior right, the pasture is overgrazed, it degrades, and all lose.

This author has personal experience with common use of pastures and the outcome is the opposite of the fable. During the Great Depression, occasionally the grazing lands of bankrupt farmers on the prairies of the West were organized into "grazing districts" and are known by that name. The error in the fable is that while each has rights to common use of the pasture they each have equal rights and none have superior rights.

The rules of these grazing districts were that each had an allotted number of cattle they could pasture in a grazing district and there were severe penalties, even confiscation of excess cattle, if a member exceeded his or her allotted share. The result, private land with unrestricted title is typically overgrazed throughout the West as ranchers maximize their income by mining the topsoil through overgrazing while the soils of those grazing districts were conserved through cattle numbers staying within the carrying capacity of the grazing land.

Where did that fable come from? Just as corporations today fund think-tanks to pour out *social-control-paradigms* that protect their wealth and property (see Chapter 3) the fable of the "Tragedy of the Commons" and other such distortions of reality were created to justify the privatization of the commons during the three centuries of the establishment of the British enclosure acts and surely even earlier. The powerful have long known how to justify the continued structuring of inequalities into law through pushing a philosophy justifying their theft. Witness the imposition of Adam Smith free trade philosophy upon the world as we discussed in Chapter 2.

Throughout history, the powerful have, through subtle forms of monopolies, structured superior rights for themselves into law. Their unearned wealth both reduces the efficiency of an economy and lowers the share of wealth of others. Having been born and raised within the current legal structure, and taught with sincerity that this is the most efficient economy, few are aware that these highly inefficient subtle monopolies even exist. Most who do recognize the monopoly features feel this legal structure of property rights was necessary to accumulate capital.

The beliefs that a legal structure of subtle monopolies was, and is, necessary to accumulate capital are in error. Not only can capital be accumulated much faster in an economy with full and equal rights for all, money to build industry and infrastructure can be printed as needed (see the money chapter of any of this author's books). *Removal of subtle monopolization would not only increase your rights to land, your rights to the use of technology, your rights to finance capital, your rights to information, and your rights to your share of the profits from their productive use, it will ensure those rights.*[a]

Regaining Rights to a Modern Land Commons

Land is social wealth. It was not created by labor, all require land to live, and all should have full and equal rights to land. Those full and equal rights can be obtained and protected by a simple change in the legal structure of title to land—while the landowner retains full use rights society should collect the landrent. A nation's landrent, currently collected by subtle land monopolists under *residual-feudal* laws of their own design over the centuries, is adequate to pay all normal costs of government.[b] With that simple change, land monopolization and almost all other taxes disappear. We repeat, "No person's labor built land, thus it is properly social wealth, and, as the proper owners, society should collect the landrent." Not only is the collection of landrent by society just, it is second only to democracy as a social and legal structure for maximum economic efficiency.[c]

---

[a] As society slowly moved from feudalism—in which aristocrats claimed all rights and thus claimed all wealth—to capitalism, monopolies were the only way of accumulating capital. Under well-advanced democratic societies that is no longer true. Capital can now be accumulated much faster under a modern commons than under subtle-monopoly capitalism.

[b] Mason Gaffney and Fred Harrison, *The Corruption of Economics: With The Development of Democracy, Mind Control Became the Urgent Need: Neo-Classical Economics Was the Tool* (London: Shepheard-Walwyn, 1994), p. 183. Social Security, Railroad Retirement, Federal Employees Retirement, unemployment insurance, Medicare, and Medicaid, are—at this time—all improperly labeled as government expenses; they are actually paid-for insurance funds separate from expenses of running governments.

[c] This is a summary of the conclusions of our chapter on Henry George, J.W. Smith, *Economic Democracy: The Political struggle of the Twenty-First Century*, updated and expanded 3rd edition (www.ied.info/cc.html: The Institute for Economic Democracy, 2003), Chapter 24. Henry George, *Progress and Poverty* (New York: Robert Schalkenbach Foundation, 1981). Henry George's classic, *Progress and Poverty,* published in 1879, is the classic on this subject. All his works and many authors writing on him are available from the Robert Schalkenbach Foundation, 41 East 72nd St., NY, NY 10021 (212-988-1680), established for the purpose of keeping Henry George's philosophy alive. For up-to-date info and listserves contact Alanna Hartzok earthrts@pa.net.

With society collecting the landrent, the price of land drops to zero while its use-value actually increases. The payment of that landrent is, at first look, only slightly less costly than purchasing that land under current law. But a second look takes into consideration the elimination of all other taxes which, on balance, returns the price of land to zero. Landrent will have replaced all other taxes and all efficient producers will now have access to land; full rights to a modern land commons will have been regained.

Equally important, a landrent tax cannot be evaded and the collection system is already in place and paid for. All true producers would be able to start a business with only the capital necessary to buy buildings, machinery, and inventory. All who have done business know that these are easy to finance while purchasing subtly-monopolized land requires immense sums and is very difficult to finance.

There are enormous accounting savings when all other taxes are eliminated. Most talented accountants, federal tax agents, and a substantial number of lawyers, their support staff, and all who built and serviced their offices and equipment would be available for fully productive work, a subject addressed in our previous work.[1] Product prices would drop as sales taxes and their accounting costs disappeared. Taxes would now be paid for out of cash flow instead of being deducted from profits. All this would be gained with no increase in costs to the true producer (land monopolists are not true producers). Society collecting the landrent is a bargain for hard working and talented productive people.

Under a modern land commons, the use-value of land is distributed instantly and without cost to all members of society. That value no longer works its way though non-productive subtle land monopolists and a part slowly work its way back down to the producers of that wealth. The efficiency gains of a modern land commons under *democratic-cooperative-capitalism* would equal the efficiency gains from the invention of money.

The use-value of land actually increases. With subtle monopolization eliminated, the most efficient farmers can pay the highest landrent, so the most efficient farmers will own those farms. The most efficient industries will own their required land because they can pay the highest landrents. The most efficient businesses will own their required land because they too can pay the highest landrent. And all citizens will have rights to the land under their homes at no initial cost. The landrent paid by all, farmers, businessmen, and labor, would be offset by all having rights to land relative to their productivity and needs and by all other taxes disappearing:

> Oil, copper, iron ore, and the like, while still in the ground, are land and can very properly be privately owned so long as society is paid the landrent. The world has adequate reserves of most of these minerals. It is only richer deposits and cheaper labor in developing world countries that make their minerals more available. Under Adam Smith unequal free market philosophy, *the developed world's more expensive deposits are not mined until the undeveloped world's*

cheap deposits are exhausted. Ecological taxes or surcharges on rich mineral deposits to equalize production costs between developed regions with their expensive mineral deposits and the developing world and their cheap minerals ... is really landrent.[2]

The first option for restructuring landrent taxes: Landowners invested their money honestly and they should not be forced to shoulder the cost of a change in tax structure which changes property rights and thus changes monetized values. Homeowners and businesses are compensated instantly through greater efficiency and the elimination of all other taxes. Farmers, large landowners, and landlords are only partially compensated. They can be fully compensated through Bonds.

A second option: When the business cycle hits bottom and land prices return to almost zero, as it always has in the past, the change in tax structure can be made almost painlessly by increasing landrent taxes, and lowering other taxes, in step with increased economic activity as the economy recovers. Every increase in landrent would be offset by a decrease in other taxes. At these times the economy needs money and this is the opportune moment to change to a landrent tax and compensate landowners with bonds. Retirees must be compensated through higher retirement payments. Compensation for the low-paid is addressed throughout this book.

A third easy and painless way to replace all current taxes: A .0005 (1/20 of 1%) transaction tax on the circulation of money will equal the U.S. state and federal annual income/expenses. This tax was studied by the Congressional Research Service of the Library of Congress and found to be feasible. Tax lawyer John A. Newman proposed this transaction tax to the American Congress in 1988 and Paul Bottis is continually proposing it to the American Congress (http://www.taxmoney-notpeople.com and http://www.madashellclub.com). A transaction tax is far more efficient than the current tax systems but a landrent tax is more efficient yet.

One generation after society collecting the landrent is established it will be the norm and today's tax structure would fade into history. If it would have been possible to restructure *residual-feudal* property rights to a modern commons at the time of the reformation, most the wars since would have been avoided.

Regaining Rights to a Modern Technology Commons

"Behind the abstraction known as 'the markets' lurks a set of institutions designed to maximize the wealth and power of the most privileged group of people in the world, the creditor-rentier class of the first world and their junior partners in the third."[3]

Society's tools (technology) are subtly monopolized through the legal structure of patents and the stock market is the legal framework through which those monopoly profits are harvested:

That stock markets are crucial to raising investment capital in a modern economy is a myth. Most stock traders have no contact with new issues of stock and those who [do] are primarily taking an already established private company public. Most corporate investment needs are financed from profits, liberal depreciation schedules, and borrowing. As currently structured, investing in stock markets is primarily a bet on which corporation will most successfully expand its share of national and world markets. These are not investments in production.[4]

Adam Smith recognized that capital is a part of the commons and properly belongs to labor and that the current monopoly structure increases costs: "Produce is the natural wages of labor. Originally the whole belonged to the labourer. If this had continued all things would have become cheaper, though in appearance many things might have become dearer."[5] Nowhere is this clearer than in the subtle monopolization of technology through the structure of patent laws. This can be understood by analyzing the immediate savings of restructuring patent laws and replacing *residual-feudal exclusive* property rights with conditional titles of a modern commons..

While leaving old patents intact and requiring a contract, everybody should be able to use any new patent through voluntarily paying a royalty. Older patents will soon run out, all patents will then be available for use by anyone, and, through competition, patent overcharges will disappear. Even as subtle monopolists and their overcharges disappear, inventors will be better paid even as products become cheaper. With full rights to use any technology through paying reasonable royalties, efficient and valuable technology will have been returned to a modern commons for all to use.

The developer of a patent should also be well paid. Therefore, patent laws should be expanded to include development patents that also are available for all to use through paying a reasonable royalty. Both the inventor and the developer are now protected by patents, just as now, but they cannot monopolize. This is right by the philosophy of Adam Smith; the only protection to the producer would be the highest quality production at the lowest possible price.

The extent of a patent's use would be much easier to calculate than keeping records on patent use. Thus an even cheaper and much more efficient patent system would be society analyzing patent use and paying the inventors a capitalized cash payment instead of that annual payment. By simply recording their use of a technology under patent, producers are now free to use any patent. With full rights and true free trade replacing the current subtle-monopoly *residual-feudal* system, prices will drop precipitously even as product quality is maximized.

Subtle-monopoly profits are currently harvested through stock market capitalized values. With all companies having rights to use any technology, creative destruction of industries through others utilizing superior technology will be replaced by all companies using the latest and most efficient technology. Creative destruction will now be internal within industries rather than new industries utilizing new technology causing the shutting down of others' perfectly good industries (capital destroying capital). The cost to society of well-run industries shutting down will be replaced by those industries retooling, continuing to operate, and calmly expanding to other regions in step with the increase in buying power in those regions. The logistics of being near resources and markets replaces subtle monopolization of key technologies taking over markets.

Maximum profits indicate a lack of competition. As industries rationalize, so do markets. With calm secure industries making minimum (yet adequate), not maximum, profits in truly-competitive, truly-free, markets as opposed to maximum profits in subtly-monopolized markets, the market for options, futures, selling short, all derivatives, and the enormous sums they claim, will either disappear or shrink to a tiny fraction as in today's markets. Those immense excess profits are money symbols of the nation's production of true value claimed by non-producers. Under the modernized laws of the commons, full values are still produced but those values are distributed to all citizens at no unnecessary costs as former subtle monopolists become fully productive. Under *democratic-cooperative-capitalism* nonproductive speculators and monopolizers transform into productive investors and managers or become a part of the productive labor force.

By all producers being able to use the most efficient technology, the use-value of a technology will go to the most efficient producers. The nations best and brightest who previously intercepted wealth through monopolization, as opposed to producing wealth, can now be productively employed. This would require a sharing of productive jobs and all can now work 2-to3 days per week for the same standard of living. Through the sharp drop in prices the use-value of technology is distributed equally and instantly to each relative to the expenditure of their productive labors. That wealth no longer works its way through a subtle monopoly for a part to slowly work its way back down to true producers. The efficiency gains of a modern technology commons within *democratic-cooperative-capitalism* will equal the invention of the printing press.

Eliminate subtle monopolization through *residual-feudal exclusive* patents and the price of drugs will drop to possibly 25%, of today's prices and in many instances much more.[a] The efficiency gains and gains in living standards are truly enormous when full rights are attained within a modern commons under *democratic-cooperative-capitalism*.

---

[a] J.W. Smith, *Economic Democracy: The Political Struggle of the Twenty-First Century*, updated and expanded 3rd edition (www.ied.info/cc.html: The Institute for Economic Democracy, 2003), Chapter 25 addresses patents, stock markets, and the enormous savings to society from elimination of subtle-monopolization of technology through residual-feudal patents in depth.

Currently patent profits are harvested through the stock markets. Eliminate subtle monopolization through *residual-feudal* patents and a society eliminates those enormous unearned profits. As production and profits will be stable, stock prices will be stable. Investments in new technology however will be as speculative as today and, for the alert and truly talented (not the monopolist), very profitable.

Regaining Rights to a Modern Money Commons

Outlining an honest banking system will expose the simplicity of money.[a] A part of the money created by powerful nations are banked outside their borders and become currencies for international trade. Through suspension of access to central bank reserves, targeted banks lose the right to credit and debit in that currency. (American President George Bush is using this power to cut off all dollar transactions for overseas banks that do not cooperate in following the terrorist money trail.) If a weak nation prints (creates) money, that currency is immediately discounted, effectively denying those regions the right to create money. The creation of money is a crucial right of a modern commons. To develop industrially and gain control of their destiny, a region of weak nations must ally together for strength and create their own trading currency.[b]

All wealth is created by combining natural resources (land), labor, and industrial technology (capital). Most the world's resources and labor are in the developing world. If a developing region were truly free, their central bank could create the money to build the industry and mine, harvest, or purchase the necessary resources. More money would have to be created to finance the first production of that industry (labor, energy, et al.). The industry, developed natural resources, products produced, and the wealth created by the economic multiplier as that money circulates within the economy, provide the value to back the money created.

That primary-created money productively spent circulates within the economy (the economic multiplier creating more money [circulation-created money]) to energize more production. If that first primary-created money is insufficient for a fully functioning economy, more money should be created and added to the circulating money to build banks, businesses and stores.

---

[a] J.W. Smith, *Economic Democracy*, updated and expanded 3rd edition (www.ied.info/cc.html: The Institute for Economic Democracy, 2003), Chapter 26 addresses the history of money and an honest country, regional, and world banking system in depth.

[b] To understand the enormous power the dollar has at this time over other nations' currencies and America's fear of other nations trading in their own or other currencies read W. Clark, "The Real Reason for the upcoming War with Iraq," http://www.ratical.org/ratville/CAH/RRiraqWar.html.

The new values created back both the primary-created money and circulation-created money.

A modern economy requires electric power stations, roads, sewer systems, water systems, et al. In step with the ability of industrial production to produce products to soak up the region's new buying power, more money must be created to build social infrastructure. To the extent that infrastructure is built with primary-created money, there is no debt. When money is understood, an increase or decrease in its primary creation can fine-tune an economy to the maximum capacity of resources and labor.

Economists can easily calculate any surplus buying power that may occasionally develop. An increase in loan margin requirements will quickly soak up that surplus money. As a region develops, money creation, both primary and circulation created, will have to be within the capacity of the earth to recycle wastes and to protect natural resources and environment for future generations

All banks should be required, as now, to keep a percentage of their deposits with the central bank. When the economy needs more money, the central bank increases the loan making ability of needy banks via recording an increase in those banks central bank deposits. As only an increased accounting entry was made and there was no deduction entered from another account, that increase is primary-created money.

Assuming the reserve requirement is 10% and remembering that one banks debit is another banks deposit, banks collectively could loan out nine times (900%) the increase in their reserves. That nine times increase, deducted from one account and added to another account at each point in its circulation, is circulation-created money. By increasing or decreasing reserve requirements, a central bank can precisely control the creation, or destruction, of money.

Bankers will have to be knowledgeable about, and loan appropriately for, community needs. Needs of regions and communities should be calculated and each region and each community should have equal rights to both savings and created money. Note: These are community banks with loyalties to a community and a region, their loyalty is not to shareholder profits. They are not banks siphoning savings from the farthest reaches of a nation to maximize profits through monopolization and speculation. Through increasing or decreasing interest rates on productive capital investments or for consumer credit, an economy can be balanced.

Subject to change to balance the economy, all checking accounts should receive a 3% real interest rate on average balances. As this is well above the long-term average real interest rate, there need be no savings accounts. A person's checking account is simultaneously their savings account.

Instead of the historic accumulations of capital through subtle monopolization of land, technology, and money, higher-risk finance capital can be made available through assigning a share of created money for risk capital and/or applying a surcharge on those loans to cover risk. Through repayments of principal plus interest, plus the right to a share of created money, this capital accumulation fund will expand in step with the expansion of an economy.

Most loans will be funded from normal savings against collateralized equity. But productive individuals with special expertise and projects of productive merit will have access to this high risk capital accumulation fund to develop the millions of ideas necessary for the progress of science, industry, and society. The capital accumulation fund loan should be to both the owner and his/her workers.

With 70-to-80% of stock reserved for employees, talented workers can study the prospectus, agree to 10-to-20% of their wages deducted to pay for his/her share of stock, and they become owner employees. Having first mortgage, and backed by both equity and a part of cash flow, the initial loan would be secure. Instead of most profits going to money monopolists, highly productive citizens broadly diffused throughout the economy will accumulate capital. A computerized stock market would bypass expensive brokers and sell shares directly to the public:

> Most workers would stay on the job, but, once the new business was secure and their new stock had capitalized value, the talented ones would search out another prospectus, help develop another business, train more workers, gain more capitalized value, and move on again. Labor would be both mobile and highly productive just as capital is now and the most productive of those workers would be the accumulators of capital. This would be mobilization of labor without the dispossession that has been so typical of past capitalization processes. Labor would have the same rights to gains in efficiencies of technology as investors now have. The talented would be in high demand by the developers of industry.
>
> Besides collateral protection, there are three flows of money that make those loans secure—landrent, profits, and a share of wages. Society's collection of landrent could, and should, permit it to accept a larger share of the risks of new entrepreneurs. Every success increases the use-value, and thus the rental value, of that land. The risk of uncollateralized investment loans could also be offset by a surcharge on the interest to go into an insurance fund. With these restructured borrowing rights, many more people would qualify for investment capital than under equity loans. If entrepreneurs were successful, they and their workers, through the shares purchased, would own that capital honestly, as opposed to the current custom of capitalizing values through subtle monopolization of social wealth.
>
> Those searching for a higher return—and confident they have found good investments—could directly employ their capital. Those who wished to, and who could find the opportunity to lend their savings at a higher rate, would be free to do so. But they could no longer obtain high profits by simple tribute for the use of subtly monopolized capital. Those who once bid for money market funds would now have to compete for loans on their projects' productive merits. This would eliminate pure speculation with social funds while retaining that right with personal funds.[6]

For maximum care for all its citizens, regional directors would be umpires overseeing their region's financial rights, while local directors would oversee state, county, and community funding rights. A minimum housing standard could be set and that goal reached as could goals for roads, parks, schools, and public buildings.

With infrared thermogram images of palm, artery, vein, eye pattern, and signature scanning confirming identity, local credit unions, an integral part of the banking system, would issue consumer credit much as credit cards do now but at a fraction the interest rates.

Creating a Constant-Value Currency

A developing region needs to protect its trading currency against both inflation and deflation. The average price of a broad range of commodities stays relatively constant over time. A constant-value currency can be attained by tying its value to

> a basket of thirty or more of the most commonly used commodities—gold, wheat, soybeans, rice, steel, copper, etc.... The essential difference [between speculation and arbitrage in commodity and currency markets] is that the arbitrageur buys and sells [contracts of different maturity dates] simultaneously [on different markets] while the speculator buys and sells at different times. The effect of arbitrage on price movements is to stabilize them; the effect of speculation is to intensify them. If arbitrage were to be conducted on a large enough and wide enough scale, speculation would become less and less enticing. But perhaps even more than this, if it were to be promoted and practiced by an independent international agency such as the bank-of-issue I am calling for on the magnitude this would make possible, it would stabilize prices to such a degree that stabilization as a serious problem would disappear. Stabilization would make speculation peripheral instead of central in the determination of the prices of basic commodities of the world.[7]

Instead of 10% of its funds sitting idle, a bank (or the Central Bank where those reserves are deposited) should purchase a broad range of commodity contracts with those reserves. The values of the world's commodities now back the value of that trading currency. With risk eliminated, international traders will write contracts in, and accept and make payments in, that constant-value currency. Those bankers, now also commodity traders, would do no speculating. They would only sell contracts approaching delivery dates and purchase new contracts. Once established, incoming and outgoing money will balance as commodity contracts are bought and sold.

With world travelers and world traders flocking to commodity-backed constant-value currency, other nations would quickly back their currencies with commodity contracts. To not do so would risk traders abandoning their currency. Thus any nation or region establishing commodity-backed money will force all the world's central banks to tie their currencies to the value of commodities. The "national character of currencies would be of no consequence, since they would be but different tokens representing the same commodities.... We will have Gresham's law operating in reverse; good money will be driving bad money out of circulation."[8]

Commodity speculation will disappear and the percentage of a nation's currency invested in commodities will lower as other nation's reserves are invested. All trades will match equal-value currency transfers, speculation in currency will disappear, and all contracts will equal the value of all commodities in the field, in transit, and in storage. On balance, each currency would be valued and backed by its nation's production.[a]

With commodity-backed, equal-value currency widely used, countries would have to use their currency-creating powers productively. Debasing their currency by printing money for nonproductive purposes would be producing no value and their currency would immediately be discounted in the markets. With a currency securely tied to the value of a broad basket of commodities, external powers could not siphon away the wealth of weak nations through discounting their currency and thus deflating its value:

> With stable constant values, individuals not using those commodities or currencies in their businesses would no longer borrow society's finance capital to speculate in commodity markets, nor would they do so with their own cash. Protected by constant-value money backed by the world's commodities, true producers would not need to speculate. Speculation in commodity and currency markets would cease and the funds of both speculators and true producers would be available for true investment. Commodity prices, thus consumer prices, would decrease by whatever amount was once siphoned away by these gamblers and confidence in constant-value money would increase efficiencies in international trade, creating even more values. Individual commodities could suffer temporary losses in value but average values would remain stable and those stabilized values would virtually eliminate world economic collapses.[9]

By tying money to commodities one has only gained a part of full trade rights. Equality in commodity trades requires weak countries being equally paid for their labor and resources. When equally and fully paid—and assuming quality management, access to markets, access to technology, etc— poor nations can immediately start accumulating wealth. True equality requires equality in trades.

Once the labor of all nations are roughly equally paid and subtle monopolization of land, technology, and finance capital are eliminated, money will be a measure of productive labor value, exactly as it was when

---

[a] The central bank could keep those reserves invested in contracts. Inflation and deflation can also be eliminated, and thus a stable value currency created, by indexing wages and contracts to the price changes (which will be minimal) of a broad basket of commodities.

complex accounting of time-units of productive labor evolved into money in Sumeria over 5,000 years ago.[a]

Once the waste of wars, the waste of capital destroying perfectly good capital, and the waste of labor and capital of subtle monopolies are eliminated, a modern economy will function with much lower capital costs and less than half the current workforce.

To avoid unemployment, the remaining productive jobs should be shared, thus reducing the workweek to 2-to-3 days per week. This would be full and equal rights which will eliminate poverty which in turn will eliminate terrorism, the subject of this book.

Once tied to the value of a broad basket of commodities, money will have been returned to a modern commons for use by all. Once subtle monopolization has been eliminated, the value of commodities will be equal to the value of the labor that produced them.[b] Money now represents the value of productive labor just as it did when invented over 5,000 years ago.[c] A modern money commons within *democratic-cooperative-capitalism* will increase economic efficiency equal to the efficiency gains of electricity.

Notes

[1] Smith, *The World's Wasted Wealth 2* and *Cooperative Capitalism: A Blueprint for Global Peace and Prosperity*.

[2] J.W. Smith, *Economic Democracy: The Political Struggle of the Twenty-First Century*, updated and expanded 3rd edition (www.ied.info/cc.html: The Institute for Economic Democracy, 2003), Chapter 24.

[3] Doug Henwood, *Wall Street* (New York: Verso, 1997), p. 7.

[4] Smith, *Economic Democracy*, updated and expanded 3rd edition, Chapter 25.

[5] Adam Smith, *Wealth of Nations* (New York: Random House, 1965), p. 64.

[6] Smith, *Economic Democracy*, updated and expanded 3rd edition, Chapter 26.

[7] Ralph Borsodi, *Inflation* (Great Barrington, MA: E.F. Schumacher Society, 1989), p. 73.

[8] Ibid, p. 8.

[9] Smith, *Economic Democracy*, updated and expanded 3rd edition, Chapter 26.

[a] One will search books on money in vain for the simple fact that money originated as what it should be, a measure of productive labor value. Once society advanced from money as a symbol of labor value to money as a medium of exchange, most of the sense of true value which money properly represents was lost. An honest banking system returns money to its original meaning, a measure of productive labor value. Miezyslaw Dobija and Martyna Sliwa, "Money as an Intellectual Adventure," pages 131-85, especially p. 135 in Stefan Kwiatkowski and Charles Stowe's *Knowledge Café for Intellectual Product and Intellectual capital* (Warsaw, Poland: Leon Kozminski, 2001).

[b] Keep in mind that capital is but stored labor and proper profits are only the earnings of that stored labor and the wages of the managers of that capital.

[c] A Tobin tax, a tax on the $1.5-trillion a day currency markets to shrink speculations is not necessary. With currency values matching commodity values there will be no speculation.

9. Reclaiming the Information Commons

> "A regime of global governance is needed in which world markets are managed so as to promote the cohesion of societies and the integrity of the states. Only a framework of global regulation—of currencies, capital movements, trade and environmental conservation—can enable the creativity of the world economy to be harnessed in the service of human needs." –John Gray, *False Dawn*, p. 199

Communication technology in the developed world is so efficient that the total communications traffic of America is handled on less than 5% the currently installed fiber-optic/satellite communication system. That potential communication efficiency outlines current monopolies in bold relief. Avoiding *residual-feudal* subtle-monopolization is the key to fast development of any regions that ally together for development.

As a region electrifies, the first household item purchased will typically be a television set. Looking towards educating their citizens well at 5-to-15% the cost in the developed world, priority should be given to establishing a satellite/fiber-optic communication system in the developing world and beaming education programs to their citizens.

Forty to 50 communication bands should be assigned for the region's education with each class taught multiple times throughout the day. The best educators in the region, several at each grade level for each subject, will produce documentary education—edited for maximum simplicity, clarity, and comprehension—for all classes of all ages, preschool, primary school, middle school, high school, and universities.

With their lessons free on TV and in a database downloadable to video-recorders, these high-quality teachers will be spending less time teaching than any one of the thousands of teachers they replace. Every teacher for every student in every class will be a gifted teacher. Through the fictions and omissions of history being challenged, researched, and corrected, their students will be much better educated. Teachers become role models for students and many students will strive to emulate these great teachers.

Education is a deeply felt universal need; most students will watch those education programs intensely. Those who cannot afford video-recorders or pencils and paper will acquire a keen memory, many will graduate equal with their peers, and that early memory training will be an asset throughout their life. Students will be able to work at home, or at a job for the survival of the family, and study in their free time. Adults could educate themselves in their free time. At little cost the already educated could further advance their education.

Timidity, feelings of inferiority, peer pressure, obsolete textbooks, overcrowded classrooms, moderately competent teachers, and the occasional incompetent teacher—great impediments to education in current schools—would not restrict these children's education. Parental interaction, advice, and support will greatly enhance a child's education.[a] The cost of building and maintaining schools, purchasing textbooks, paying teachers, and transporting children to and from school is avoided. Facilities must be built for the occasional subject that will require hands-on learning for that small part of class time.

Testing stations should be established to issue certificates of scholastic achievement. When students feel they have advanced to the next level, they will go to the testing station and take the appropriate test. The brightest students will advance one grade every four months or faster. Many will have the knowledge of Ph.D.s at an age when today's students enter college.

Judgments would be made while still young and idealistic. All this would be gained while enjoying the irreplaceable quality time between parent and child. Some talented students who do not have parental support would find a surrogate family by immersing themselves in education.

Eliminating Political Corruption by the Wealthy and Powerful

Currently only politicians in office or the wealthy have access to a region's citizens. Ten-to-20 TV channels should be reserved for all politicians with a sincere following to reach all of the people. With free access to the masses, any funding of politicians would be recognized for the corruption that it is and every politician would be watching other politicians' funding practices so they could be defeated in the next election. Most politicians are fundamentally honest and would rather not be beholden to wealth to fund their campaigns anyway.

As the public could now be reached cheaply with a message of purchased votes, corruption would rapidly decline. Few politicians would risk the voters' penalties through accepting election funds. Election funding would immediately be recognized for what it really is, buying votes within the law-making process, and made illegal.

---

[a] A full reading of this author's work will alert one that the economies of today are over 50% distribution by unnecessary labor. A democratic-cooperative capitalist society we are outlining would have large amounts of free time. Parents could spend many of those free hours working with their children and advance them even faster than we outline.

An unseen and unfelt Money Transaction Tax

The cost of an efficient modern communications industry can be covered by an infinitesimal (.0005, 1/20 of 1%) transaction tax on the circulation of money (see p. 146). The costs would be so small they would not even be noticed by the individual and the savings to a nation or region to utilize this tax to fund a modern communication system will be nothing less than reducing education costs to 5-to-15% of what is normal today and reduce product distribution costs by half (see below). Each of those cost reductions represent reductions in the labor and capital necessary to educate, produce, and distribute.

With the developed world frozen by custom into expensive education and distribution systems, this is the opportunity for the developing world to leapfrog the developed world and establish a truly efficient society with a workweek averaging no more than 2-to-3 days.[1]

Converting Wasted Time to Free Time

Groceries and inexpensive, small, frequently traded items will be available, as now, at the supermarket and corner store.

Big ticket, infrequently purchased items, cars, appliances, furniture, farm equipment, industrial equipment, and major tools are purchased primarily through prior knowledge and experience of use. Sales of these expensive items do not require intense advertising. Manufacturers of each product need only index their product in a video database with all pertinent information—price, energy efficiency, hours of useful life, noise level, et al.—to make an informed decision.

Every qualified producer would have the right to place his/her service or product in that databank and pay a minuscule percentage of gross sales out of cash flow for that right. With the enormous costs of advertising eliminated, small producers can compete with large corporations in many products and services. Their low prices for quality products and services would insure low prices by the major producers who normally enjoy the high prices of monopoly protection.

Buyers would study specifications, styling, engineering, and actual use of the product on their computer or television at their leisure. A purchase would be made by typing in the model, color, accessories, delivery address, and credit card number that is protected by infrared thermogram images of thumb prints, palm, artery, vein, and eye pattern, or signature scanning. The item purchased would be shipped that day from the closest distribution point or the factory.

With access to a database of products ready for shipment, small independent truckers can compete with large trucking companies. The price of major items would be reduced by much lower advertising costs (and save billions of trees), almost no sales force or banking costs, and much lower inventory and storage costs. Guarantees, maintenance, and repairs can be handled by local private industry.

Manufacturers' on-time delivery of parts to the factory that greatly reduces storage and finance capital costs will have been expanded to on-time shipping to consumers. Instead of time spent in warehouses and retail stores, the products would be immediately packaged and addressed and go directly from the factory to their home (larger items to a distribution point near the customer). On-time delivery of finished products would eliminate most wholesale and retail buildings. The cost of inventory, insurance, heat, electricity, stocking clerks, sales clerks, maintenance workers, building repairs, and security will drop precipitously.

Under the above guidelines, distribution efficiency will double, meaning distribution costs will drop by half, as a nation's ships, planes, trucks and railroads settle into a postal flow pattern just as with Christmas packages today. Purchases would be delivered just as United Parcel Service does today or consumers could, upon notification, pick up their products at a freight terminal. Products that formerly were stored for months in warehouses and showrooms will now be in transit and storage less than a week and some may drop in price by half.

With each person having to work only 2-to-3 days per week for a quality living, those with artistic abilities and dreams will have time to study and hone their skills. Music, painting, sculpturing, sports, writing, inventions—virtually every skill and the enjoyment of those arts—will expand exponentially.

That Population can be stabilized without Coercion has been proven

It is much cheaper to guarantee the elderly food and shelter in old age than it would be to care for the increased children these parents normally depend upon in their declining years.

Population stabilization is possible without any attempt to control citizens' decisions; Japan has 1.53 births per family, Germany 1.51 births, and Italy 1.29. These are birthrates that could reduce their populations by half in roughly 50 years while doubling the amenities of life for each citizen with no increase in use of resources. A steady increase in technological efficiency during the same time span could more than double the amenities of life again and all that gain would be without increasing hours of labor, consumption of resources, or pollution of the environment. With fewer members per family, the amenities per person that can be purchased on the same income rises even more steeply than these figures indicate.

Here again a modern communications system explaining the great per-capita gains possible without an increase in resource use from a reduction in population is the key. Take note: The most Catholic country in the world,

Italy, has the lowest birthrate. So the citizens of all countries will reduce their birthrates of their own free will once they realize the high quality of life possible by a reduction in births.

Restructuring to a modern land, technology, money, and information commons within *democratic-cooperative-capitalism* would increase economic efficiency equal to the invention of money, the printing press, and electricity. Use-values are distributed without waste through fully productive labor. Money no longer flows through subtle monopolies and a part work its way back to true producers. Living standards rise rapidly. As wasted labor disappears labor time drops equally rapidly. The drop in the GNP measures the previous wasted labor and wasted capital within the previous subtly-monopolized economy.

Notes

[1] J.W. Smith, *Cooperative Capitalism: A Blueprint for Global Peace and Prosperity.*

Conclusion: Give Full Rights to all People and Terrorism Disappears

No society will admit to imposing an injustice upon others. After many centuries in which the line of demarcation between the Christian and Muslim regions of the world moved back and forth, those religious leaders will not even admit there is a struggle. But that struggle can be historically traced through to the present time and the successes and losses measured.

With each religion claiming over 1.2-billion followers, the battle for souls is relatively equal. But when the winners of wars establish the rules of unequal trade, that winner will be wealthy and the loser will be poor. By any measure—economic, technological, military power, standard of living, life expectancy—the Christian West has emerged thoroughly triumphant over the last 500 years. As addressed in the opening chapter, the Muslim world, which had relative equality with the Christian world for the first 800 years of this epic battle, has been vanquished and their people politically dominated, economically exploited, and impoverished.

For dependent societies, all avenues leading to their gaining control of their destiny—economic, financial, or military—are blocked. After all, those are the three methods of gaining, and retaining control, of the *wealth-producing-process*. With the *imperial-centers-of-capital* in control of the Western world's beliefs, any who would seriously challenge the current world political and trade structure are quickly branded an enemy to all humankind and either neutralized or eliminated.

This leaves billions of people unable to control their destiny and in poverty. Of those billions, the angriest will resort to their only remaining weapon, terrorism.

The Muslim religion and the Christian religion both have fanatic followers. Indeed, religion in extreme form breeds fanaticism, and oppression transforms it into terrorism. Any assault by a Christian nation on a segment of the Muslim religion will trigger the loyalty response in even the mildest mannered of other Muslims. The same is true of Christians; witness the mass outpouring of Christian loyalty when New York's World Trade Center and the Pentagon were destroyed. Not only was the American flag flying from most homes, Churches reported greater attendance and greater purchases of religious writing and artifacts.

America had no choice but to respond to that massive terrorist attack on the World Trade Center, the Pentagon, and many other points around the world. However, eliminating current terrorists will hardly solve the problem. The cause of their impoverishment has not been removed. If the control of their destiny by the *imperial-centers-of-capital* is not addressed, and especially as their poverty increases while the wealth of those imperial centers increase, the Muslim world will rally around their heroes and, through their religion, form an allied bloc. If America is going to free itself and the world from terrorism, the world's resources, the *wealth-producing-process*, and the wealth produced must be shared on a much more equitable basis.

Under *democratic-cooperative-capitalism*, as opposed to the current subtle-monopoly capitalism, developing the Undeveloped World and eliminating poverty will, through abandonment of wars and elimination of the waste of inefficient subtle monopolization, be self-financing.

Only half of America's current expenditure on arms turned to producing industries for the developing world would produce industries as fast as the developing world could absorb them. With those industries (3.7% of the wealth of a balanced economy) and balanced regions allied together as a producing/trading bloc, those nations could produce their own social wealth (96.3% of all wealth).

Five Primary Guidelines for a World at Peace

1. Developing nations must ally together so as to negotiate with equal power with the allied imperial centers;
2. equal pay for equal work;
3. sharing those remaining productive jobs (meaning each need work only 2-to-3 days per week);
4. elimination of the subtle monopolizations of land, technology, and finance capital;
5. and addressing population issues and sustainable development so that the earth's capacity to provide resources for all and the environment to absorb wastes is protected.

Equal pay for equal work provides roughly equal buying power to all who are employed. Sharing the remaining productive jobs would employ all able-bodied workers which, along with equal pay for equal work, would immediately melt the *invisible economic borders* which currently guide the manufactured wealth, produced primarily by the low paid, into the hands of the well paid. Grossly underpaid workers would no longer be toiling to produce products and unearned profits for the powerful and wealthy. Each person in society will be equally paid for equally-productive labor and/or earning honest profits.

As development of the poor regions improves and living standards increase, addressing population issues in order to avoid overstressing the resource and ecological capacity of the earth will be even more important. With the most Catholic country in the world, Italy, having a birth rate per family (1.29) and Germany and Japan's birth rates also well below replacement rates (1.51 and 1.53), that is an attainable goal.

The buying power for a healthy economy comes from adequate wages paid to productive labor. Those earnings are spent for family needs and that money is spent again and again as it is passed from hand to hand to purchase necessary food, fiber, shelter, and services (the multiplier factor). Thus care must be taken by both the developed and developing world for *each region* (not small or medium sized nations) to produce most of their own food and consumer products and provide most of their own services.

With the wealthy developed world sincerely promoting equality in world trade through relinquishing their monopoly on resources, technology, and finance capital, and with that newly-produced wealth relatively equally shared in the developing region through equality in wages and with equal access to jobs, poverty will quickly be alleviated and terrorism will subside.

Democratic-Cooperative-Capitalism

Except for terrorist outbreaks, powerful nations currently control the world. That control is the opposite of what is preached (*peace, freedom, justice, rights, and majority rule*) by those same nations. If terrorism is to be eliminated, this offer by the powerful for equality of rights and elimination of poverty must be made, sincerely, to all nations of the world:[a]

- The wealthy world will turn their war industries towards producing industrial technology for any nation or region of the world that agrees to eliminate terrorism; that agrees to reduce their military to a level that provides internal security but leaves no offensive capabilities; and that agrees to provide full political and economic rights to all its citizens, including women and minorities. These rights to include: a constitutional government, democratic elections, freedom of speech, freedom of religion, and separation of church and state.

    As this is exactly what most destabilized emerging nations were in the process of constructing, agreement on these conditions for

---

[a] To stop fast expanding socialism, this is essentially the unwritten post WWII agreement between America and the shattered Western Europe, Japan, and the Southeast Asian tiger economies.

developmental aid will be quickly accepted.ᵃ Industries and access to markets would go only to those who agreed to these conditions. The authoritative dictatorships that the *imperial-centers-of-capital* have placed in power and kept in power throughout the world for two centuries by the imperial centers will quickly melt away once that sincere offer is made.ᵇ

- All military weapons beyond that necessary for internal security should be turned over to a fully democratized United Nations and destroyed. In trade, the powerful nations will assign their military forces to a restructured, fully democratic, United Nations command, in step with the demilitarization of the world, and those forces shall guarantee the borders of all nations. All weapons of mass destruction in all nations should be destroyed.
- A restructured, fully democratic, United Nations should be chartered with the responsibility to oversee world peace and all nations should agree to place a worldwide embargo against any nation which attacks or subverts any other nation—or against any nation which attempts to retain or build its own military capacity to wage war.
- Any honest accounting would show the wealthy world in enormous debt to the developing world through centuries of imperialism, slavery, and structural exploitation designed to create indebtedness through *plunder-by-trade*. Thus all unjust Third Word debts should be cancelled.
- Markets should be free between regions of equal development and equal pay. Trade between countries and regions unequally paid for equally-productive labor should be balanced through equalizing surcharges.
- To take control of their destiny, regions should establish their own central bank and trading currency.
- The level playing field so crucial to efficient economics should be leveled upwards. Through equalizing surcharges natural resources should be priced relative to mining or harvesting of those same resources or substitute commodities in the developed world. Labor values should be calculated and equalizing surcharges collected on exports of manufactured products.

ᵃ This process will be quick as we saw previously in the rapid development of those nations which were given access to resources, technology, and Western markets so as to stop fast expanding socialism.
ᵇ For an in depth analysis of developing the world to a sustainable level and eliminating poverty and terrorism, read Part III of this author's *Economic Democracy: The Political Struggle of the Twenty-First Century*, updated and expanded 3ʳᵈ edition (www.ied.info/cc.html: The Institute for Economic Democracy, 2003).

- Funds collected from these tariffs on international trade should go towards building industries and economic infrastructure in the lower-paid regions and for renewable energy capitalization, developing environmentally sound products, designing and implementing ecologically sustainable lifestyles, rebuilding soils, and cleaning up and revitalizing the ecosystems of both the developing and developed world. Protections should be lowered in step with the equalizing of industrial technology, capital accumulation, labor skills, and the wages paid equally-productive labor.

  With the cost of minerals in the United States at 1.7% of GNP and the cost of fuel 2%, economies can handle these equalization surcharges.[1] Through those same surcharges (or call then resource-depletion taxes), the price of minerals and carbon fuels in the developing world should be increased to a level near that of the lower grade deposits in the developed world. The recycling of minerals would then be profitable and renewable energy would be competitive. The consumption of the world's oil and coal will be slower, pollution pressures will be lower, and all countries will develop faster.

  Those incentives and disincentives will conserve resources, reduce pollution, and protect the environment. Once equalizing surcharges are established and all have access to technology, *the entire world* will be able to quickly develop to a sustainable level. What appears more expensive to the few in the affluent developed world is really far cheaper to the billions in the entire world.

- To prevent diversion of funds, money should not be distributed directly to developing nations or regions. Fulfillment of contract is the essence of a successful economy. Any industry or infrastructure built with developing world money or with equalizing surcharge funds shall be built by contract and the contractors paid from those funds. Since they now have the tools of production, these regions will be building their own infrastructure and eventually their own industries.

- Once nations or regions are roughly equal in technology and labor roughly equally paid, labor-equalizing surcharges should be eliminated and fair and honest free trade will flow between nations and between regions. We will have turned "win-lose" and "lose-lose" trade wars into "win-win" equalizing managed fair trade and from there into honest and equal free trade.

- There should be a balance between industry and resources. A nation or region short on resources should be allotted a higher level of industrialization. (Japan provides the ideal example.) Once

all nations and regions are roughly equal in world trade, equalizing surcharges should be converted to a resource-depletion tax to fund rebuilding soils and revitalizing the world's ecosystems.
- As has already been successfully tested, one-year-old trees in biodegradable, aerodynamic, pointed cylinders can be planted at the rate of 800,000 trees a day per plane (keywords "Moshe Alamaro", "reforest"). Newly planted grass grows beautifully in North Africa when fenced off from goats and sheep. Technology has been developed to grow extensive ground cover in 1-to-3 years on steep, barren, infertile road cuts. The technology is here to reforest and regenerate the earth and a resource-depletion tax is the proper source of funds.[2]
- Patent laws should be restructured, as per Chapter 8, so all can use a technology simply by paying an appropriate royalty. Destruction of industries and communities through industries moving offshore would cease—even as competition between and within regions increased. Prices would fall and living standards would rise.
- And, to protect everyone's rights and freedom, the world's intelligence services should remain operative and alert. As opposed to being the planners of most of the world's most violent acts of terrorism, these agencies should be mandated to cooperate in preventing terrorist attacks or acts of war anywhere in the world. As opposed to today's demanding job of suppressing breaks for freedom which is the source of most state terrorism, that mandated change alone will eliminate most terrorism.

Much of the world's current "retail" terror is a response to the "wholesale" terror of intelligence agencies of powerful nations. Restructuring to true rights and freedom for all in the world as addressed in these rules for peaceful world development, and all people having some control of their own destiny, will eliminate most terrorism.

Powerful Nations giving up their Superior Rights

Powerful nations respond only to another equal power. However, just laying out how the wealth of the weak is appropriated by the powerful and outlining the simplicity of eliminating poverty by full and equal rights for all, if this knowledge is broadly distributed, provides that power and severely weakens these mighty powers.

It remains for all developing nations of a region to ally together to gain their freedom, just as the powerful nations have allied together although this reality is never openly acknowledged. Once they agreed to work and negotiate as a team, the world's weak nations will have power. With that power they can negotiate to trade resources for technology, as per the guidelines for world development above, and they can negotiate for equality of pay for equally-productive work. To not do so is to stay in poverty and watch their natural wealth be continually transformed into someone else's manufactured and capitalized wealth.

Equal rights within the *wealth-producing-process* (economic rights) are just as important as political rights. With political rights you are politically free but may still be ill-fed, ill-clothed, and poorly housed. Add equal economic rights for all people to the democratic rights they now have through efficient and productive *democratic-cooperative-capitalism* and all people can be well-fed, well-clothed, and live in a comfortable home.

Certainly those powerful nations will manufacture excuses as they always have (the leaders of these new breaks for freedom are killers, dictators, and terrorists) and send in the military to suppress these allied breaks for freedom. But, if these newly allied nations firmly hold their ground; a few hundreds of millions will no longer be able to preach peace, freedom, justice, rights, and majority rule while simultaneously using their military to suppress those very same rights for billions of people.

Mahatma Gandhi of India pointed the way. When the workers of India stood up together, refused to fight and refused to work, the British had to leave. All wealth is processed from natural resources and those resources are primarily in the impoverished world. If the developing world refuses to work those mines, cut those forests, pump that oil, drive those trucks, or load those ships, the powerful nations will have no choice except to negotiate in good faith.[a]

But before people can organize they must fully understand why they are poor while others are rich. Our research provides those simple reasons WHY and also maps the road out of poverty. *Democratic-cooperative-capitalism* is that road.

In Chapter 3 we documented the expenditures of hundreds of billions of dollars by the *imperial-centers-of-capital* to protect their wealth and power through controlling the beliefs of the world. But that war of words is a war they cannot win if we seriously engage them in that battle. The truth is too simple and too obvious.

For the masses to gain the knowledge to win this war of words, we ask that each who come across our research and gain this understanding to inform their personal contacts and have them inform all who trust their judgment. Many have, or sense, these fundamentals of poverty already; they just have not learned how to articulate them. A quick read of our research will provide the articulation tools to go head to head with those imposing upon the world the very philosophy that is creating poverty. It is a debate

---

[a] Germany's industrial sector was occupied by France after WWII. When German labor refused to work, France was forced to abandon the occupation.

the powerbrokers and their negotiators cannot win once the masses and their negotiators are armed with the simple tools of truth.

Form study groups to look deeply into every aspect of why there is poverty and how to eliminate it. Professors, organize your peers and students to study this in depth.[a] If all this were to happen, this knowledge will sweep across the world and not even the powerful nation's *Mighty Wurlitzer* could stop it. The truth is too simple and too sensible.

Being fully free is having full and equal economic rights. If the world's poor share this knowledge among themselves, and especially if developing world universities and governments accept the job of informing the masses, no amount of propaganda and bluster can stop the world from gaining their full rights and rising out of poverty.

There is no left in the American political system, only a right and an extreme right and that nation is moving further right all the time. This thesis is not to the left, it is in the middle. We are not proposing government ownership of industry as some socialists do. We are proposing restructuring private property rights to provide full and equal rights to all and maximize the efficiencies of the *wealth-producing-process*. The solid logic and the enormous gains possible under *democratic-cooperative-capitalism* permits the misnamed left (really the middle) to regain their voice.

These are Historic Moments

We all know the story of the king whose tailor promised him clothes made of gold, could not create the gold thread, dressed him in invisible gold clothes, faithful courtiers admired his non-existent clothes, and soon the whole kingdom marveled at his beautiful gold clothes. It took an innocent child to see the naked king and say, "The king has no clothes."

For 50 years the *imperial-centers-of-capital* have dressed themselves in the fine clothes of peace, freedom, justice, rights, and majority rule. But this allied empire has no clothes. Throughout those same 50 years *policies-of-state* of that empire has been anything but peace, freedom, justice, rights, and majority rule.

Continually we are being told the empire is dressed in gold clothes. The unrest of the masses in times of crisis (Napoleon freeing Europe, the French Revolution, the Great Depression, the Vietnam War) and the possibility of it being pointed out that the empire has no clothes (was not being truthful and/or was not properly caring for its citizens) forced powerbrokers to give more rights to the people. The need for allies to create a barrier to fast expanding socialism forced these same powerbrokers

---

[a] Books with a clear focus and easily understood will be listed and promoted through our cooperative capitalism project. Rights are available for publishing in your region or in translations. For information, please check the endpages.

to dress themselves in the fine clothes of equal rights for nations. Thus Friedrich List protection was provided to key nations.

Once that struggle was won, however, those protections were substantially withdrawn. This has forced Japan to the edge of collapse and shrank the standard of living of the Asian Tigers. Argentina's economy has shrunk 60%, Brazil Uruguay, and a few other Latin American Countries are threatened with collapse. Russia is down 50% and the economies of nations of Eastern and Central Europe range from serious to a substantial loss of living standards.

Originally strengthened by the collapse of the periphery causing money to flee to the imperial center, powerbrokers are now trying to stave off a collapse of that center through gaining control of Iraq's oil, lower the price of oil to $10 to $20 a barrel, and give a boost to the world economy.

These are historic moments. If a further collapse cannot be stopped and the empire's armies are busy hopping all over the globe to keep all countries in line, the empire will stand exposed. Many will see the light and say, "The Empire is not for peace, freedom, justice, rights, and majority rule. The empire is for maintaining control of our resources and the *wealth-producing-process*."

When that can be said on the evening news—just as news anchor Walter Cronkite said it about the Vietnam War, forcing the powerbrokers to make peace—people will in unison see that the empire has no clothes just as the kingdom spoke in unison that the king has no clothes once that small child spoke the obvious.

If we do not stand up and speak openly about the obvious, the world may not break free. The two options are: freedom for all or the mighty military of the imperial centers controlling the world's resources, controlling the *wealth-producing-process*, and imposing poverty on weak nations. That second option is not necessary, eliminate the waste of that control process (in both internal economies and in world trade) and there is enough on this earth for everybody.

Restructuring to an efficient Internal Economy

An economic structure is a machine designed to care for a society's citizens. Just as more efficient machines reduce costs, a more efficient economic structure cheapens costs and produces better products. The elimination of subtle monopolies is the key to an efficient internal economy:

- Eliminating *residual-feudal* land titles through society collecting the landrent would instantly distribute land rights to every person, while eliminating all other taxes, and increasing economic efficiency equal to the invention of money.

- Elimination of *residual-feudal* patent titles, along with a job for each worker and equal pay, would instantly and equitably distribute the values produced by technology. The gain in efficiency would be equal to the invention of the printing press.
- Elimination of the subtle monopolization of finance capital would provide equal access to finance capital for all productive entrepreneurs and all productive businesses. The gain in economic efficiency would be equal to the invention of electricity.
- And elimination of the monopolization of information through returning a share of the communication wavelengths back to the modern commons for use by all again creates a massive increase in economic efficiency.
- As shown by how easily the world could be developed to a sustainable level and poverty eliminated in only 50 years, those efficiency gains are equal to the invention money, the printing press and electricity.

Enormous Savings Possible abandoning Subtly-Monopolized Economies

The challenge will be that there are not enough resources and the standard of living of the developed world will drop if the imperial centers shared their good fortune. If the American throw-away-society is the model, that would be true. Even using highly optimistic estimates on efficiency gains lowering resource use, by following the American model less than half the world's population attaining America's standard of living would consume the earth's annual resource production.

But it is possible to increase the quality of life rapidly even as per-capita consumption of resources is rapidly reduced. The current world of subtle-monopoly capitalism based on *residual-feudal exclusive* property rights in land, technology, and finance capital is not nearly as efficient as claimed. In reality it is inefficient to the extreme.

That same inefficiency operates throughout a subtly-monopolized economy. Insurance, law, medicine, and the welfare system could be restructured to eliminate 70% of costs with no loss of benefits.[3] Those costs are expenditures for unnecessary labor. As demonstrated in this author's previous books and summarized in this book, the subtle monopolization of land, technology, finance capital, and information under capitalism entails equally large amounts of unnecessary (wasted) labor.

Once one understands the reality of subtle-monopoly capitalism's distribution by unnecessary labor under the falsely claimed efficiencies of falsely labeled free-enterprise capitalism, one can walk into any city, look up at the huge glass skyscrapers, go in and look at the name plaques on the doors, and realize that whole buildings are there only as part of a system of interception of wealth (those *residual-feudal* monopolies), not its production.

Chapter 9's analysis on the efficiencies possible for the developing world in education and retail distribution exposes the same wasted labors in those sections of a subtly-monopolized economy. All the support industries that build, clean, and service the unnecessary share of those buildings are themselves a waste; as are the industries that produce the unnecessary furniture and equipment. Wasted labor in a subtly-monopolized capitalist economy is fully 50% and employing that unnecessary labor operating these subtle-monopolies through which wealth is intercepted wastes large amounts of capital.

The developed world is today locked into this horribly expensive and wasteful distribution system (wealth interception system) that simply cannot be restructured under the economic and political laws that have been designed over the centuries to subtly monopolize the *wealth-producing-process* and lay claim to the wealth produced. Each person's earnings are tied to the arteries of commerce as currently structured, so a society will not, and cannot, change except in a crisis extreme enough to trigger such a revolution.

Though the wealthy world cannot quickly change, the day will come when the world will realize the very philosophy being imposed upon them is what is creating their poverty and a change will be imperative. When that day arrives and that change is made, all that is currently wasted within *imperial-centers-of-capital*, including those enormous military expenditures, will be available to produce beneficial goods and services to meet the true needs of a peaceful society.

Restructuring all Societies to a Life of Leisure

Assuming the above offer is sincerely made; emerging nations can avoid being locked into the West's enormously wasteful distribution system. With a modern communication system it is possible to educate the citizens of the developing world even better than the industrialized world at from 5-to-15% the current cost. Utilizing the same efficient communications systems for consumer choices will lower distribution costs by possibly 50%.

Utilizing those efficiencies, these now-free nations would have the option of developing a properly efficient economy with large amounts of free time for everyone. Workers would have the choice of working five days a week for five months with their pay spread over the full year. They could work a full year and take over a year off with pay. Or they could work two days a week the year round.

Peace through Full Citizenship and Full Rights

Armenians, the Kurdish people, and many other minorities defeated centuries ago have lived on their land for thousands of years. Many of the borders of those nations were arbitrarily drawn so as to weaken and control those societies, even to deny them any semblance of self-government. Once organized economically, those regions can organize politically as one nation with full rights for all ethnic groups as per the rules for world development above. Either this will happen or the world is on a fast slope to disaster. Many efforts at just such consolidations have been made in past history but all have been thwarted by external destabilizations.

The Irish, Palestinians, and a few others are battling within established states or nations. Those Protestants are Scottish people who had their lands taken from them by England and forcibly resettled to Ireland centuries ago. So neither the Catholic Irish who have been on that land for tens of thousands of years or the Scotch Irish who have been there for a few hundred years are to blame. It is Britain, the leading imperial nation of the colonial era who owes an apology and reparations to both. Once that happens, hopefully both proud people can shake hands and remain proud cooperative competitors as they abandon terrorism.

The Palestinian displacement from their land and the rise of Israel is recent history. All people should democratically control their own destiny within the borders of their own nation. As the lack of control of their own nation is where anger, and thus the risk of a major war is highest, these shattered people would, after being given formal statehood, be good candidates to be the first allotted adequate industry and access to world markets. For a standard of living much higher than they could ever otherwise have hoped to attain, and with the world guaranteeing the borders of their nation, these embattled souls could make a positive contribution to a peaceful and just new world order by recognition of Israel and publicly and actually abandoning terrorism.

As the standard of living rises throughout the world under the above-outlined rules of development, calmer and wiser heads shall govern those nations and those terrorists will eventually fade into history.

If the terrorist attacks of 9/11/2001 on America serve to focus minds on an equitable, peaceful, friendly, and prosperous world, perhaps those martyrs will not have died in vain.

Understanding economics becomes easy when we realize that the classical economists were protecting wealth and power. They consistently insisted that labor should be paid just enough to reproduce itself and that all wealth produced by increased efficiencies of technology should go to capital even as they ignored that this primitive accumulation of capital went first and foremost to grand castles and high living.[4]

Only a few philosophers—Gerard Winstanley in the 16th-Century, Jean Jacques Rousseau in the 17th-Century, Johann Herder in the 18th-Century, and Karl Marx in the 19th-Century—spoke to the rights of labor.[5]

As the common people fought for equal rights, the power-structure protected itself by trumpeting each gain of rights as full and equal rights. But those excess rights of capital promoted by classical economists have never been fully set aside, the full and equal rights promoted by a minority of philosophers has never been attained, and it is this lack of full rights which creates the poverty and violence of today's world.

Provide equal rights through the suggested slight changes in the structure of property rights eliminates the current unacknowledged subtle land, technology, and money monopolies that are the essence of today's world economy. Without cost and without waste use-values are distributed to all. The quality of life rises rapidly even as the hours of required labor and the GDP drop precipitously. The drop in GDP measures the previously wasted labor, capital, and resources of a subtly monopolized economy. The GDP then rises as people utilize their new free time to develop their many artistic talents or to simply socialize with friends.

Under a modern commons within *democratic-cooperative-capitalism*, the just rights of private property are fully protected, individualism and competition are strengthened, and money no longer flows through subtle monopolies to the interceptors of wealth. Society's production is instead—through the mechanism of equal pay for equal labor and equal sharing of productive jobs—distributed instantly and without cost to the producers of wealth. Under those rules of equality, the need for massive military forces and their attendant massive slaughters disappear.

Those owning and working within the superstructure of those subtle monopolies are the world's brightest and most talented. That is why they attained those positions and they will unanimously dispute their redundancy even as a few of them finance and guide the enormous propaganda process—as outlined in Chapter 3—which protects their excess rights. Under a system of full and equal rights with a sharing of productive jobs, these talented and brilliant people will be producing wealth instead of intercepting wealth.

September 11th, 2001 which triggered the War on Terror will unquestionably prove to be a major milestone on mankind's long and difficult road towards true civilization. Which path we pursue is ultimately up to us. This time, we must not allow ourselves to be blinded or deceived by either our trusted leaders or the treacheries of past history.

The most important aspect of regaining rights to a modern commons within *democratic-cooperative-capitalism* is that private ownership is retained and even strengthened, yet subtle monopolists disappear, and the wealth created by nature (not that created by labor and capital [stored labor]) is instantly distributed to all and this while working less for a higher standard of living.

Distribution of wealth would be through fully productive labor, fully productive capital, and the instant and costless distribution of use-value within a modern commons. Full and equal rights means none would live in poverty. GNP and the average workweek would fall by one-half or more even as the average living standards rise. The fall in GNP measures the previously wasted labor, wasted capital, and wasted resources within the economy. The money no longer flows through low-productivity monopolies to provide a high living to those not producing.

The efficiencies of subtle-monopoly capitalism we have heard about for generations are fictions protecting the monopolization of wealth and power. Economic efficiency has always been greater under *conditional* private ownership of what nature produces (*democratic-cooperative-capitalism*) than under monopolies created by *residual-feudal exclusive* private titles.

It is the arteries of commerce running through these unproductive subtle monopolies and the battles over monopolization of resources and the *wealth-producing-process* that wastes enormous amounts of labor, resources, and capital. Many are forced to the margins of the flow of commerce and some are excluded altogether. The expansion of full private property rights, individualism, and competition to all people under *democratic-cooperative-capitalism* (a relatively small change in the legal structure of capitalism) brings all within the economic system, eliminates that waste, and creates an efficient, productive, peaceful society.

World peace is not complicated. All that is necessary is that powerful nations "***Be who they say they are and do what they say they do.***"

Notes

[1] Herman E. Daly, *Steady-State Economics* (San Francisco: W.H. Freeman, 1977), p. 109. See also Brian Milani, *Designing the Green Economy: The Postindustrial Alternative to Corporate Globalization* (New York: Rowman & Littlefield, 2000).

[2] Alan Weisman, "Nothing Wasted, Everything Gained," *Mother Jones*, March/April, 1998, pp. 56-59; William Kötke, *The Final Empire* (Portland, OR: Arrow Point Press, 1993), p. 36; Stephanie Mills, *In Service of the Wild: Restoring and Reinhabiting Damaged Land* (Boston: Beacon Press, 1995); John J. Berger, Ed., *Environmental Restoration: Science and Strategies for Restoring the Earth* (Washington, DC: Island Press, 1990); William E. McClain, *Illinois Prairie: Past and Future: A Restoration Guide* (Springfield, IL: Illinois Department of Conservation, 1986); Jonathan Turk et. al., *Ecosystems, Energy, Population* (Toronto: W.B. Saunders Co., 1975); Alan Dregson, Duncan Taylor, editors, *Ecoforestry: The Art and Science of Sustainable Forest Use* (Gabriola Island, BC: New Society Publishers, 1997); Michael Pilarski, *Restoration Forestry: An International Guide to Sustainable Forestry Practices* (Durango, CO: Kivaki Press, 1994); A Report by The International Institute for Environment and Development and The World Resources Institute, *World Resources 1987: An Assessment of the Resource Base That Supports the Global Economy* (New York: Basic Books, 1987), p. 289; Alan Weisman, "Columbia's Modern City," *In Context* (No 42, 1995), pp. 6-8; Lester Thurow, *Head to Head* (New York: William Morrow, 1992), p. 223; Jeremy Rifkin, *Entropy: Into the Greenhouse World* (New York: Bantam Books, 1989), p. 220.

[3] J.W. Smith, *The World's Wasted Wealth 2* (www.ied.info/cc.html: The Institute for Economic Democracy, 1994); Smith, *Cooperative Capitalism*, 2003.

[4] Michael Perelman, *The Invention of Capitalism: Classical Political Economy and the Secret History of Primitive Accumulation* (London: Duke University Press, 2000), especially p. 91: Thomas C. Patterson, *Inventing Western Civilization* (New York: Monthly Review Press, 1997).

[5] Perelman, *The Invention of Capitalism*, Chapter 3.

Appendix I: A Practical Approach for Developing Poor Nations and Regions

Europe has cheap, fireproof, rammed-earth homes over 300 years old. Most regions have massive numbers of unemployed labor and can, working as a modern commons, build high-quality, rammed-earth homes with fired (ceramic) interiors cheaply. (Some regions will use other building materials stone, straw bale, wood, et al. (run a Google Internet search).

A university would bring in experts to train the first homebuilders. These newly-trained experts would train others on the job. The experts would be paid but the worker's pay would be their training as master homebuilders. Assuming five workers to a crew, every three houses built would train five more experts, expanding the homebuilding project exponentially. Industries would be built to produce the doors, windows, plumbing, carpets, roofs, ceilings, and furniture and those industries would expand exponentially along with the home building.

Though these homes will be built cheaply they have full use-value. As the project matured labor building some of those homes would be paid. In other homes the master builder would be paid to train more volunteer workers. These newly-trained volunteers can build more homes utilizing more volunteers. They would build homes for themselves, family, and friends. Thus they are paid indirectly but are well-paid.

As real value is being produced, money can be created by that nation or region up to the value of those homes, businesses and inventory. This provides the money to build the industries, regional businesses, and inventory necessary to service that developing community.

Simultaneous with building homes a country or region must develop a prosperous agriculture. Farms, equipment, and the food produced have value and, as it is locally produced, money can be created for that development. All resources should be processed into high value-added products both for regional consumption and export. As economic activity increases and community values rise, buying power increases to purchase that production.

Money can be created to build industries and infrastructure. A development region can be expanded to include an oil-producing region.

But soon that country or region will need technology and industries that are firmly under the control of the imperial centers. It is at this point that regions must ally together to negotiate equally with the imperial centers to trade access to resources for access to technology. To not ally together would be to see the wealth created transferred to those imperial centers via unequal pay for equally-productive labor, resources purchased below full value, and the resulting inevitable debt traps.

Appendix II. An Hour of Work as the World Money Unit

by
Bob Blain, Ph. D.
Professor of Sociology Emeritus
Southern Illinois University Edwardsville

I propose that all money in the world be denominated in Hours of Work. Initially and immediately, each country would divide its Gross Domestic Product (GDP) by the Total Hours of Work (THW) that produced it; GDP/THW. It would use the result to evaluate the validity of its exchange rate, to track its movement, to identify disparities with other countries, to influence exchange rate adjustments by the International Monetary Fund, and to decide whether to buy or sell particular currencies. This proposal would put the denominator of all money on the same kind of equitable, stable, clear, and certain foundation as the Metric System has put all other standard units of measure.

Because the proposed unit is an hour of work, the question arises as to whether or not an hour of work is also a wage and salary standard. Let me explain the difference.

As a Currency Exchange Rate Standard

As a currency exchange rate standard, every country's money denominated in Hours of Work would exchange for equal hours of work:

$$H_{Country\ A} = H_{Country\ B}$$

Just as the length of a meter does not change when measurements pass from one country to another, so an hour of work would remain the absolute standard of equal currency exchange when the money of one country is exchanged for the money of another country.

As a Wage and Salary Standard

On the other hand, as a wage and salary standard, an Hour of Work would be subject to variation based on whatever conditions employers and employees choose to take into account. Let us use the letter D, meaning Discretionary, to represent any and all such factors. Then we can represent the amount of money that any specific person might receive for the work they do as follows:

$$D_i * H$$

This notation means that a person i would be paid some fraction of or some multiple of an Hour of money for the work he or she does. The specific value of D would be negotiated between employer and employee.

Factors included in D might be productivity, experience, ease or hardship of the work, special occasions like weekend, night, or work on holidays, and the supply of and demand for that person's skills. There might be other factors taken into account in a wage or salary negotiation between an employer and an employee as well.

The result of using D in the determination of wages and salaries would be some inequality in wages and salaries. For example, a teenager taking his or her first job in a fast food restaurant might be paid 1/2 an Hour of money per hour of work. Such a decision would reflect the principle that equally (less) productive work would be paid equally (less).

On the other hand, a person with a year's experience managing a fast food restaurant might be paid 2 Hours of money per hour of work. Such a decision would reflect the principle that equally (more) responsible labor would be paid equally (more). The same person might be paid extra for working a night shift or for working a holiday. You can see that the Discretionary factor would allow variation among wages and salaries.

Would this mean that wage and salary inequalities would remain the same as they are today? Would, in effect, nothing change except having the words "Hour of Work" printed on money?

The difference would be in *degree* of inequality. Without a known and relevant quantity denominating money as the situation exists today, inequalities are astronomical. Yesterday a 20- year-old young lady won $28-million in the lottery. She won on the first ticket she had ever purchased. The news coverage was congratulatory. How wonderful that she won such a sum. But we can ask, how much did she win? It sounds like a lot, but how much is it? With dollars, we can only guess at the real meaning of the sum. Let us convert it to hours of work.

In the year 2000, the GDP of the United States was $9,873-billion. It was produced by 135.2-million people working an average of 2030 hours a year, a total of 274.5 billion hours of work. Therefore, the United States dollar was worth $36-per hour (i.e., $9,873 / 274.5). Let us now convert $28-million to its equivalent in hours of work.

$$\$28{,}000{,}000 / \$36 = 777{,}778 \text{ Hours of Work}$$

Let us take the math one step further. The standard year of work at 40 hours per week for 50-weeks is 2,000 hours.

An Hour of Work as the World Money Unit

So let us convert the hours of work of $28,000,000 into years of work by dividing 777,778 by 2,000.

777,778 hours / 2000 per year = 389 years

That 20-year-old young lady won the equivalent of almost 400 years of income! A wage of $36 an hour amounts to $72,000 per year, a lot more than most people make in a year. Had she started to receive that income in the year 1602, 35 years before the Pilgrims landed at Plymouth Rock, she would only now (2002) receive her last paycheck.

What difference would it make to denominate money in Hours of work instead of dollars? Amounts of money would become more clearly understood for what they really mean. Would that clarity have any effect? What do you think? It certainly has an effect on me. But not to pick on this young lady, consider the athlete who recently signed a five-year contract to play baseball for $250,000,000. That sum of dollar money equals 3,472 years of income at the rate of $72,000 per year.

What do you think would have happened if negotiation for that contract had taken place in terms of Hours of Work instead of dollars? Imagine the conversation. The baseball pitcher's lawyer says to the club's owner, "My client only made 3,500 years of income in his last contract, and you know he hit a record of home runs. He has a wife and three children. He will only be able to play ball for another five years or so. And you know he brings the fans into the ballpark by the millions. We want 5,000 years of money in the new contract." I think that a lawyer with that opening to a contract negotiation would be seen as certifiably insane.

The examples of contemporary money insanity are everywhere. Let me give you one more at the upper end and then one at the lower end. In 1995, the richest 400 individuals in the United States had a net worth of $1-billion each. Convert $1 billion to years of work.

$1,000,000,000 / $36 = 27,777,778 hours of Work.
27,777,778 hours of work / 2000-per year = 13,889 years of Income!

In what condition were humans living 14,000 years ago? Probably hunters and gatherers living in caves. No domestic animals or plants, no writing, elementary language perhaps. These 400 individuals would have had to receive $72,000-income starting then, to accumulate such vast net worth for each of them.

That was net work in 1995. Four years later, by 1999, the net worth of these 400 individuals had doubled! Their new net worth then was equivalent to:

27,778 years each!

I must believe that human beings are smart enough and fair enough to understand that such huge sums of money are far beyond any amount that could be reasonably justified. I believe that we tolerate them only because they are expressed in a money unit that is undefined. An Hour of Work would cast a spotlight of glaring clarity on them and lead reasonable people to demand sensible adjustments.

Lets take one example from the other end of the spectrum, the minimum wage of $5.75 an hour. How much is that converted to hours of work?

$$\$5.75 / \$36 = 0.16 \text{ of an Hour of money per hour of work.}$$
$$.16 \text{ of an hour is 9.6-minutes of pay per hour of work.}$$

At that rate, how much pay does a person working for minimum wage receive in a year?

$$.16 * 2000 = 320 \text{ hours of money.}$$

What effect do you think receiving 320 hours of money for 2,000 hours of work would have on people now being paid minimum wage?

Do you think dramatic clarifications like these would lead to demands for dramatic adjustments? I certainly do. And they should. Money numbers without an appropriate denominator have produced hideous distortions in the distribution of income. No wonder the country that claims to be one of the most productive in the history of the world, the United States, has millions of people homeless and hungry, poorly educated, and incarcerated. We have more people in prison that any other country in the world and more than in the history of the world. The undefined dollar and the distortions it has created must be held responsible for a lot of that misery.

I have not mentioned the distortions caused by unequal currency exchange rates. Just take what I have said about inequalities within the United States and multiply them many times over and you will have some understanding of why there is so much poverty and misery throughout the world. Lets start correcting the situation. If we can find a cure for polio, if we can put men on the moon, surely we can denominate our money in Hours of Work and get the adjustments that can lead to the peace and prosperity that we all deserve.

Bibliography

ABurish, Said K. *A Brutal Friendship: The West and the Arab Elite.* New York: St Martin's Press, 1997.
Acheson, Dean. *Present at the Creation.* New York: W.W. Norton, 1987.
Adams, J. *Secret Armies.* New York: The Atlantic Monthly Press 1987.
Addison, Charles G. *The Knights Templar.* London: Longman, Brown, Green, and Longman, 1842.
Agee, Philip. *Inside the Company: CIA Diary.* New York: Bantam Books, 1975.
_____. and Louis Wolf, *Dirty Work.* London: Zed Books, 1978.
Ahmad, Feroz. "Arab Nationalism, Radicalism, and the Specter of Neocolonialism." *Monthly Review* (February 1991).
Alexander, Yonah and Michael S. Swetnam. *Osama Bin Laden's al-Queda: Profile of a Terrorist Network.* Ardsley NY: Transnational Publishers, 2001.
Altvater, Elmar, Kurt Hubner, Jochen Lorentzen, Raul Rojas,. *The Poverty of Nations.* New Jersey: Zed Books, 1991.
Alvord, Clarence Walworth. *The Mississippi Valley in British Politics: A Study of Trade, Land Speculation, and Experiments in Imperialism Culminating in the American Revolution.* New York: Russell & Russell, 1959.
Ambrose, S.E. *Ike's Spies.* Garden City, New York: Doubleday . 1981.
Ameringer, C.D. *U.S. Foreign Intelligence.* Lexington, MA: Lexington Books, 1990.
Andrew, C. *For the President's Eyes Only: Secret Intelligence and the American Presidency From Washington To Bush.* New York: HarperCollins Publishers 1995.
Arnove, Anthony. *Iraq Under Siege: The Deadly Impact of Sanctions and War.* South End Press: Cambridge, 2002.
Arrighi, Giovanni. *The Long Twentieth Century.* New York: Verso, 2000.
Avirgan, Tony, M. Honey, editors, *Lapenca: On Trial in Costa Rica.* San Jose, CA: Editorial Porvenir. 1987.
Bairoch, Paul. *Economics and World History: Myths and Paradoxes.* Chicago: University of Chicago Press, 1993.
_____. *Cities and Economic Development From the Dawn of History to the Present.* Chicago: University of Chicago Press, 1988.
Bamford, James. *Body of Secrets: Anatomy of the Ultra-Secret National Security Agency.* New York: Doubleday, 2001.
Barck, Oscar Theodore, Jr. and Hugh Talmage Lefler. *Colonial America,* 2nd ed. New York: Macmillan, 1968.
Barnett, Correli. *The Collapse of British Power.* New York: Morrow, 1971.
Barnet, Richard. *The Rockets' Red Glare: War, Politics and American Presidency.* New York: Simon and Schuster, 1983.
Barlett, Donald L., James B. Steele. *America: What Went Wrong?* Kansas City: Andrews and McMeel, 1992.
_____."Fantasy Island and Other Perfectly Legal Ways that Big companies Manage to avoid Billions in Federal Taxes," *Time* (November 16, 1998).
_____."Paying a Price for Polluters," *Time* (November 23, 1998).
_____."The Empire of Pigs," *Time* (November 30, 1998).
Beard, Charles A. *An Economic Interpretation of the Constitution.* New York: Macmillan Publishing Co, 1941.
Bello, W. *Dark Victory: The United States and Global Poverty.* San Francisco: Institute for Food and Development Policy, 1999.
Bergen, Peter L. *Holy War Inc.: Inside the Secret World of Osama Bin Laden.* New York: Simon & Schuster, 2001.
Berger, John J., ed. *Environmental Restoration: Science and Strategies for Restoring the Earth.* Washington, DC: Island Press, 1990.
"Big Lie Exposed," *Workers World,* April 12, 2001.
Blackstock, Nelson. *Cointelpro: The FBI's Secret War on Political Freedom.* New York: Anchor Foundation, 1988.
Blaufarb, D.S. *The Counterinsurgency Era: U.S. Doctrine and Performance 1950 To Present.* New York: The Free Press, 1977.
Blum, William. *Rogue State: A Guide to the World's Only Super Power.* Monroe, ME: Common Courage Press, 2000.
_____. *The CIA: A Forgotten History.* New Jersey: Zed Books Ltd., 1986.
_____. *Killing Hope: U.S. Military Interventions Since World War II.* Monroe, Me: Common Courage Press, 1995.

Borosage, R.L., Marks, J. editors. *The CIA File.* New York: Grossman Publishers, 1976.
Borsodi, Ralph. *Inflation.* Great Barrington, MA: E.F. Schumacher Society, 1989.
Bortzutzky, Silvia. "The Chicago Boys, Social Security and Welfare in Chile", *The Radical Right and the Welfare State: An International Assessment of International Social Policy and Welfare,* Howard Glennerster, James Midgley, ed. Lanham, MD: Barnes and Noble, 1991.
Brody, Reed. *Contra Terror in Nicaragua: Report of a Fact Finding Mission: September 1984-January 1985.* Boston: South End Press, 1985.
Brown, Walt. *Treachery in Dallas.* New York: Carroll & Graf, 1995.
Bulletin from the AFL-CIO Task Force on Trade (1992).
Burman, Edward. *The Inquisition: Hammer of Heresy.* New York: Dorset Press, 1992.
Burnes, James. *The Knights Templar.* London: Paybe and Foss, 1840.
Bunzl, John, *The Simultaneous Policy: An Insider's Guide to Saving Humanity and the Planet.* London: New European Publications 2002.
Buzgalin, Alexander, Andrei Kolganov. *Bloody October in Moscow: Political Repression in the Name of Reform.* New York: Monthly Review Press, 1994.
Caldwell, M. Editor Ten Years Military Terror Indonesia. Nottingham: Spokesmen Books, no date.
_____. *The Rise of Fascism.* Berkeley: University of California Press, 1982.
Carey, Alex. *Taking the Risk out of Democracy; Corporate Propaganda versus Freedom and Liberty.* Chicago: University of Illinois Press, 1995.
Castro, Fidel. *Capitalism in Crisis: Globalization and World Politics Today.* New York: Ocean Press, 2000.
Caute, David. *The Great Fear.* New York: Simon and Schuster, 1978.
Chamorro, E., "Packaging the Contras: A case of CIA Disinformation." *Monograph Series Number 2.* New York: Institute For Media Analysis, 1987.
Chester, E.T. *Covert Network: Progressives, the International Rescue Committee, and the CIA.* New York: M.E. Sharpe, 1995.
Chinweiezu. "Debt Trap Peonage." *Monthly Review* (November 1985).
Chomsky, Noam. "Oppose the War." *Z Magazine* (Feb. 1991)
Chossudovsky, Michel. "United States War Machine: Revving the Engines of World War III, *CovertAction Quarterly* (Fall 2002),
_____. "Dismantling Yugoslavia, Colonizing Bosnia." *CovertAction Quarterly* (Spring, 1996).
_____. *The Globalization of Poverty: Impacts of IMF and World Bank Reforms.* London: Zed Books, 1997.
_____. *War and Globalization: The Truth behind September 11.* Centre for Research on Globalization, 2002)
Church Committee Report. Congressional Record. 1975-76.
Churchhill, Ward. *Cointelpro Papers : Documents from the FBI's Secret Wars Against Domestic Dissent.* South End Press, 1990.
_____. *Indians Are Us.* Monroe: Common Courage Press, 1994.
_____. *A Little Matter of Genocide: Holocaust and Denial in the Americas, 1492 to the Present.* San Francisco: City Lights Books, 1997.
_____. *Agents of Repression : The FBI's Secret Wars Against the Black Panther Party and the American Indian Movement.* Boston South End Press, 1989.
The Christian Science Monitor (December 4, 1997).
Clairmont, Frederic F. *The Rise and Fall of Economic Liberalism.* Goa India: The Other India Press, 1996.
Clark, Ramsey. *Hidden Agenda: U.S./NATO Takeover of Yugoslavia.* New York: International action Center, 2002.
Clarridge, Duane R. *A Spy for all Seasons: My Life in the CIA.* New York: Scribner, 1997.
Cline, R.S. Secrets, Spies, and Scholars. Washington, DC: Acropolis Books, 1976.
Cockburn, Alexander. "Beat the Devil." *The Nation* (March 6, 1989).
Codevilla, Angelo. *Informing Statecraft.* New York: The Free Press, 1992.
Cohen, Stephen. *Failed Crusade: America and the Tragedy of Post-Communist Russia.* New York: W.W. Norton, 2000.
Coleman, Peter. *Liberal Conspiracy.* London: Collier Macmillan, 1989.
Collon, Michel. *Liars Poker: The Great Powers, Yugoslavia and the Wars of the future.* New York:: International action Center, 2002.
Commons, John R. *Legal Foundations of Capitalism.* London: Transaction Publishers, 1995.
_____. *Institutional Economics.* London: Transaction Publishers, 1995.
Cook, B. *The Declassified Eisenhower.* Garden City, NY: Doubleday, 1981.
_____. "Hitler's Extermination Policy and the American Indian." *Indian Historian* 6 (Summer 1973), 48-49.
Cook, Don. *Forging the Alliance.* London: Seeker and Warburg, 1989.
Cooley, John K. *Unholy Wars: Afghanistan, America, and International Terrorism,* 2nd edition. London: Pluto Press, 2000.
Cooper, Marc. Chile and the End of Pinochet." *The Nation* (February 26, 2001).

Bibliography

Cordovez, D, S.S. Harrison, *Out of Afghanistan: The Inside Story of the Soviet Withdrawal.* New York: Oxford University Press, 1995.
Corn, D. Blond Ghost: *Ted Shackley and the CIA's Crusades.* New York: Simon and Schuster, 1994.
Corn, David, Jefferson Morley. "Beltway Bandits." *The Nation* (April 9, 1988).
Corwin, Julie, Douglas Stranglin, Suzanne Possehl, Jeff Trimble. "The Looting of Russia." *U.S. News & World Report* (March 7, 1994).
Cottin, Heather. "George Soros, Imperial Wizard: Master-Builder of the New Bribe Sector, Systematically Bilking the World" *CovertAction Quarterly* (Fall 2002).
Covington, Sally. "Right Thinking, Big Grants, and Long Term Strategy: How Conservative Philanthropies and Think Tanks Transform U.S. Policy." *CovertAction Quarterly* (Winter 1998).
Crowther, Samuel. *America Self-Contained.* Garden City, N.Y.: Doubleday, Doran & Co., 1933
Curry, Andrew. "The First Holy War," *U.S. News & World Report,* April 8, 2002, pp. 36-42.
Daly, Herman E. *Steady-State Economics.* San Francisco: W.H. Freeman 1977.
Das, Bhagirath Lal. *WTO: The Doha Agenda: The New Negotiations on World Trade.* London: Zed Books, 2003, and his many other books.
David, Arie E. *The Strategy of Treaty Termination.* New Haven: Yale University Press, 1975.
Diamond, Jared. *Guns, Germs, and Steel: The Fates of Human Societies.* New York: W.W. Norton, 1999.
_____. *The Third Chimpanzee: The Evolution and Future of the Human Animal.* New York: HarperCollins, 1992.
DiEugenio, James and Lisa Pease. *The Assassinations: Probe Magazine on JFK, MLK, RFK, and Malcolm X.* Los Angeles: Feral House, 2003.
Dobson, John M. *Two Centuries of Tariffs: The Background and Emergence of the U.S. International Trade Commission.* Washington DC: U.S. International Trade Commission, 1976.
Donner, Frank J. *The Age of Surveillance: The Aims and Methods of America's Political Intelligence System.* New York: Random House, 1981.
Dregson, Alan, Duncan Taylor, Editors. *Ecoforestry: The Art and Science of Sustainable Forest Use.* Gabriola Island, BC: New Society Publishers, 1997
Eckes, Alfred E., Jr. *Opening America's Markets: U.S. Foreign Trade Policy Since 1776.* Chapel Hill: University of North Carolina Press, 1995.
Emerson, S. Secret Warriors. New York: G.P. Putnam, 1988.
Endicott, Stephen, Edward Hagerman. *The United States and Biological Warfare: Secrets from the Early Cold War and Korea.* Bloomington, IN: Indiana University Press, 1998.
Erickson, J. *The Road to Berlin.* New Haven: Yale University Press, 1983.
Etzold, Thomas H., John Lewis Gaddis. *Containment: Documents On American Policy and Strategy, 1945-50.* New York: Columbia University Press, 1978.
Fallows, James. "How the World Works." *The Atlantic Monthly* (December 1993).
Faux, Jeff. "The Austerity Trap and the Growth Alternative." *World Policy Journal* (Summer 1988).
Feffer, John. "The Browning of Russia." *CovertAction Quarterly* (Spring 1996).
Felix, David. "Latin America's Debt Crisis." *World Policy Journal* (Fall 1990).
Fingleton, Eamonn. *In Praise of Hard Industries: Why Manufacturing, not the Information Economy, is the Key to Future Prosperity.* New York: Houghton Mifflin, 1999.
Flaherty, Patrick. "Behind Shatalinomics: Politics of Privatization," *Guardian* (October 10, 1990).
Fleming, D. F. *The Cold War and Its Origins.* 2 vol. New York: Doubleday, 1961.
Flexner, James Thomas. *George Washington: The Forge of Experience.* Boston: Little Brown and Co., 1965.
Foner, Philip S. *From Colonial Times to the Founding of the American Federation of Labor.* New York: International Publishers, 1947.
Forbes, Jack D. *The Indian in America's Past.* Englewood Cliffs, NJ: Prentice Hall, 1964.
Ford, Peter. "Regime Change: A Look at Washington's Methods and Degrees of Success in Dislodging Foreign Leaders," *The Christian Science Monitor,* January 27, 2003,
Francis, David R. "Debt-riddled Russia to Ask for Forgiveness." *The Christian Science Monitor* (April 5, 1999).
Frazier, H., ed. *Uncloaking the CIA.* New York: The Free Press, 1978.
Freeland, Chrystia. *Sale of the Century: Russia's Wild Ride From Communism to Capitalism,* New York: Crown Publishers, 2000.
Fresia, Jerry. *Toward an American Revolution: Exposing the Constitution and Other Illusions.* Boston, South End Press, 1988.
Fromkin, David. *A Peace To End All Peace.* New York: Avon Books, 1989.
Furiati, Claudia. *ZR Rifle: The Plot to Kill Kennedy and Castro.* Melbourne: Ocean Press, 1994.
Gaffney, Mason, Fred Harrison. *The Corruption of Economics: With The Development of Democracy, Mind Control Became the Urgent Need: Neo-Classical Economics Was the Tool.* London: Shepheard-Walwyn, 1994.
Galeano, Eduardo. *Guatemala: Occupied Country.* New York: Monthly Review Press, 1969.

Gardner, Lloyd C. *Safe for Democracy*. New York: Oxford University Press, 1984.
Garrison, Jim. *On the Trail of the Assassins*. New York: Sheridan Square Press, 1988.
Garvin, G. Everybody Has His Own Gringo: The CIA and the Contras. New York: Brassey's,1992.
Garwood, Darrell. *Under Cover: Thirty-Five Years of CIA Deception*. New York: Grove Press, 1985.
George, Henry. *Progress and Poverty*. New York: Robert Schalkenbach Foundation,1981.
George, Susan. *The Lugano Report: On Preserving Capital in the Twenty-First Century*. Sterling, VA: Pluto Press, 1999.
A Fate Worse Than Debt. Rev. New York: Grove Weidenfeld, 1990.
_____. *The Debt Boomerang*. San Francisco: Westview Press, 1992.
Gervasi, Sean. "Germany, U.S., and the Yugoslavian Crisis." *CovertAction Quarterly* (Winter 1992-93).
Gibbs, D., *The Political Economy of Third World Intervention: Mines, Money and U.S. Policy in the Congo Crisis* Chicago, IL: The University of Chicago Press, 1991.
Gill, Stephen. The Geopolitics of the Asian Crisis." *Monthly Review* (March 1999).
Gill, William J. *Trade Wars Against America: A History of United States Trade and Monetary Policy*. New York: Praeger, 1990.
Gleijeses, P. *Shattered Hope: The Guatemalan Revolution and the United States*, 1944-1954. Princeton, New Jersey, Princeton University Press, 1991.
Gohari, M.J. *The Taliban: Ascent to Power*. New York: Oxford University Press, 2000.
Goodson, Larry P. *Afghanistan's Endless War: State failure, Regional Politics, and the Rise of the Taliban*. Seattle: University of Washington Press, 2001.
Gorbachev, Mikhail. *Perestroika*. New York: Harper & Row, 1987.
Gordon, John Steele. *Hamilton's Blessing: The Extraordinary Life and Times of Our National Debt*. New York: Walker and Co., 1997.
Gowan, Peter. *The Global Gamble: Washington's Faustian Bid for World Dominance* (New York: verso, 1999).
_____. "Old Medicine in New Bottles." *World Policy Journal* (Winter 1991-92).
Gray, John. *False Dawn*. New York: The New Press, 1998.
Greider, William. *Who Will Tell the People?* New York: Simon and Schuster, 1992.
Griffin, Michael. *Reaping the Whirlwind: The Taliban Movement in Afghanistan*. Sterling, VA: Pluto Press, 2001.
Grinde, D. "Cherokee Removal and American Politics." *Indian Historian* 8 (Winter 1975), 33-42.
Griswold, Deirdre. "Marxism, Reformism and Anarchism: Lessons from a Steel Mill in Slovakia." *Workers World* (December 14, 2000).
Groden Robert J., Harrison Edward Livingstone. *High Treason: The Assassination of President John F. Kennedy and New Evidence of Conspiracy*. New York: Berkeley Books, 1990.
Grose, Peter. *Gentleman Spy : The Life of Allen Dulles*. Boston: University of Massachusetts Press, 1996.
Guma, Greg. "Cracks in the Covert Iceberg." *Toward Freedom* (May 1998).
Gunson, P., A. Thompson, G. Chamberlain. *The Dictionary of Contemporary Politics of South America*. New York: Routledge, 1989.
Gup, Ted, *The Book of Honor: Covert Lives and Classified Deaths at the CIA*. New York: Doubleday, 2000.
Hartung, William D. "Why Sell Arms?" *World Policy Journal* (Spring 1993).
Hawken, Paul. *Natural Capitalism: Creating the Next Industrial Revolution*. New York: Little Brown and Company, 1999.
Hatal, William H. Richard J. Verey. "Recognizing the 'Third Way.'" *The Christian Science Monitor* (March 3, 1999).
Heckscher, Eli F. *Mercantilism,* 2 vol. New York: The Macmillan Company, 1955.
Heidenry, D. *Theirs Was the Kingdom: Lila and Dewitt Wallace the Story of the Reader's Digest*. New York: W.W. Norton, 1993.
Henwood, "Clinton and the Austerity Cops." *The Nation* (November 23, 1992).
Herman, Edward S. *The Real Terror Network*. Boston: South End Press, 1982
_____. and F. Broadhead. *Demonstration Elections: U.S. Staged Elections in the Dominican Republic, Vietnam, and El Salvador,* Boston: South End Press, 1984 .
Hersh, Burton. *The Old Boys: The American Elite and the Origins of the CIA*. New York: Charles Scribner's Sons, 1992.
Heuvel, Katrina vanden. Editorial, *The Nation* (August 10-17, 1998).
Hines, Colin, Tim Lang. Jerry Mander, Edward Goldsmith, eds. *The Case Against the Global Economy and For A Turn Toward the Local*. San Francisco: Sierra Club, 1996.
Hunt, H.J. *Undercover: Memoirs of an American Secret A*gent. New York: Berkeley Publishing, 1974.
Irwin, Douglas A. *Against the Tide: An Intellectual History of Free Trade*. Princeton, N.J.: Princeton University Press, 1996.
Isaacson, Walter, and Evan Thomas, *The Wise Men*. New York: Simon and Schuster, 1986.
Jacobs, Dan. *The Brutality of Nations*. New York: Alfred A. Knopf, 1987.

Bibliography

Jai-eui, Lee. *Kwangju Diary: Beyond Death, Beyond the Darkness of Age.* Los Angeles: University of California, 1999.

Jaimes, A. *The State of Native America.* Boston: South End Press, 1992.

Jayko, Margaret. *FBI on Trial: The Victory in the Socialist Workers Party Suit against Government Spying.* New York: Pathfinder Press, 1989.

Jeavons, John. *How to Grow More Vegetables Than You Ever Thought Possible On Less Land Than You Ever Imagined: A Primer On The Life Giving Biointensive Method Of Organic Horticulture.* Berkeley, CA: Ten Speed Press, 1991.

Jeffreys-Jones, R. *The CIA & American Democracy.* New Haven CT: Yale University Press, 1989.

Jennings, F. *The Invasion of America.* Chapel Hill: University of North Carolina Press, 1975.

Johnson, Chalmers. *Blowback: The Costs and Consequences of the American Empire.* New York: Henry Holt & Company, 2000.

Johnson, Emory R. *History of Domestic and Foreign Commerce of the United States.* Washington DC: Carnegie Institute of Washington, 1915.

Jonas, Susanne. *The Battle for Guatemala: Rebels, Death Squads, and U.S. Power.* San Francisco: Westview Press, 1991.

Joynt, Carey B., and Percy E. Corbett. *Theory and Reality in World Politics.* Pittsburgh: University of Pittsburgh Press, 1978.

Jukes, Jeffrey. *Stalingrad at the Turning Point.* New York: Ballantine Books, 1968.

Kagarlitsky, Boris. *Square Wheels: How Russian Democracy Got Derailed.* New York: Monthly Review Press, 1994.

Kahin, McT. *Subversion as Foreign Policy: The Secret Eisenhower and Dulles Debacle in Indonesia.* New York: New Press. 1995.

Kaku, Michio and Daniel Axelrod. *To Win A Nuclear War.* Boston: South End Press, 1987.

Kaplan, David and Michael Schaffer. "Losing the Psywar." *U.S. News & World Report* (October 8, 2001).

Elie Kedourie. *England and the Middle East.* London: Bowes and Bowes, 1956.

Kelley, Sean. *America's Tyrant: The CIA and Mobutu of Zaire.* Washington DC: American University Press, 1993.

Kennedy, Paul. *The Rise and Fall of the Great Powers.* New York: Random House, 1987.

Kernaghan, Charles. "Sweatshop Blues." *Dollars and Sense* (March/April, 1999).

Kessler, R. *Inside The CIA: Revealing The Secrets Of The World's Most Powerful Spy Agency.* New York: Pocket Books, 1992.

Ketchum, Richard M., ed. *The American Heritage Book of the Revolution.* New York: American Heritage Publishing, 1971.

Kettle, Michael. *The Allies and the Russian Collapse.* Minneapolis: University of Minnesota Press, 1981.

Kielinger, Thomas, Max Otte. "Germany: The Presumed Power." *Foreign Policy* (Summer 1993).

Klare, Michael T. *Resource Wars: The New Landscape of Global Conflict.* New York: Henry Holt and Company, 2001.

_____. and P. Kornbluth. *Low Intensity Warfare.* New York: Pantheon Books, 1988.

Knightley, Philip. *The First Casualty.* New York: Harcourt Brace Jovanovich, Publishers, 1975.

Kohn, Stephen M. *American Political Prisoners: Prosecution under the Espionage and Sedition Acts.* Westport: Praeger Publishers, 1994.

Komisar, Lucy. "Documented Complicity: Newly Released Files Set the Record Straight on U.S. Support for Pinochet." *The Progressive* (September, 1999).

Koning, Hans. *The Conquest of America: How the Indian Nations Lost Their Continent.* New York: Monthly Review Press, 1993.

Kornbluth, Peter. *Nicaragua, The Price of Intervention: Reagan's War Against the Sandinistas.* Washington DC: Institute for Policy Studies, 1987.

_____.and M. Byrne. *The Iran-Contra Scandal: The Declassified History.* New York: A National Security Archive Documents Reader, The New Press. 1993.

Korten, David. *When Corporations Rule the World.* West Hartford, CT: Kumarian Press and San Francisco: Berret-Koehler, 1995

Kötke, William H. *The Final Empire: The Collapse of Civilization and the Seed of the Future.* Portland, OR: Arrow Point Press, 1993.

Kotz, David. "Russia in Shock: How Capitalist 'Shock Therapy' is Destroying Russia's Economy." *Dollars and Sense* (June 1993).

Kraus, Michael. *The United States to 1865.* Ann Arbor: University of Michigan Press, 1959.

Kropotkin, Petr. *Mutual Aid.* Boston: Porter Sargent Publishers Inc., 1914.

_____. *The State.* London: Freedom Press, 1987.

Kurtzman, Joel. *The Death of Money.* New York: Simon and Schuster, 1993.

Kwiatkowski, Stefan and Charles Stowe. *Knowledge Café for Intellectual Product and Intellectual capital.* Warsaw, Poland: Leon Kozminski, 2001.

_____. *Endless Enemies: The Making of an Unfriendly World.* New York: Congdon & Weed, 1984.

Labeviere, Richard. *Dollars for Terror: The United States and Iran.* New York: Algora Publishing, 2000.

Landay, Jonathan S. "Study Reveals U.S. Has Spent $4 Trillion on Nukes Since '45." *The Christian Science Monitor* (July 12, 1995).

Lane, Charles Theodore Stanger, Tom Post. "The Ghosts of Serbia." *Newsweek* (April 19, 1993).

Lane, Mark. *Plausible Denial: Was the CIA Involved in the Assassination of JFK?* New York: Thunder Mouth Press, 1991.

Lappé, Frances Moore. *World Hunger: Twelve Myths.* New York: Grove Press: 1998.

Layne, Christopher. "America's Stake in Soviet Stability." *World Policy Journal* (Winter 1990-91).

_____. "Rethinking American Grand Strategy." *World Policy Journal* (Summer 1998).

Lea, Henry Charles. *The Inquisition of the Middle Ages.* New York: Citidel Press, 1954.

Lens, Sidney. *Permanent War.* New York: Schocken Books, 1987.

List, Friedrich. *The National System of Political Economy.* Fairfield, NJ: Augustus M. Kelley, 1977.

Litvinoff, Barnet. *The Burning Bush.* New York: E.P. Dutton, 1988.

Livingston, Harrison Edward. *Killing the Truth: Deceit and Deception in the JFK Case.* New York: Carroll & Graf, 1993.

Loftus, John. *The Belarus Secret.* New York: Alfred A. Knopf, 1982.

Lohbeck, K. *Holy War, Unholy Victory: Eyewitness to the CIA's Secret War in Afghanistan.* Washington DC: Regnery Gateway, 1993.

Logan, John A. *The Great Conspiracy: Its Origin and History, 1732-1775.* New York: A.R Hart & Co., 1886.

Longworth, Richard C. *Global Squeeze: The Coming Crisis of First-World Nations.* Chicago: Contemporary Books, 1999.

MacDonald, William, ed. *Documentary Source Book of American History, 1606-1926,* 3rd ed. New York: Macmillan, 1926.

Mackay, Neil. "Bush Planned Iraq 'Regime Change' Before Coming President." *The Sunday Herald* (Scotland), September 15, 2002.

Magoffin, Ralph V.D. and Frederic Duncalf. *Ancient and Medieval History.* New York: Silver Burdett and Company, 1934.

Makhijani, Arjun. *From Global Capitalism to Economic Justice.* New York: Apex Press, 1992.

Manz. Beatriz. *Refugees of A Hidden War: The Aftermath of Counterinsurgency in Guatemala.* New York: State University of New York, 1988.

Marchetti, Victor, John D. Marks. *The CIA and the Cult of Intelligence.* New York: Knopf 1974; Dell Publishing, 1980.

Marcuse, Peter. "Letter from the German Democratic Republic." *Monthly Review* (July/August 1990).

"Mark Twain on Henry George" at gopher://echonyc.com:70/00/Cul/HGS/archimed

Marks, P. *In a Barren Land.* New York: William Morrow and Company, 1998.

Marrs, Jim. *Crossfire: The Plot That Killed Kennedy.* New York: Carroll and Graf, 1989.

Marsh, Nadia, M.D. "U.S. Med Students Arrive in Cuba." *The Workers' World* (April 19, 2001).

Marshall, J., P.D. Scott, J. Hunter. *The Iran-Contra Connection.* Boston, MA: South End Press, 1987.

Martin, D. *Wilderness of Mirrors.* New York: Harper and Row, 1980.

Mayer, Milton. *They Thought They Were Free.* Chicago, University of Chicago Press, 1955.

Mayers, David. *George Kennan.* New York: Oxford University Press, 1988.

Maynes, Charles William, "A New Strategy for Old Foes and New Friends." *World Policy Journal,* (Summer 2000).

McCann, T. *An American Company: The Tragedy of United Fruit.* New York: Crown Publishers, 1976.

McClain, William E. *Illinois Prairie: Past and Future: A Restoration Guide.* Springfield, IL: Illinois Department of Conservation, 1986.

McClintock, Michael. *Instruments of Statecraft: U.S. Guerrilla Warfare, Counter Insurgency, and Counter Terrorism 1940-1990.* New York: Pantheon, 1992.

_____. *The American Connection: State Terror and Popular Resistance in Guatemala.* London: Zed Books, 1985.

_____. *The American Connection: State Terror and Popular Resistance in El Salvador.* London: Zed Books, 1985.

McGehee, Ralph W. *Deadly Deceits.* New York: Sheridan Square Press, 1983.

_____. CIABASE, Box 5022, Herndon, VA 22070; http://come.to/CIABASE/.

McNeill, William H. *The Pursuit of Power.* Chicago: University of Chicago Press, 1982.

Mechin, Jaques Benoist-, *The End of The Ottoman Empire.* ISBN 3-89434-008-8, no publisher or date noted.

Milani, Brian. *Designing the Green Economy: The Postindustrial Alternative to Corporate Globalization.* New York: Rowman & Littlefield, 2000.

Miller, John C. *Origins of the American Revolution.* Boston: Little Brown and Co., 1943.

Miller, N. *Spying for America.* New York: Paragon House, 1989.

Mills, Stephanie. *In Service of the Wild: Restoring and Reinhabiting Damaged Land*. Boston: Beacon Press, *1995*.
Minnick, Wendell. *Spies and Provocateurs: A Worldwide Encyclopedia of Persons Conducting Espionage and Covert Action, 1946-1991*. Jefferson, North Carolina: McFarland,1992.
Moffitt, Michael. "Shocks, Deadlocks, and Scorched Earth: Reaganomics and the Decline of U.S. Hegemony." *World Policy Journal* (Fall 1987).
Mohammad, Yousai, M. Adkin. *The Beartrap: Afghanistan's Untold Story*. London, England: Leo Cooper, 1992.
Mollison, Bill. *Permaculture: A Designers' Manual*. Tyalgum, Australia: Tagari Pub., 1988.
Monbiot, George. "A Discreet Deal in the Pipeline" (*The Guardian*, 15 February 2001).
Morison, Samuel Eliot and Henry Steele Commanger, *Growth of the American Republic*, 5th ed. New York: W.W. Norton, 1959.
Morgan, Dan and David B Ottaway. "In Iraqi Oil Scenario, Oil is Key Issue: U.S. Drillers Eye Huge Petroleum Pool." *Washington Post*, September 14, 2002.
MacKenzie, Angus and David Weir. *Secrets: The CIA's War at Home*. Berkeley: University of California Press, 1997.
Mumford, Lewis. *Technics and Civilization*. New York: Harcourt Brace Jovanovich, 1963.
Murphy, Austin. *The Triumph of Evil: The Reality of the USA's Cold War Victory*. Italy: European Press Academic Publishing, 2000.
Murphy, Dan. "Indonesia Confronts Unruly Past." The Christian Science Monitor (November 20, 2000)
Nadudere, Dan. *The Political Economy of Imperialism*. London: Zed Books, 1977.
Nair, K. Devil and His Dart: How the CIA is Plotting in The Third World. New Delhi: Sterling Publishers, 1986.
Namier, Sir Lewis and John Brooke, *Charles Townsend*. New York: St. Martin's Press, 1964.
Neilson, Francis. *How Diplomats Make War*. New York: Robert Schalkenbach Foundation, 1984.
Newman. John A. and Paul Bottis (http://www.taxmoney-notpeople.com and http://www.madashellclub.com
Newman, Richard J, "A Kosovo Numbers Game," *U.S. News & World Report* (July 12, 1999).
Oberman, Heiko A. *The Roots of Anti-Semitism*. Philadelphia: Fortress Press, 1984.
Ostrogorsky, George. *History of the Byzantine State*. New Jersey: Rutgers University Press, 1969.
Palast, Greg. *The Best Democracy that Money can Buy: The Truth about Corporate Cons, Globalization, and High-Finance Fraudsters,* London: Penguin Books, 2003.
Parakal, P.V. *Secret Wars Of CIA*. New Delhi: Sterling Publishers Private Limited, 1984.
Parenti, Michael. *History as Mystery*. San Francisco: City Light Books, 1999.
_____. *To Kill a Nation*. New York: Verso, 2000.
Parnas, David Lorge. "Con: Dayton's a Step Back—Way back," *Peace* (March/April 1996).
Pastor, Robert A., Ed. *A Century's Journey: How the Great Powers Shape the World*. New York: Basic Books, 1999.
Pearson, Hugh. *The Shadow of the Panther: Huey Newton and the Price of Black Power in America*. Perseus Press, 1995.
Pepper, William F. *An Act of State: The Execution of Martin Luther King*. New York: Verso, 2003.
Perelman, Michael. *The Invention of Capitalism: Classical Political Economy and the Secret History of Primitive Accumulation*. London: Duke University Press, 2000.
Peterson, Scott . *"In War, Some Facts Less Factual."* The Christian Science Monitor September 6, 2002.
Peterzell, J. *Reagan's Secret Wars*, CNSS Report 108. Washington, DC: Center for National Security Studies, 1984.
Petras, James. "Argentina: Between Disintegration & Revolution." *CovertAction Quarterly* (Fall 2002).
Pitt, William Rivers with Scott Ritter. *War on Iraq*. New York: Context Books, 2002.
Phillips, D.A. *The Night Watch*. New York: Atheneum, 1977.
Pilarski, Michael. *Restoration Forestry: An International Guide to Sustainable Forestry Practices*. Durango, CO: Kivaki Press, 1994.
Pirenne, Henri. *Economic and Social History of Medieval Europe*. New York: Harcourt, Brace, 1937.
Pepper, William F. *An Act of State: The Execution of Martin Luther King*. New York: Verso, 2003.
Polanyi, Karl. *The Great Transformation*. Boston: Beacon Press, 1957.
Pool, James, Suzanne Pool. *Who Financed Hitler?* New York: The Dial Press, 1978.
Powell, Bill. "Iraq, We Win, Then What." *Fortune* (November 25, 2003).
Powers, T. *The Man Who Kept The Secrets*. New York: Alfred A. Knopf, 1979.
Prados, John. *The Presidents' Secret Wars*. New York: William Morrow, 1986.
_____. *The Presidents Secret Wars*, revised. Warwick: Elephant Paperbacks, 1996.
_____. *The Hidden History of the Vietnam War*. Chicago: Elephant Paperbacks, 1995.

_____. *Keepers Of The Keys A History Of The National Security Council From Truman To Bush*. New York: William Morrow, 1991.
"Proud Russia on Its Knees." *U.S. News & World Report* (February 8, 1999).
Prouty, L.F. *JFK: The CIA, Vietnam, and the Plot to Assassinate John F. Kennedy*. New York: Birch Lane Press, 1992.
_____. *The Secret Team*. Englewood Cliffs, NJ: Prentice-Hall, 1973.
Quigley, John. *The Ruses for War: American Interventionism Since World War II*. Buffalo: Prometheus Books, 1992.
Raanes, Tuva. "A Divine Country All on Its Own." *World Press Review*, October 2002.
Rai, Milan. *War Plan Iraq*. London: Verso Press, 2002.
Raghavan, Chakravarthi. *Recolonization: GATT, the Uruguay Round & the Developing World*. London: Zed Books, 1990.
Rashid, Ahmed, *Taliban: Militant Islam, Oil and Fundamentalism in Central Asia*. New York: Yale University Press, 2001.
Rayack, Elton, *Not So Free to Choose: The Political Economy of Milton Friedman and Ronald Reagan*. Westport, Conn: Praeger, 1986.
Renard, George. *Guilds of the Middle Ages*. New York: Augustus M. Kelly, 1968.
A Report by The International Institute for Environment and Development and The World Resources Institute,
Richelson, J. *American Espionage and The Soviet Target*. New York: William Morrow, 1987.
_____. *The U.S. Intelligence Community*. Cambridge, MA: Ballinger Publishing Company, 1985.
Ridenour, R. *Back Fire: The CIA's Biggest Burn*. Havana, Cuba: José Marti Publishing House, 1991.
Rifkin, Jeremy. *Biosphere Politics*. San Francisco: HarperCollins, 1992.
_____. *Entropy: Into the Greenhouse World*. Rev. ed. New York: Bantam Books, 1989.
Roberts, J.M. *The Triumph of the West*. London: British Broadcasting Company, 1985.
Robinson, Linda. "America's Secret Armies," *U.S. News & World Report* (November 4, 2002).
_____. "What didn't we do to get rid of Castro." *U.S. News & World Report* (October 26, 98).
Robinson, William I. *A Faustian Bargain: U.S. Intervention in the Nicaraguan Elections and American Foreign Policy in the Post-Cold War Era*. Boulder, CO: Westview Press, 1992.
Rodman, Peter. *More Precious Than Peace*. New York: Charles Scribner & Sons, 1994.
Roosevelt, Kermit. *Countercoup: The Struggle for the Control Of Iran*. New York: McGraw-Hill, 1979.
Rositzke, H. *The CIA's Secret Operations*. New York: Thomas Y. Crowell Company, 1977.
Ross, Michael. "Yeltsin: POWs 'Summarily Executed.'" *The Spokesman Review* (November 12, 1992).
_____. *The Age of Triage*. Boston: Beacon Press, 1983.
Rzheshevsky, Oleg. *World War II: Myths and the Realities*. Moscow, U.S. USSR: Progress Publishers, 1984.
Sale, Kirkpatrick. *The Conquest of Paradise*. New York: Alfred A. Knopf, 1991.
Samaray, Catherine. *Yugoslavia Dismembered*. New York: Monthly Review Press, 1995.
Saunders, Frances Stoner. *The Cultural Cold War: The CIA and the World of Arts and Letters*. New York: The Free Press, 1999.
Schlesinger, Stephen. "The CIA Censor's History." *The Nation* (September 7, 1997).
Schor, Juliet B. "Workers of the World Unwind." *Technology Review* (November/December 1991).
_____. *The Overworked American*. Basic Books, 1991.
Schrecker, Ellen. *No Ivory Tower: McCarthyism in the Universities*. New York: Oxford University Press, 1986.
Simon, Jean-Marie. *Guatemala: Eternal Spring Eternal Tyranny*. New York: W.W. Norton, 1988.
Simpson, Christopher. *Blowback*. New York: Weidenfeld & Nicolson, 1988.
Sipols, Vilnis. *The Road to Great Victory*. Moscow, USSR: Progress Publishers, 1985.
Sklar, Holly, *Washington's War On Nicaragua*. Boston: South End Press, 1988.
Smith, Adam. *The Wealth of Nations*. New York: Random House, 1965.
Smith, J.W. *Economic Democracy: The Political Struggle of the Twenty-First Century*, updated & expanded 3rd edition. www.ied.info/cc.html: The Institute for Economic Democracy, 2003.
_____. *Cooperative Capitalism: A Blueprint for Global Peace and Prosperity*. www.ied.info/cc.html: The Institute For Economic Democracy, 2003
_____. *The World's Wasted Wealth 2*. www.ied.info/cc.html: The Institute For Economic Democracy, 1994.
Smith, Mathew. *Say Goodbye to America: The Sensational and Untold Story Behind the Assassination of John F. Kennedy*. London: Mainstream Publishing, 2001.
Stannard, D. *American Holocaust*. Oxford: Oxford University Press, 1992.
Statistical Abstract of the United States. Washington DC: U.S. Government Printing Office, 1990, 1992.
Stelzer, Gus. *The Nightmare of Camelot: An Exposé of the Free Trade Trojan Horse*. Seattle, Wash.: PB publishing, 1994.
Stephanson, Anders. *Kennan and the Art of Foreign Policy*. Cambridge: Harvard University Press, 1989.

Bibliography

Stiglitz, Joseph. *Globalization and its Discontents* New York: WW Norton, 2002
Stockwell, John. *In Search of Enemies.* New York: W. W. Norton, 1978.
_____. *The Praetorian Guard.* Boston: South End Press, 1991.
Stone, I.F. *The Hidden History of the Korean War.* Boston: Little, Brown, 1952.
Stone, Oliver. Movie JFK.
Strange, Susan. *The Retreat of the State: The Diffusion of Power in the Global Economy,* Cambridge, UK: Cambridge Studies in International Relations number 49, 1998.
Summers, Anthony. *Conspiracy.* New York: Paragon House, 1989.
Swearingen, M. Wesley. *FBI Secrets : An Agent's Exposé.* Boston: South End Press, 1995.
Tabb, William. *The Amoral Elephant: Globalization and the Struggle for Global Justice in the Twenty-First Century.* New York: Monthly Review Press, 2001.
Taheri, Amir. *Nest of Spies: America's Journey to Disaster in Iran.* New York: Pantheon Books, 1988.
Taylor, Edmond. *The Fall of the Dynasties: The fall of the Old Order, 1905-1922.* New York: Dorset Press, 1989.
Thomas, E. *The Very Best Men.* New York: Simon & Schuster, 1995.
Thomas, Peter D.J. *The Townshend Duties Crisis: The Second Phase of the American Revolution, 1776-1773.* Oxford: Clarendon Press, 1987.
Thomas, Rich. "From Russia, With Chips," *Newsweek* (August 6, 1990).
"Three Marketeers, The." *Time.* (February 15, 1996).
Thurow, Lester C. *Head to Head: The Coming Economic Battle Among Japan, Europe, and America.* New York: William Morrow, 1992.
_____. *The Future of Capitalism: How Today's Economic Forces Shape Tomorrow's World.* England, Penguin Books, 1996.
Treverton, G. *Covert Action: The Limits of Intervention in the Post-War World.* New York: Basic Books, 1987.
Tuchman, Barbara. *The March of Folly.* New York: Alfred A. Knopf, 1984.
Turk, Jonathan, Janet T. Wittes, Robert Wittes, Amos Turk. *Ecosystems, Energy, Population.* Toronto: W.B. Saunders Co., 1975.
Twentieth Century Fund. *The Need to Know: The Report of The Twentieth Century Fund Task Force on Covert Action and American Democracy.* New York: The Twentieth Century Fund Press, 1992.
United Nations Commission on the Truth in El Salvador. *From Madness To Hope: The 12-Year War In El Salvador.* U.N. Security Council (1993).
United Nations Human Development Report. 1991, 1998.
United Nations Truth Commission on Guatemala. U.N Security Council (1995, 1999).
"U.S. Becomes Biggest Dealer of Arms in Worldwide Market." *Spokesman Review* (October 15, 1992).
Vandenberg, Arthur Hendrick. *The Greatest American.* New York: G.P. Putnam's and Sons, 1921
Vanek, Jaroslav. The Labor Managed Economy. London: Cornell University Press, 1977.
Volkman, Ernest, Blaine Baggett. *Secret Intelligence.* New York: Doubleday, 1989.
Volman, Dennis. "Salvador Death Squads: A CIA Connection?" *The Christian Science Monitor* (May 8, 1984).
Wachtel, Howard M. "Labor's Stake in WTO." *The American Prospect* (March/April 1998).
Wallerstein, Immanuel. *The Origin of the Modern World System.* 2 vol. New York: Academic Press, 1974.
Watson, B., S. Watson, G. Hopple. *United States Intelligence: An Encyclopedia.* New York: Garland Publishing, 1990.
Weatherford, Jack. *Indian Givers.* New York: Fawcett Columbine, 1988.
Wedel, Janine R. "The Harvard Boys Do Russia," *The Nation.* (June 1, 1998).
Weiner, T. *Blank Check*: The Pentagon's Black Budget. New York: Warners Books, 1990.
_____. Nothing Wasted, Everything Gained:." *Mother Jones* (March/April, 1998).
Weissman, Steve. *The Trojan Horse.* Rev. ed. Palo Alto: Ramparts Press, 1975.
Westerfield, H. B. editor. *Inside CIA's Private World: Declassified Articles from the Agency's Internal Journal 1955-1992.* New Haven CT. Yale University Press, 1995.
Willan, Philip. *Puppetmasters: The Political Use of Terrorism in Italy.* London: Constable, 1991.
Williamson, Ann. "An Inconvenient History."
   http://www.geocities.com/Athens/7842/wcessay04.htm.
Williams, Eric. *From Columbus to Castro.* New York: Vintage Books, 1984.
Williams, William Appleman. *The Contours of American History.* New York: W.W. Norton, 1988.
_____. *The Tragedy of American Diplomacy.* New York: W. W. Norton, 1988.
Winks, Robin W. *Cloak & Gown: Scholars in the Secret War, 1939-1961.* New York: Quill, 1987.
Wise, David, Thomas B. Ross. *The Espionage Establishment.* New York: Bantam Books, 1978.
Wright, Robin. *Sacred Rage: The Wrath of Militant Islam.* New York: Simon & Schuster, 1985.
Yallop, David A., *In God's Name.* New York: Bantaam Books, 1984.
Yeoman, Barry "The Stealth Crusade." *Mother Jones,* May/June 2002.

Index

Academy Awards, blacklisted, 41
Acheson, Dean, *Present at the Creation*, 49
Afghanistan, 21-22, 53, 71, 78, 96-99, 114
Africa, 6, 11-13, 15-16, 75-76, 94, 98, 120, 165
Agent provocateurs, 52, 76, 107
Al-Qaeda, 21-22, 70, 96
Al-Aqsa Mosque, 20
Albania, 97, 104, 106-10
Alexandrette, 14
Algeria, 14-16
Allende, Salvadore, President, 45, 73
Alsop, Joe and Stewart, 40
American Enterprise Institute, 43
American Federation of Labor, 41
American Legislative Exchange Council, 43
American Revolution, 60, 61
American Spectator, The 42
Angola, 39, 75
Arab, 11, 16-19, 69, 129
Arbenz, Jacobo, 73
Argentina, 35, 120, 129, 131, 168
Armstrong, Leslie, jury foreman, 55
Asian tigers, 6, 35, 116, 120, 123, 132, 168
Assassination, 40, 45, 53-57, 73, 95
Athens, 12, 131
Australia, 6, 32
Austria, 14-16, 89, Austro-Hungarian, 15
Ayatollah Khomeini, 68
Azerbaijan, 109
Bahrain, 18
Balkan, 11, 14-15, 108-09, 114
Bangladesh, 134
Banking system, 149, 152, 154,
Batista, 75
Battle of the Bulge, 85
Battle of Tours, 12
Bay of Lepanto, 12
Bay of Pigs, 55
Beirut, 14
Belgium, 51
Belgrade Center for Human Rights, 113
Berlin, 14-15, 40
Berlin, Isaih, 41
Bessarabia, 84
Biafra, 73
Bin Laden, Osama, 21-22, 96
Bismarck 35
Black Death, 28
Blain, Bob, 175
Bologna railway station, 51
Borsodi, Ralph, xvii, 138
Bosnia-Herzegovina, 104
Bosporus, 15, 17
Botswana, 75, 126
Bottis, Paul, 146
Brazil, 35, 66, 120, 129, 133, 168
Bretton Woods, 124

Britain, 4-5, 14-18, 27-31, 34-35, 50, 61, 67-69, 72, 85, 140, 171, Navigation Acts-28, MI6, 67
Brzezinski, Zbigniew, 98
Bulgaria, 15, 110, 114
Bush, President George, 52, 70, 149, First President Herbert Bush, 94
Butler, General Smedley, 54
Byzantine, 11-12
Cable Splicer, 52
Cambodia, 72
Canada, 32, 113, 124
Capital; accumulation, 24-25, 36, 68, 133, 136, 137, 141, 151, 164, 171
Carter, President Jimmy, 96, 98
Carthage Foundation, 42
Casey William, 71
Caspian Sea, 22, 109
Castro, Fidel, 55, 75, 77-78, 88-89
Cathars, 59-60
Ceku, Agim, 104
Central Europe, 111, 115-16, 168
Center for Anti-War Action and Media, 113
Center for Democracy Foundation, 113
Center for International Private Enterprise, 113
Central Intelligence Agency (CIA), 21, 38-56, 67-78, 90, 95-98, 104
CHAOS, 52
Charles G. Koch foundation, 42
Chase, Stuart, 138
Chechnya, 71, 96, 110
Chile, 27, 39, 45, 73-74, 102
China, 6, 11-12, 33-35, 49-50, 80, 112, 115, 118, 131, 134, 140
Christianity, 10-13, 17, 20, 59-60, 80, 104-05, 108-10, 115-16, 160
Clark, General Wesley, 107
Claude R. Lambe charitable foundations, 42
Clay, Henry, 31
COINTELPRO, 52, 56, 107
Colby, William, CIA Director, 40
Cold War, 5, 40-41, 45-53, 58-62, 78, 81, 84, 88, 94, 108-12, 132, 139-40
Coleman, Peter, 39-41
Columbus. 12
Commons, The, 9, 122-23, 143-49, 154-55, 159, 169, 172-74
Communism, 40, 44, 71, 78, 87, 108-09, 114, 123
Comparative advantage, 26, 68, 128, 137
Conference of San Remo, 17
Congo, The, 39, 75
Congress for Cultural Freedom, 39-41, 50
Constant-value currency, 153
Constantine, Roman emperor, 11, 59
Constantinople, 11, 14
Continental blockade system, 30

Index

Coordinating Committee for Multilateral Export Controls (Cocom), 88
Count Berchtold, 16
Covert warfare, 6-7, 15, 26, 39-41, 48-51, 54-55, 67, 72, 81, 96, 98, 106, 110-13, 126, 132, 136
Covington, Sally, 43
Crimea, 14
Croatia, 103-10, 114
Crusades, 10, 20
Cruzada, 12
Cuba, 27, 39, 55, 63, 75-78, 80, 102, 126
Currency Exchange Rate Standard, 175, 178
Currency Act of 1764, 31
Cyprus, 89
Czarist, 16, 44, Secret Police, 61
Czechoslovakia, 116
Damascus, 14
Dark Ages, 13
David H. Koch foundation, 42
Dayton Accords, 103-04
Death squads, 46-47, 55-56, 73-74, 105, 114
Deflation, 35, 152-53
Dengue fever. 76
Denmark, 21
Diamond, Jared, 13
Dinarides Thrust, 109
Dominican Mendicant Order, 59
Dupin, 30
Dutch, 11, 28, 50
Eagleburger, Lawrence, 103
East Germany, 76, 120
East Timor, 110
Eastern Europe, 11, 12, 81, 84-88, 102, 110-12, 114-16, 120
Eastern Front, 85
Eastern Orthodox Christianity, 10-11, 104-05, 108-10, 114-16
ECHELON, 21, 51
Economic multiplier, 8, 91-92, 111, 121, 128, 135-37, 149, 162
Economic warfare, 6-7, 120, 126, 128, 132-33
Egypt, 11, 14-16, 80
El Salvador, 39, 74
Elliot, Michael, 103
Embargo, 1, 66, 70, 68, 72, 75, 103, 110-11, 127, 136, 163
Emperor Franz Josef, 16
Enabling Act, 52, 62
England, English, 11, 14-15, 28-31, 69, 85, 171, 176
Environment, 20, 40, 125, 136-38, 150, 155, 158, 161-64
Equalizing surcharge, 136-38, 146, 150-51, 163-65
Estonia, 84
Ethiopia, 110
Ethnic cleansing, 104-10
European Community (EC), 88
European Movement of Serbia, 113
European Union, 88, 124, 135, 138
Exchange Rate Standard, 175

Far East, 12
Fascism, 52, 62, 85
Federal Bureau of Investigation (FBI), 52-55, 107
Federal Reserve, 33, 49
Financial Times, 92
Financial warfare, 6-7, 102, 128-35
Finland, 84
Florence, 27
Foreign Operations Appropriations Bill, 103
Foreign policy, 2-3, 16, 36, 44, 45, 49-52, 66, 71, 80, 119-20
Fort Benning, 46
Fourteen Points, 16
Fox, Vicente, President, 47
France, 11, 14-18, 28, 30, 40, 51, 60, 85, 89, 104, 127, Revolution, 13, 60, 97, 122, 167
Free Congress Foundation, The, 43
Free Trade Area of the Americas (FTAA), 124, 126-27, 130
Freeland, Chrystia *Sale of the Century,* 92-93
Furiati, Claudia, *ZR Rifle,* 55-58
G-17, 113
G7, the seven leading Western countries, 88
Gandhi, Mahatma, 46-47, 69, 166
Garden Plot, 52
General Agreement on Trades and Services (GATS), 124, 126-27, 130
General Agreement on Trades and Tariffs (GATT), 124-27, 130
Genocide, 106-08
Genoese, 12
Genscher, Hans Dietrich, 103
George, Henry, 44, 144
Georgia, Russian, 96, 109
German BND, 97, 104
Germany, 14-16, 25, 30, 41, 49-52, 60-62, 76, 84-89, 94, 97, 103-06, 109-16, 120, 140, 158, 162
Gill, Professor Stephen, 33
Gladio, Operation, 51
Gowan, Professor Peter, 33-35, 87-88
Grand Strategies, 26, 40, 49, 50, 91, 110, 115
Gray, Professor John, *False Dawn,* 34, 155
Great Depression, 123, 132, 143, 167
Greece, 12, 15, 50, 110, 138
Greenspan, Alan, 33
Greider, William, 130, 137
Gresham's law, 153
Guatemala, 73-74
Gulf War, 68, 70-71, 78, 110
GUUAM, 109
Gypsies, 105, 108
Habsburg, 16
Hague, The, 74, 114
Haider, 14
Hampton, Fred, 53
Hanseatic traders, 28
Harbor Freight, 118-120
Harry Bradley Foundation, 42
Harvard Institute for International Development, 90, 92

Heartland Institute, The, 43
Heckscher, Eli F., 25
Heiju, 78
Henry Salvatori Foundation, 42
Herder, Johann, 172
Hess, Rudolf, 85
High Representative (HR), 103
Hijack, 1, 10, 71, 78
Hitler, 38, 51-52, 62, 85, 104-05, 114
    thousand-year Reich, 111, Enabling Act,
    52, 62
Holland, 21
Holocaust, 104
Holy Alliance, 12
Hook, Sidney, 41
House Select Committee on Assassinations,
    54, 55
House Un-American Activities Committee,
    41, 52
Humanitarian Law Center, 113
Hungary, 15-16, 88, 110
Hunt, E. Howard, 55-56
Hussein, Saddam 70
Illuminati, Bavarian, 60-61
India, 14, 49, 166
Indian, American, 13
Indonesia, 6, 32, 50, 71-72, 110
Inflation, 49, 68, 103, 129, 131, 152-53
Inquisition, 47, 59-62
International Monetary Fund (IMF), 33, 81,
    88, 102, 104, 114-16, 126-27, 130
International Criminal Tribunal (ICTY), 74
International Workers of the World,
    Wobblies, (IWW), 52
Iran, 27, 66-72
Iran-Iraq War, 69-70
Iraq, 1, 16-22, 27, 53, 68-72, 79, 97, 109-10,
    117, 168
Irish, 171
Israel, 1, 11, 70, 74, 171
Italy, 15-18, 51, 54, 85, 158-59, 162
Jacobs, Dan, 63
Jaffa, 14
Jalal al-Din al-Afghani, 17
Japan, 6, 32-35, 41, 49, 51, 57, 69, 85, 87, 90,
    116, 120-24, 132, 134, 158, 162, 164, 168
Jaques Benoist-Mechin, 14
Jerusalem, 14, 20, 80
Jihad, 98
JM Foundation, 42
John M. Olin Foundation, 42
Kehoe, Judge James W., 55
Kemal, Mustapha, 16
Kennedy, Bobby, 57
Kennedy, President John F., 54-57, 77
Kerensky, 44
Khomeini, Ayatollah, 68
King Feisal, 17
King Philip IV, 60
King, Martin Luther, 46, 54, 56, 69
Kissinger, Henry, 67

Knights Templar, The, 60
Koestler, Arthur, 41
Korean War, 50, 52, 77-79
Korten, David C, 45, 125
Kosovo Liberation Army (KLA), 97, 104-07
Kosovo, 97, 104-13
Krehm, William, 118
Kuwait, 17, 70
Kuznet's Curve, 126, 132
Lane, Mark, 54-58, 103
Lantern Council, 59
Lappé, Frances Moore 127
Latin America, 41, 47, 77, 116, 168
Latvia, 84, 105
Layne, Christopher, 16
League of Nations, 16, 18
Lebanon, 16, 74
Lemnitzer, General Lyman, 63, 76, 78
Lenin, 16, 46-47
Liberty Lobby, 55, 64
Libya, 15-16, 27, 72, 68
Lippman, Walter, 40
List, Friedrich, 4, 6, 28-30, 33-35, 86, 168
Lloyd George, Prime Minister, 17-18
Lord Brougham, 31
Luce, Henry, 41
Lumumba, Patrice, 75
Luther, Martin 13
Lynde Foundation, 42
MacArthur, General Douglas, 78
Macedonia, 97, 104
Madagascar, 50
Mafia, 51, 89
Maher, Bill, 2
Malaysia, 6, 32, 50
Manhattan Institute, The, 43
Marshall, General George C., 86
Marshall Plan, 41, 86, 88
Marx, Karl, 172
McCarthyism, 41, 45-46, 50-52, 58
McGehee, Ralph, 47, 49-50
Men Who Killed Kennedy, The (documentary), 58
Mercantilism, 4-5, 17-18, 25-27, 30, 57, 67, 90,
    128
Mesopotamia, 11
Methuen treaty of 1703, 28
Mexico, 47, 69, 116, 129, 133
Middle East, 6, 10, 14-20, 41, 66-70
Military Professional Resources MPRI, 97,
    104
Milosevic, President, 105, 112, 114
Mobutu, Joseph, 75
Moffit, Michael, 133
Mohammed, 11, 66
Money, Constant-value-153, deflation-35,
    152-53, inflation, 49, 103, 129, 131, 152,
    labor value, 25, 130, 136, 153, 163
Money Transaction Tax, 93, 146, 157
Montenegro, 15, 112, 114
Mossadeq, Dr. Mohammed, 66
Most Favored Nation (MFN), 124
Mozambique, 39, 75

Index

Mujahideen, 96
Multilateral Agreement on Investments (MAI), 124-27, 130
Multilateral Trading Organization (MTO), 125
Mumford, Lewis, 27
Mussolini, 51-52
Namibia, 75
Napoleon, 30-31, 61, 110, 167, Napoleonic Codes, 110
National Empowerment Television, 43
National Endowment for Democracy (NED), 89, 113
National Interest, The, 42
Nat. Security Council, 49, 73, 78, 96, 98, 102
National Union for the Total Independence of Angola (UNITA), 75
Neibuhr, Reinhold, 41
NetNewsNow, 43
New Criterion, The, 42
Newman, John, 146
Nicaragua, 27, 39, 74, 102
Nigeria, 73, 129
Nixon, President, 67
Nobel Prize, 126
Normandy, 85
North American Free Trade Agreement (NAFTA), 124, 126-27, 130
North Atlantic Treaty Organization (NATO), 22, 104-15, 139-41
North Korea, 21, 27, 28, 78-80
OECD, 129
Office of Strategic Studies (OSS), 50
Operation Ajax, 67
Operation Gladio, 51
Operation Northwoods, 78
Operation Statewatch, 51
Organization of Oil Exporting Countries (OPEC), 67, 70, 128-29
Osama Bin Laden, 21-22, 96
Oswald, Lee Harvey, 54
Ottoman Empire, 11-17
Pakistan, 21, 96
Palast, Greg, 57, 112, 126
Palestine, 1, 16, 20, 74, 171
Panama, 46
Panmunjom peace negotiations, 79
Patriot Act, 52, 62
Peace of Versailles, 31
Pentagon, 1, 4, 10, 21, 44, 53, 58, 69, 71, 95-98, 104, 107, 132, 160
Persia, 11, 15, 68
Peter the Great, 12
Phillip M. McKenna Foundation, 42
Pike Committee, 40
Pinochet, General, 73-74
Pirenne, Henri, 25
Pitt, William, 30
Plans for war: Bushwhacker, Broiler, Sizzle, Shakedown, Dropshot, Trojan, Pincher, and Frolic, 95
Plunder-by-trade, 3, 5, 10, 25, 27, 36, 163
Poland, 84, 88
Polanyi, Karl, 15
Policy Fax, 43
Popular Movement for the Liberation of Angola (MPLA), 75
Portugal, 12, 28, 138
Pratt, Geronimo, 53
Propaganda, 3-5, 22, 36-41, 45-49, 54-55, 62, 69, 73, 78, 95-98, 105-12, 121, 167, 172
Protocols of The Learned Elders of Zion, 61
Prouty, L Fletcher, 54, 57-58
Public Interest, The, 42
Pujol, Emilio Perez, 107
Puppet Masters: The Political Use of Terrorism in Italy, 54, 57
Qatar, 18
Quadrilateral Group of Trade Ministers, (QUAD), 124
Queen Isabella, 12
Radio Free Europe, 41
Radio Liberty, 41
Rambouillet, 104-06
Reichstag fire, 51-52, 62
Reinhold Neibuhr, 41
Resource-depletion tax, 137, 164--65
Reuters, 41
Rhee, Syngman, 78
Richardson, Bill, 109
Roman Empire, 11-12, 80, 108
Romania, 105, 110
Roosevelt, Kermit, 67
Roosevelt, President Franklin D, 54
Rothmyer, Karen, 43
Rousseau, Jean Jacques, 172
Rubin, Robert, 33
Russell, Bertrand, 41
Russia, 12-18, 25, 35, 44, 77, 84-98, 104, 109-10, 115, 120, 168
Rwanda, 110
Sachs, Jeffrey, 90-91
Salonica, 14
San Remo, Conference of, 17
Sarah Scaife Foundation, 42
Saudi Arabia, 17
Saunders, Frances Stoner, 40
Savak, 67, 69
Savimbi, Jonas, 75
Say, J. B., 30
Schlesinger, Arthur, 41
School of the Americas, School of Assassins, School of Coups, 46
Salenica, 14
Serbia, 15-16, 104-15
Siena, 27
Singapore, 6
Slave, 11, 115, 163
Sliwa, Martyna, 154
Slovakia, 116-17
Slovenia, 104, 110, 114
Smith Richardson Foundation, 42
Smith, Adam, 4-5, 27-30, 33-36, 86, 89-90, 126, 137, 143-47
Smyrna, 14, 16

Socialist Workers Party (SWP), 52
SOCOM, Special Operations Command, 97, 121
Soros, George, 89, 113
South Africa, 75, 94
South America, 6, 73
South Korea, 6, 32-33, 78-79, 87, 123, 134
Southeast Asia, 33, 116, 132, 140, 162
Soviet Union, 6, 19, 22, 33, 35, 39, 49, 51, 61, 69, 75, 77, 81, 84--98, 103, 112-16, 120, 128, 131, industrial capacity, 84-86, Secret agreement Exposed, 18-19
Spain, Spanish, 11-12, 22, 28, 69, 74, 89, 107, 138
Spotlight, 55
State Policy Network, 43
Stiglitz, Joseph, 126
Stone, I.F., 79
Stone, Oliver, 58
Structural adjustment, 29, 33, 36, 102, 114-16, 126-27, 130, 136
Subsidize, 40, 45, 74, 127
Sudan, 110
Suez Canal, 13-14
Suharto, 72
Sukarno, 71-72
Suleiman the Magnificent, 11
Sumeria, 154
Summers, Larry, 33
Taiwan, 6, 32-33, 87, 123
Taliban, 78, 97, 99, 114
Terrorism, Wholesale, 3, 33, 36, 39, 50, 52, 72, 81, 90, 140, 158, 165
Thailand, 6, 134
The Reason Foundation, The, 43
Theodosius, Emperor, 11, 59
Think-Tanks, 30, 41-45, 112-13, 143
Third Reich, 35
Thrips-palmi, 76
Thurow, Professor Lester, 118, 130
Tobin Tax, 154
Tragedy of the Commons, 143
Transaction tax, 93, 146, 157
Trepca mining/manufacturing complex, 109
Triple Alliance, 16
Truman, Harry, President, 49, 52
Tunisia, 14-16
Turkistan, 11
Turkey, 14-16
U.S. Steel, 116
Ukraine, 109, 114, 127-28
Union for Total Independence (UNITA), 75
United Arab Emirates, 18
United Fruit Company, 73
United Nations, 109, 138, 140, 163
Uruguay, 120, 168
Ustase, 105, 114
Uzbekistan, 109
Vasco da Gama, 12
Veblen. Thorstein, 138
Venetian, 12
Vienna, 12, 16

Vietnam, 39, 50, 52, 54, 66, 72-73, 95, 167-68
Voice of America, The, 41
VSZ steel complex, 116-17
Wachtel, Howard, 124
Waldensians, 59-60
Wall Street, 35
Waller stein, Immanuel, 25
War Crimes Tribunal, 115
War of 1812, 31
Warren Commission, 54
Watergate, 55
Weishaupt, Professor Adam, 60
Western Europe, 12, 49, 84-88, 95, 109-11, 114, 116, 122-23, 135, 162
Western Front, 85
Western Hemisphere Institute for Security Operations, 46
Willan, Philip, 54, 57
Wilson, President Woodrow, 18, Fourteen Points-16
Winstanley, Gerard, 172
Wisner, Frank, 40
Wobblies, IWW, 52
World Bank, , 102, 114-16, 124-27, 130
World Money Unit, 175
World Trade Center bombing, 1, 4, 10, 21, 53, 58, 69, 71, 76, 95, 98, 108, 132, 140, 160
World Trade Organization (WTO), 124-27, 130
World War I, 4-5, 15-17, 32, 34, 52, 84
World War II, 4-5 16, 18-22, 32-35, 38, 46, 50, 61, 66, 71-72, 85-88, 104-05, 108, 122, 125, 139, 140, 162, 166
World War III, 140
Yeltsin, President Boris, 92, 94
Young Socialist Alliance (YSA), 52
Yugoslavia, 2, 16, 27, 39, 53, 78, 97, 99, 102-15
Zambia, 75, 128
Zimbabwe, 75
ZR Rifle: The Plot to Kill Kennedy and Castro, 55, 57

ABOUT THE AUTHOR

With a Ph.D. in political economics, J.W. Smith has written broadly and lectured widely at conferences around the world. This is the second edition of his 4th book on the causes and cures of world poverty.

J.W. Smith not only takes a different view from most economists his deep research pushes dense and impossible to understand neoliberal economics off the table and replaces it with sensible economics that we can all understand. As he says, "neoliberal economics makes sense only within borders of an empire. As soon as one steps outside those borders they make no sense at all. How could it? It is designed to lay claim to the wealth of the periphery of empire?"

Smith's 20 years of deep study of economic history builds a new school of thought. Where else do you read how wealth accumulation increases or decreases exponentially with the differential in pay between equally productive labor? That evolving from plunder by raids to plunder by trade became the signature of "civilized" nations? That Adam Smith free trade was specifically designed to entrench this system of laying claim to others wealth? Or that no nation ever developed under that philosophy? The exposure of these realities provide a new foundation upon which to understand the world.

That understanding of economic history leads us to Smith's explanation of how Western "democracies" evolved from feudalism and today's property rights laws retain the essentials of those feudal exclusive rights to nature's bounty. The concept these monopoly rights which exclude the weak from their rightful share follows naturally.

Smith provides the historic foundation to understand how Western "democracies" evolved from feudalism, that property rights still retain feudal exclusive rights to nature's bounty, and that it is these monopoly rights excluding the weak from their rightful share as the powerful continue the privatization of the commons that impoverishes so many people.

Smith looked deeply under the blanket of imposed belief systems protecting the power structure and its stolen wealth and concluded the debris of custom and law are the barriers preventing Western societies from evolving into peaceful and far more productive societies.

Smith's explanation of how the elimination of those monopolies through expanding individual rights and competition through a modern commons increasing economic efficiency equal to the invention of money, writing, and electricity providing all with a quality life working only two to three days per week; all while protecting the earth's resources and ecosphere, provides a ray of light on what we must do for a peaceful and prosperous world.

If you wish to join, or financially support, one of our groups, please do so through a check to addresses at the web sites below or paying a membership fee through PayPal and simultaneously emailing us your name and address. That payment and email will automatically register you as a member. Go to www.ied.info/resources.html or www.ied.info/cc.html for further updates. Please join us:

The Institute for Cooperative Capitalism
1st World, $30 Students/3rd World $10
Creating a blueprint for global peace and prosperity
www.paypal.com/ - account: cc@ccus.info
www.ccus.info/

The Institute for Economic Democracy
1st World, $30 Students/3rd World $10
Sustainable development research: peace and prosperity for all
www.paypal.com/ - account: ied@ied.info
www.ied.info/

Global Literacy Outreach: 1st World, $30 Students/3rd World $10
Illuminating the darkness of illiteracy
www.paypal.com/ - account: glo@gloliteracy.org
www.gloliteracy.org/

International Philosophers for Peace
1st World, $30 Students/3rd World $10
Developing a just social, economic, & political basis for peace and human well-being. www.paypal.com/, account: ippno@ippno.org
wwwippno.org/

Action Institute for Literacy and Human Resource Development
1st World, $30 Students/3rd World $10
Education through Project Learning Communities (PLC)
www.paypal.com/, account: plc@ailahurd.org
www.ailahurd.org/

The Hour Money Institute for Global Harmony
1st World, $30 Students/3rd World $10
Dedicated to establishing an hour of work as the money unit worldwide
www.paypal.com/, hourmoney@hourmoney.org
wwwhourmoney.org/

Network On Democracy Over Empire
1st World, $30 Students/3rd World $10
Dedicated to egalitarian democracies replacing the global imperial system
www.paypal.com/, accounts: wdavis@kent..edu
wwwwaltedavis.info/

Global Issues (www.globalissues.org)
A very active supporter but does not take donations at this time

Translation rights are available in your region, www.ied.info/cc.html.
ied@ied.info

Discount for groups as an educational/money-earning project; Discounts to classrooms/University Bookstores, www.ied.info/cc.html.
ied@ied.info

We are available to present these concepts to your class or group. A potential this can be handled at no cost to you, www.ied.info/cc.html.
ied@ied.info